Integrated Korean

Beginning 1

Integrated Korean

Beginning 1

Young-mee Cho   Hyo Sang Lee   Carol Schulz   Ho-min Sohn   Sung-Ock Sohn

KLEAR Textbooks in Korean Language

© 2000 University of Hawai'i Press
All rights reserved
Printed in the United States of America
10 09 08 07 06   11 10 9 8 7

This textbook series has been developed by the Korean Language Education and
Research Center (KLEAR) with the support of the Korea Foundation.

Library of Congress Cataloging-in-Publication Data

Integrated Korean : beginning 1 / Young-mee Cho... [et al.].
    p. cm. — (KLEAR textbooks in Korean language)
  ISBN-13: 978-0-8248-2174-6 (cloth : alk. paper) — ISBN-13: 978-0-8248-2342-9 (pbk. : alk. paper)
  ISBN-10: 0-8248-2174-2 (cloth : alk. paper) — ISBN-10: 0-8248-2342-7 (pbk. : alk. paper)
    1. Korean language—Textbooks for foreign speakers—English. I. Cho, Young-mee.
II. Series.

PL913.I58 2000
495.7'82421—dc21   00-039298

Camera-ready copy has been provided by the authors.

University of Hawai'i Press books are printed on acid-free paper
and meet the guidelines for permanence and durability of the Council
on Library Resources.

Printed by The Maple-Vail Book Manufacturing Group

CONTENTS

Beginning 1

PREFACE

Unlike cognate languages of English such as Spanish, French and German, the Korean language is one of the most difficult languages for English speakers to learn because of the profoundly distinct cultural features, the entirely different sound patterns and vocabulary, the unique writing system with indigenous letters, the predicate-final sentence structure, the word structure with extensive agglutination of suffixes, the intricate hierarchical system of honorifics, and so on. To optimize and maximize English speakers' learning of this truly foreign language, therefore, we need textbooks that are based on the most sound pedagogical principles and approaches, on the one hand, and adequately deal with the vast linguistic, sociolinguistic, and cultural differences between Korean and English, on the other. The *Integrated Korean* series was designed and developed to meet diverse student needs with the above requirements in mind.

Integrated Korean consists of four levels: Beginning (main text 1 and 2 and workbook 1 and 2), Intermediate (main text 1 and 2 and workbook 1 and 2), Pre-Advanced (main text 1 and 2), and Advanced (main text 1 and 2). Each level is expected to be covered by two semesters or three quarters, assuming five class hours per week for the Beginning and Intermediate levels and three class hours per week for the Pre-Advanced and Advanced levels.

The lessons in *Integrated Korean* are sequenced in terms of the proficiency levels that students are expected to achieve. For each lesson, special efforts were exerted to properly integrate all five language skills (listening, speaking, reading, writing, and culture), to provide authentic situations and materials as much as possible, to explain detailed grammatical patterns, vocabulary items, and cultural aspects from a contrastive perspective, to provide students with relevant examples and exercises for each grammar point, and to include extensive student-centered communicative and task/function activities.

The Beginning and Intermediate levels are designed to train students to master the basics of the language and perform appropriate spoken and written communication in the interpersonal mode in most essential daily life situations. Following a schematic overview of the language and the Han'gŭl writing system, each lesson begins with a page of lesson objectives, which is followed by model conversations, a related narration, new words and expressions, culture, grammar points, and tasks/functions, in that order. For students' easy reference, extensive appendices, including predicate conjugation, useful semantic classes, a grammar index, and glossaries (Korean-English and English-Korean) are provided. Students' factual knowledge and basic language skills learned from the main texts are further reinforced through extensive drills and skill-building activities in the workbooks, as well as via CD-ROMs, which will be available later for further listening practice. In the Pre-Advanced and Advanced levels, a wide variety of interesting authentic materials on Korean culture and society is introduced to train students to achieve advanced levels of proficiency not only in interpersonal but also in interpretive and presentational communication.

On behalf of the Korean Language Education and Research Center (KLEAR), I extend my heartfelt thanks to the following individuals who, functioning as main authors of different volumes of *Integrated Korean,* worked most devotedly and tirelessly over a long period until the final versions were produced:

> Sungdai Cho, Stanford University
> Young-mee Cho, Rutgers University
> Jiha Hwang, Harvard University
> Eun-Joo Lee, University of California, Los Angeles
> Hyo Sang Lee, Indiana University
> Young-Geun Lee, University of Hawai'i at Manoa
> Carol Schulz, Columbia University
> Ho-min Sohn, University of Hawai'i at Manoa
> Sung-Ock Sohn, University of California, Los Angeles
> Hye-sook Wang, Brown University

The following Korean-language specialists gratefully cooperated on the project in various functions, such as providing dialogue samples, reading materials, or initial sample lessons, and reviewing draft versions:

> Andrew Byon, University of Hawai'i at Manoa
> Sunny Jung, University of California, San Diego
> Gwee-Sook Kim, Princeton University
> Sek Yen Kim-Cho, State University of New York at Buffalo
> Young-Key Kim-Renaud, George Washington University
> Haejin Koh, University of Hawai'i at Manoa
> Dong Jae Lee, University of Hawai'i at Manoa
> Jeyseon Lee, University of Michigan
> Miseon Lee, University of Hawai'i at Manoa
> Sunae Lee, University of California, Santa Barbara
> Sangsuk Oh, Defense Language Institute

Kyu J. Pak-Covell, Defense Language Institute
Duk-Soo Park, University of Sydney
Yong-Yae Park, Seoul National University
Joe J. Ree, Florida State University
Yoo Sang Rhee, Defense Language Institute
Seok-Hoon You, Korea University
Soo-ah Yuen, University of Hawai'i Kapiolani Community College

I am also grateful to many research assistants who helped the main authors. Special thanks go to Jeannie Kim and Haejin Koh, who translated the dialogues, narrations, and other Korean materials into English, and to the commercial artist, Julie Sohn, who did some two thousand line drawings at nominal cost. Throughout the entire project, Eun-Joo Lee functioned as managing assistant. With amazing ability, energy, and patience, she efficiently handled all the materials as they were developed or repeatedly revised and prepared the final camera-ready versions, while at the same time taking care of other project-related chores. Indeed, her contribution deserves special recognition.

The *Integrated Korean* series and all its sister volumes (*Composition, Chinese Character Studies, Selected Readings, Modern Literature Reader, Modern Short Stories, Language in Culture and Society,* and *Grammar and Usage Dictionary*) are the outcome of seven years of extremely strenuous collaborative work by many Korean-language experts under KLEAR's Korean Language Textbook Development Project. This monumental project was initiated and financially supported by the Korea Foundation. KLEAR owes a great deal to the past and present presidents of the Korea Foundation and their staffs, especially to its former president Son Chu Hwan, who was instrumental in launching this project in 1994. I would also like to express my sincere thanks to the members of the Korea Foundation's textbook review committee for their valuable comments at the initial stage of the project and to the KLEAR board members for their continued support throughout the project. Last but not least, I would also like to extend my sincere appreciation to the National Foreign Language Center in Washington, D.C., for providing four KLEAR members with Andrew Mellon fellowships for the preparation of the original project guidelines in 1994, to the Center for Korean Studies and Department of East Asian Languages and Literatures of the University of Hawai'i for providing office space as well as moral support, and to the University of Hawai'i Press for publishing the KLEAR textbooks.

Ho-min Sohn, KLEAR President

INTRODUCTION

What Kind of Language Is Korean?

This unit provides students with essential information on the linguistic features of Korean. The McCune-Reischauer system is followed in romanizing Korean expressions. Han'gŭl is provided for students who are familiar with the script.

1. Speakers
Korean is a language spoken
  a. as a native language by 67 million Korean people living on the Korean peninsula, including 23 million North Koreans and 44 million South Koreans;
  b. as a heritage language by 5.6 million overseas Korean residents, among them 2 million in China, 2 million in the United States, 0.7 million in Japan, and 0.5 million in the former Soviet Union;
  c. as a foreign language by an ever-increasing number of non-Koreans worldwide.

In terms of the number of speakers, Korean is rated eleventh among over 3,000 languages in the world.

2. Dialects
The Korean language consists of seven geographically based dialects:
  a. Central dialect (Seoul and vicinity), the standard language (*p'yojun-ŏ* 'Standard Language') of South Korea;
  b. *Ch'ungch'ŏng* dialect, spoken in the Ch'ungch'ŏng province areas located between the central and southern dialect zones;
  c. *Chŏlla* dialect, spoken in the southwest;
  d. *Kyŏngsang* dialect, spoken in the southeast;
  e. *P'yŏngan* dialect (P'yŏngyang and vicinity), the standard language (called *munhwa-ŏ* 'Cultured Language') of North Korea;
  f. *Hamgyŏng* dialect, spoken in the northeast;
  g. *Cheju* dialect, spoken on the island of Cheju.

Superimposed on these geographical divisions is a sociopolitical dialectal difference between North and South Korea due to the division of the country in 1945. North

Koreans have replaced thousands of Chinese character-based words with newly coined native words while using many expressions laden with Communist ideology. On the other hand, South Koreans use a large number of loanwords borrowed recently from English.

MAP OF DIALECTAL ZONES

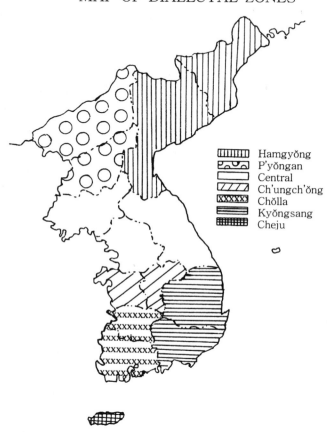

⊞⊞⊞	Hamgyŏng
ꛂꛂ	P'yŏngan
☐	Central
⧄⧄	Ch'ungch'ŏng
✕✕✕✕✕	Chŏlla
☰☰☰	Kyŏngsang
⊞⊞⊞	Cheju

Despite such geographical and sociopolitical dialectal differences, Korean is relatively homogeneous, with excellent mutual intelligibility among speakers from different areas. Mass media and formal education based on standard speech greatly contribute to the standardization of the language. Since North Korea's P'yŏngyang-based "Cultured Language" contains many elements of South Korea's Seoul-based "Standard Language", the linguistic divergence between the two Koreas is not as great as often claimed.

3. Relationship to other languages

The closest sister language of Korean is Japanese, although they are not mutually intelligible, and their relationship is much weaker than that between, say, English and French. Some scholars claim that Korean and Japanese are remotely related to the so-called Altaic languages such as native Manchu, Mongolian, and the Turkic languages. Thus, Korean and Japanese are often called Altaic languages.

Although Korea and Japan are geographically, historically, and culturally close to China, Korean and Japanese are not part of the same language family as Chinese, and therefore are not grammatically related to Chinese. However, both Korean and Japanese have borrowed a large number of Chinese words and characters throughout the course of their long historical contact with various Chinese dynasties. Such borrowed Chinese words and characters have become integral parts of the Korean and Japanese vocabularies. Since identical words and characters evolved independently in the three countries, their current pronunciations are considerably different. For example, the Chinese character words for 'Korea' and 'college' are pronounced differently in the three countries, as approximately transcribed below:

	'Korea'	'college'
Mandarin Chinese	*han-kwo*	*ta-she*
Korean	*han-guk*	*tae-hak*
Japanese	*kan-koku*	*dai-gaku*

Korea also borrowed from Japan a large number of words that the Japanese created based on Chinese characters (e.g., *yŏnghwa* 'movie', *iryoil* 'Sunday', *kwahak* 'science', *ipku* 'entrance', *yaksok* 'promise'). Numerous words have also been created by Koreans with Chinese characters as building blocks (e.g., *p'yŏnji* 'letter', *sikku* 'family members', *samch'on* 'uncle', *ilgi* 'weather', *oesang* 'on credit'). All of these Chinese character-based words are called "Sino-Korean" or "Chinese-character" words.

Since the end of World War II, Korean people have been in contact with many foreign countries and have borrowed from them thousands of words, the majority of which are English. During the thirty-five-year occupation of Korea by Japan, a considerable number of native Japanese words were also borrowed. At the same time, many Western words that the Japanese had borrowed were re-borrowed into Korean through Japanese. All such borrowed words are termed "loanwords."

4. Vocabulary

The Korean vocabulary is composed of three components: native words and affixes (approximately 35 percent), Sino-Korean words (approximately 60 percent), and loanwords (approximately 5 percent). Native words denote daily necessities (food, clothing, and shelter), locations, basic actions, activities, and states, lower-level numerals, body parts, natural objects, animals, etc. The native stock includes thousands of sound symbolic (onomatopoeic and mimetic) words and idioms and proverbs that reflect traditional culture and society. Most of the particles and affixes in Korean are from the native stock.

Due to their ideographic and monosyllabic nature, Chinese characters are easily combined and recombined to coin new terms as new cultural objects and concepts are created. Even the name of the country (*han-guk* 'Korea') is a Sino-Korean word, as we have seen above. So are most institutional terms, traditional cultural terms, personal names, and place names (except for *Seoul*, which is a native word).

There are about 14,000 loanwords in Korean, of which almost 90 percent are from English. Loanwords such as the following are commonly used in daily life, facilitating cross-cultural communication to a certain extent.

Loanword	**Pronunciation**	**Spelling**
apartment	*ap'at'ŭ*	아파트
ballpoint pen	*polp'en*	볼펜
boiler	*poillŏ*	보일러
cake	*k'eik'ŭ*	케이크
coffee	*k'ŏp'i*	커피
computer	*k'ŏmp'yut'ŏ*	컴퓨터
condo(minium)	*k'ondo*	콘도
elevator	*ellibeit'ŏ*	엘리베이터
engine	*enjin*	엔진
fax	*p'aeksŭ*	팩스
golf	*kolp'ŭ*	골프
hotel	*hot'el*	호텔
ice cream	*aisŭk'ŭrim*	아이스크림
motorcycle	*ot'obai* .	오토바이
opera	*op'era*	오페라

orange juice	*orenji jusŭ*	오렌지주스
sports	*s'ŭp'och'ŭ*	스포츠
stress	*s'ŭt'ŭresŭ*	스트레스
super(market)	*syup'ŏ*	슈퍼
taxi	*t'aeksi*	택시
television	*t'ellebijŏn*	텔레비전

Notice that the sounds of the original words are slightly modified in the loanwords according to the available sound pattern of Korean. If the words are pronounced as native speakers of the original forms normally do, they are not loanwords, but foreign words.

5. Word order

Korean, like Japanese, is a verb- or adjective-final language. The verb or adjective usually comes at the end of the sentence or clause, while all other elements, including the subject and the object, appear before the verb or adjective. In the English sentence *John plays tennis with Mary at school*, for example, *John* is the subject because it appears before the verb and denotes an entity which the rest of the sentence is about and *tennis* is its object because it appears immediately after the verb and denotes an entity that directly receives the action of the verb *plays*. The other elements (*with Mary* and *at school*) follow the object. The Korean word order would be *John school-at Mary-with tennis plays*. Notice here that while English prepositions always occur before a noun or a pronoun, Korean particles (equivalent to English prepositions) always occur *after* the element they are associated with, as in *school-at* and *Mary-with*. Korean particles are all postpositions.

Korean is often called a "free word order" language because it permits the elements before the verb or adjective to be scrambled for emphatic or other figurative purposes, as long as the verb or adjective retains the final position. Thus, for example, the neutral order of *John school-at Mary-with tennis plays* may be changed to *school-at Mary-with John tennis plays*; *Mary-with tennis John school-at plays*; *tennis John school-at Mary-with plays*; etc.

6. Situation-orientated language

Korean is often called a situation-oriented language in that contextually or situationally understood elements (including subject and object) are omitted more frequently than not. Observe the following expressions in comparison to their

English counterparts and notice that the subject does not appear in any of the Korean expressions.

a. *annyŏnghaseyo?* 안녕하세요?   How are you?
   are peaceful

b. *komapsŭmnida.* 고맙습니다.   Thank you.
   am thankful

c. *ŏdi kaseyo?*   어디 가세요?   Where are you going?
   where go

Inserting the pronoun 'you' or 'I' in the above Korean expressions would sound awkward in normal contexts, unless 'you' or 'I' is emphasized or contrasted with someone else.

7. Macro-to-micro language

Korean, like Japanese, is a "macro-to-micro" language, in that the universe is represented in the order of a set (macro) and its members (micro). Thus, for example, Koreans say or write the family name first and then the given name, optionally followed by a title; say or write an address in the order of country, province, city, street, house number, and personal name; and refer to time with year first and day last.

a. *Kim Minsu kyosu-nim*   김민수 교수님   Prof. Minsu Kim
   Kim Minsu Professor

b. *Sŏul Chung-gu P'il-tong 1*   서울 중구 필동 1   1 P'il Street,
   Seoul Chung-district P'il-street 1   Chung District,
                                                         Seoul

c. *2000-nyŏn ir-wŏl i-il*   2000년 일월 이 일   January 2, 2000
   2000-year 1-month 2-day

8. Honorific expressions

Korean may be called an honorific language, in that different forms of expressions and different speech levels are used depending on the person you are talking to as well as the person you are talking about. While interpersonal differences in terms of relative age, kinship, social status, etc., are largely ignored in the structure and use of English, they are systematically encoded in the structure and use of Korean. For instance, compare the English and Korean in a father and son saying good night.

English Son: *Good night, Dad.*
Father: *Good night, John.*

Korean Son: *abŏji, annyŏngi chumuseyo.* 아버지 안녕히 주무세요.
father peacefully sleep
Father: *nŏ do chal chara.* 너도 잘 자라.
you also well sleep

Notice in English that son and father use the same expression except for the address terms, a kinship term by the son and a given name by the father. In Korean, on the other hand, they use entirely different expressions. Not a single element is shared. Under no circumstances may the son use any part of his father's utterance in saying good night to his father, and vice versa. Honorific and plain forms appear in the following categories.

Address/reference terms

Korean has an extensive set of address and reference terms that are sensitive to degrees of social stratification and distance between speaker and addressee and between speaker and referent. The most frequently used terms for a social superior or an adult distant equal are composed of an occupational title followed by the gender-neutral honorific suffix *-nim* 님 (lit. honorable). The full or family name may precede this.

Kim Minsu kyosu-nim   김민수 교수님   Prof. Minsu Kim
Kim sŏnsaeng-nim   김 선생님   Teacher Kim
kyosu-nim   교수님   Professor

There are several title words. The most frequently used one among young company colleagues or to an adult junior is the gender-neutral noun *ssi*. This noun is attached to a full name or a given name, as follows.

Kim Yujin ssi	김유진 씨
Yujin ssi	유진 씨

To address or refer to a child, either a full name without any title word or a given name alone is used. Such a bare name is never used to an adult except by his/her own parent or teacher. When addressing a child by a given name, the particle *a* 아 (after a consonant) or *ya* 야 (after a vowel) is used.

Kim Yujin	김유진	(address/reference)
Minsu	민수	(address/reference)
Yujin-a!	유진아	(address)
Minsu-ya!	민수야	(address)

Honorific and humble words

A small number of commonly used words have two forms, one plain and the other honorific. The honorific forms are used for an adult equal or senior, whereas the plain forms are used for a junior or child, as illustrated below.

Plain		Honorific		
pap	밥	*chinji*	진지	'rice, meal'
chip	집	*taek*	댁	'house'
irŭm	이름	*sŏngham*	성함	'name'
nai	나이	*yŏnse*	연세	'age'
mŏk-ta	먹다	*chapsusi-da*	잡수시다	'eat'
cha-da	자다	*chumusi-da*	주무시다	'sleep'
it-ta	있다	*kyesi-da*	계시다	'stay'

There is also a small number of humble verbs used to express deference to a senior person.

Plain	Humble
chu-da 주다 'give to a junior' *po-da* 보다 'see a junior'	*tŭri-da* 드리다 'give to a senior' *pwep-ta* 뵙다 'see a senior'

Pronouns

Korean has both plain and humble first person pronouns ('I'): *na* 나 (plain singular), *uri* 우리 (plain plural); *chŏ* 저 (humble singular), *chŏ-hŭi* 저희 (humble plural). *Chŏ* and *chŏ-hŭi are* used when talking to a senior or a socially distant adult.

There are several second person pronouns ('you') such as *nŏ* 너 (singular) and *nŏ-hŭi* (plural) addressed to children. No second person pronoun may be used to refer to an adult equal or senior. Thus, one continuing cultural observation is that Korean does not have a second person pronoun for an adult equal or senior. The only alternative is to use address/reference terms as second person pronouns, for example, *(Kim) sŏnsaeng-nim* (김) 선생님 'you teacher (Kim)'.

Speech levels

Korean has six speech levels that indicate the speaker's interpersonal relationship with the addressee. These speech levels are indicated by sentence-final suffixes attached to verbs and adjectives. These suffixes are illustrated below with the declarative (statement) sentence type. There are also interrogative (question), imperative (command, request), and propositive (suggestion) suffixes.

a. deferential style	-*(sŭ)mnida*	습니다/ㅂ니다
b. polite style	-*ŏyo/-ayo*	어요/아요
c. blunt style [infrequent]	-*so/-o*	소/오
d. familiar style [infrequent]	-*ne*	네
e. intimate style	-*ŏ/-a*	어/아
f. plain style	-*ta/-da*	다

For example, *mŏk-sŭmnida* 먹습니다, *mŏg-ŏyo* 먹어요, *mŏk-so* 먹소, *mŏng-ne* 먹네, *mŏg-ŏ* 먹어, and *mŏng-nŭn-da* 먹는다 all mean '(someone) eats', expressed in different speech levels. Younger speakers use only the deferential, polite, intimate, and plain levels.

The most common level used to an adult is the polite one, which is less formal than but just as polite as the deferential level. While the deferential level is used mostly by male speakers, the polite level is widely used by both males and females in daily conversation. Both the polite and the deferential levels are used to address a socially equal or superior adult, but in general, the polite level is favored between close adult friends. Even in a formal situation, both the deferential and polite levels are usually used by the same speaker in the same conversation. In formal occasions such as news reports and public lectures, only the deferential level is used.

The intimate level, which is also referred to as the "half-talk" level (polite form minus *-yo* 요), may be used by an adult to a student, by a child of preschool age to his or her family members, including parents, or between close friends whose friendship began in childhood or adolescence.

The plain level is typically used by any speaker to any child, to younger siblings, children, or grandchildren regardless of age, to a daughter-in-law, between intimate adult friends whose friendship started in childhood, and in writing for a general audience. This level is frequently intermixed with the intimate level.

Subject honorific suffix

When the subject of a sentence is an adult equal or a senior, the so-called subject honorific suffix *-(ŭ)se* (으)세 before the polite ending *-yo* 요, or *-(ŭ)si* (으)시 before other suffixes, is attached to the verb or adjective, as follows:

a. *annŏngha-**se**-yo.*   (polite)   안녕하**세**요?   How are you?
   be peaceful

b. *annŏngha-**si**-mnikka.* (deferential) 안녕하**십**니까?   How are you?
   be peaceful

Nonverbal behavior

Nonverbal behavior parallels hierarchical verbal expressions. For example, one bows to a senior person such as a professor when arriving or leaving. The senior person does not bow to a junior. A junior person is required to behave properly in the presence of an ingroup senior, e.g., he or she is not to smoke in front of an ingroup senior.

9. Words and word classes

Sentences consist of words. For example, the sentence *chŏ nun han'gugŏ sŏnsaengnim ieyo* 저는 한국어 선생님 이에요 'I am a teacher of Korean' consists of five words: *chŏ* 저 'I', *nŭn* 는 'as for', *han'gugŏ* 한국어 'the Korean language', *sŏnsaengnim* 선생님 'a teacher', and *ieyo* 이에요 'is, are, am'. A word may consist of a single meaning unit, as in *chŏ* 'I' and *nŭn* 'as for', or may contain one or more additional elements such as suffixes, as in *han'gugŏ* 'the Korean language' (*han'guk* 'Korea' + suffix *-ŏ* 'language'), *sŏnsaengnim* 'a teacher' (*sŏnsaeng* 'a teacher' + suffix *-nim* 'Mr./Ms.'), and *ieyo* 'is, are, am' (*i* 'be' + sentence-ending suffix *-eyo* [polite level]). Based on how they function in sentences, all words are classified into the following classes and subclasses. These word classes and subclasses are given in each lesson under "New Words and Expressions."

1. **Nouns** (naming all kinds of objects, function as the grammatical subject or object of a verb or adjective):
   common nouns, e.g., *irŭm* 이름 'a name', *ch'aek* 책 'a book'
   proper nouns, e.g., *han'guk* 한국 'Korea', *Sŭt'ibŭ* 스티브 'Steve'
   counters, e.g., *kwa* 과 (counter for lessons), *mari* 마리 (counter for animals)
   loanwords, e.g., *k'ŭllaesŭ* 클래스 'a class', *pilding* 빌딩 'a building'
2. **Pronouns** (substitute for nouns or noun equivalents): e.g., *na* 나 'I' (plain), *chŏ* 저 'I' (humble), *uri* 우리 'we', *muŏt* 무엇 'what', *nugu* 누구 'who', *ibun* 이분 'this person (he/she)', *igŏs* 이것 'this (thing)'
3. **Numbers** (indicate numbers, including native and Sino-Korean words): native numbers, e.g., *hana/han* 하나/한 'one', *tul/tu* 둘/두 'two'; Sino-Korean numbers, e.g., *il* 일 'one', *i* 이 'two', *sam* 삼 'three'
4. **Verbs** (denote action or progress): e.g., *kada* 가다 'to go', *kongbuhada* 공부하다 'to study', *mŏkta* 먹다 'to eat', *poepta* 뵙다 'to see (a senior)'
5. **Adjectives** (denote state, either physical or psychological): e.g., *annyŏnghada* 안녕하다 'to be well', *mant'a* 많다 'to be much, many', *chot'a* 좋다 'to be good'
6. **Copulas** (a special subclass of adjectives, denoting equation, identification, or definition): e.g., *ita* 이다 'to be', *anita* 아니다 'to not-be'
7. **Adverbs** (modify a verb, an adjective, another adverb, a clause, a sentence, or a discourse): e.g., *aju* 아주 'very much', *yojum* 요즘 'these days', *chal* 잘 'well', *a* 아 'ah!', *ne* 네 'yes, I see', *anio* 아니오 'no'

8. **Pre-nouns** (occur only before a noun, and include demonstratives and expressions of quality and quantity): e.g., *i* 이 'this', *ku* 그 'that (near you or the subject of discussion)', *chŏ* 저 'that over there', *ŏnŭ* 어느 'which (one)', *musŭn* 무슨 'what kind of', *myŏt* 몇 'how many'

9. **Conjunctions** (connect two sentences): e.g., *kŭrigo* 그리고 'and', *kŭrŏnde* 그런데 'by the way', *kŭraesŏ* 그래서 'so'

10. **Particles** (following a noun or noun equivalent, indicate its grammatical relation or delimit its meaning): e.g., *i/ka* 이/가 (subject), *e* 에 'at, on, in', *ŭn/nŭn* 은/는 'as for', *to* 도 'also', *man* 만 'only'

Korean verbs and adjectives cannot stand alone; they must be followed by a sentence- or clause-ending suffix. For example, *mŏk-* 먹 'eat', *annyŏngha-* 안녕하 'be well', and *i-* 이 'be' cannot be used without an ending suffix, as in *mŏgŏyo* 먹어요 'eats', *annyŏnghaseyo* 안녕하세요 'How are you?' and *ieyo* 이에요 'is, am, are'. A bare verb or adjective form without a suffix is called a verb stem or an adjective stem. As dictionary entries, all verb and adjective stems are followed by the dictionary citation marker *-ta/-da* 다, as in *mŏkta* 먹다 'to eat', *annyŏnghada* 'to be well', and *ida* 'to be'. These are called dictionary forms.

10. The sound pattern

Korean speech sounds and the pattern of sound combinations are extremely different from English, Chinese, and Japanese. In English, for example, not only the plosive consonant sounds *p, t, ch, k,* and *s* but also their voiced counterparts *b, d, j, g,* and *z* occur in initial position in words, as in *pill/bill, tie/die, cheer/jeer, Kate/gate,* and *seal/zeal.* Korean does not allow such voiceless/voiced contrasts in initial position in words. Instead, Korean allows a three-way voiceless contrast (plain/aspirate/tense) in plosive consonants, a two-way contrast (plain/tense) in fricative consonants *s/ss* ㅅ/ㅆ, and no contrast (only plain) in the fricative consonant *h* ㅎ, as illustrated below.

a. plosive consonants:

pul	불	'fire'	*p'ul*	풀	'grass'	*ppul*	뿔	'horn'
tal	달	'moon'	*t'al*	탈	'mask'	*ttal*	딸	'daughter'
cha	자	'sleep'	*ch'a*	차	'kick'	*tcha*	짜	'salty'
kae	개	'dog'	*k'ae*	캐	'dig'	*kkae*	깨	'sesame'

   b. fricative consonants:

   si 시 'poem'   *ssi* 씨 'seeds'
   hae 해 'sun'

In addition to the above fifteen plosive and fricative consonants, Korean has the
"liquid" consonant *l* (pronounced as flap *r*, like Japanese and Spanish *r*, in initial
position or between vowels) and the nasal consonants *m* ㅁ, *n* ㄴ, and *ng* ㅇ.
   Thus, a total of nineteen consonants exists in Korean, as diagrammed below
(with the corresponding Korean alphabetic symbols):

Place Manner	LIPS	GUM RIDGE	HARD PALATE	SOFT PALATE	THROAT
PLOSIVE plain aspirate tense	*p* ㅂ *p'* ㅍ *pp* ㅃ	*t* ㄷ *t'* ㅌ *tt* ㄸ	*ch* ㅈ *ch'* ㅊ *tch* ㅉ	*k* ㄱ *k'* ㅋ *kk* ㄲ	
FRICATIVE plain tense		*s* ㅅ *ss* ㅆ			*h* ㅎ
LIQUID		*l* ㄹ			
NASAL	*m* ㅁ	*n* ㄴ		*ng* ㅇ	

These nineteen consonants alter their sound values depending on their position in a
word. For example, *p* ㅂ, *t* ㄷ, *ch* ㅈ, and *k* ㄱ become voiced *b, d, j,* and *g,*
respectively, between voiced sounds, as in *abŏji* 아버지 'father', *pada* 바다 'sea',
and *sagwa* 사과 'apple'. *hak* 학 'study' in *hak-saeng* 학생 'student' changes to
hang in *hang-nyŏn* 학년 'school year' because the following consonant is nasal.
Kkoch' 꽃 'flower' in *kkoch'-i* 꽃이 'flower (subject)' changes to *kkot* in *kkot-tto*
꽃도 'flower also' or when it occurs by itself, and to *kkon* in *kkon-man* 꽃만
'flower only'. These and numerous other sound-alternating phenomena will be
observed and drilled in great detail throughout this volume. Notice in all of the
above examples that Korean orthographic spellings are not changed despite the
sound alternations.

There are eight vowel sounds in standard Korean, as represented below:

TONGUE POSITION	FRONT	BACK	
	unrounded	unrounded	rounded
HIGH MID LOW	*i* ㅣ *e* ㅔ *ae* ㅐ	*ŭ* ㅡ *ŏ* ㅓ *a* ㅏ	*u* ㅜ *o* ㅗ

Front/back and high/mid/low refer to tongue positions, and unrounded/rounded refers to the shape of the lips in producing the relevant vowels.

There are two semivowels, *y* and *w*. Examples: *yŏngŏ* 영어 'English', *hakkyo* 학교 'school', *syup'ŏ* 슈퍼 'supermarket', *wŏryoil* 월요일 'Monday', and *kwa* 과 'lesson'.

The syllable structure of spoken Korean is outlined in (a) below, where parentheses stand for optional appearance. Only the vowel is a required element in a spoken syllable. The dot (.) stands for a spoken syllable boundary.

a. .(consonant) (semivowel) VOWEL (consonant).

b. *i*   이 'this'   *yŏl* 열 '10'   *kŭ* 그 'that'
  ot   옷 'clothes'   *pyŏl* 별 'star'

c. *Sŏ.ul* 서울 'Seoul'   *sŏn.saeng.nim* 선생님 'teacher'
  i.rŭm 이름 'name'

While English allows up to three consonants in syllable-initial and syllable-final positions, as in "strike" and "tasks," Korean allows only one consonant in those positions. Thus, for example, the single-syllable English word *strike* is borrowed into Korean as a five-syllable loanword, *sŭ.t'ŭ.ra.i.k'ŭ* 스트라이크, with the insertion of the vowel *ŭ* 으 to make it conform to Korean syllable structure. Similarly, the final *s* ㅅ in the Korean word *kaps* 값 'price' in *kaps-i (kap.ssi)* 값이 'price (subject)' becomes silent before a consonant or when the word occurs alone, because a spoken syllable does not allow two consonants after a vowel, thus: *kap.tto* 값도 'price also' and *kap* 값 'price'.

11. Writing systems

Currently Korean is written by means of a mixed script of the Korean phonetic alphabet called Han'gŭl 한글 (meaning "the great writing") and Chinese characters. Han'gŭl is used to represent all Korean vocabulary, including native words, Sino-Korean words and loanwords, and any foreign words. Chinese characters are used only to represent Sino-Korean words. For centuries before Han'gŭl was created by King Sejong the Great, the fourth king of the Chosŏn dynasty, and his royal scholars in 1443, only Chinese characters had been used. Koreans are truly proud of Han'gŭl, one of the most scientific writing systems that has ever been created.

The current trend shows increasing use of Han'gŭl spellings over Chinese characters. Even in newspapers and scholarly books, use of Chinese characters is extremely limited. Chinese characters are often useful in differentiating the meanings of identically pronounced and spelled Han'gŭl words.

Unlike Chinese characters, which represent meanings of words, and Japanese characters, which represent syllables, the characters of the Han'gŭl alphabet represent individual sounds such as consonants and vowels. Details of Han'gŭl orthography are presented in "Han'gŭl and Pronunciation," below.

12. Learning Korean

Arabic, Chinese, Japanese, and Korean are among the most difficult languages for native English speakers to learn because of the vast differences between English and these languages in vocabulary, pronunciation, grammar, and writing system, as well as in the underlying tradition, culture, and society. English speakers require three times as much time to learn these "difficult" languages than to learn "easy" languages, such as French or Spanish, to attain a comparable level of proficiency. Indeed, English-speaking students who study Korean deserve praise for undertaking such a difficult but invaluable language, which has enormous cultural, academic, economic, and strategic significance.

한글 Han'gŭl and Pronunciation

In this unit, students learn how the individual letters and syllable blocks of the Korean alphabet, Han'gŭl (한글), are written and pronounced, how the Korean alphabetic letters are ordered in dictionaries, word lists, and indexes, and how correct pronunciations are obtained from a variety of Han'gŭl spellings by means of a simple set of pronunciation rules. Students will also learn how to romanize Han'gŭl according to the McCune-Reischauer system of romanization, which is widely used by scholars, library cataloguers, and the educated public in English-speaking countries.

1. 한글 Han'gŭl

1.1 Introduction

Korean speech sounds are graphically represented by Han'gŭl letters. The individual consonant and vowel letters of Han'gŭl are combined into syllable blocks to spell Korean words and sentences. For example, the consonant sound *h* is represented by the Han'gŭl letter ㅎ, the vowel sound *a* by the letter ㅏ, and the consonant sound *n* by the letter ㄴ. The three letters ㅎ, ㅏ, and ㄴ are combined as the syllable block 한 to be pronounced *han*, which means 'one' or 'great' in Korean.

　　Similarly, the consonant *k* or *g* is represented by ㄱ, the vowel *ŭ* by ㅡ (pronounced somewhat like English *u* in p*u*t and *oo* in g*oo*d), and the consonant *l* (like English *l* in p*l*ease) by ㄹ. These letters are combined as 글 and pronounced *kŭl* or *gŭl*. This syllable means 'writing' or 'script'. The two syllable blocks 한글 are pronounced as *han.gŭl*, which means 'the great writing', the literal name of the Korean alphabet.

ㅎ	+	ㅏ	+	ㄴ	=	한	han
ㄱ	+	ㅡ	+	ㄹ	=	글	kŭl/gŭl
한	+	글			=	한글	han.gŭl

Remember that a syllable must contain one and only one vowel. Since the word 한글 has two vowels, it has two syllables.

Notice in the above that ㄱ is pronounced as either *k* or *g*. When ㄱ is preceded and followed by "voiced" (vocal-cord vibrating) sounds such as a vowel or *n, m, ng,* or *l,* it is pronounced as the voiced sound *g,* as in 한글 *han.gŭl* where ㄴ *n* and ㅡ *ŭ* are voiced sounds. Otherwise it is pronounced as a voiceless *k,* as in the independently pronounced 글 *kŭl* or 학 *hak.* Similarly, the letter ㄹ is associated with two sounds, *l* and *r* (flap *r* like American English *t* in *water* and Japanese and Spanish *r*). It is pronounced as *l* when it appears at the end of a syllable, as in 글 *kŭl.* It is pronounced as *r* between two vowels, as in 나라 *na.ra* 'country'. We will see more on the pronunciations of ㄹ later.

Practice 1   Transcribe the following syllable blocks in Roman letters in the spaces provided.

할	날	낙	각	간
근	흔	늘	는	흑
가난	그늘	한근	나는	극한
하늘	나를	그가	가락	흔한

Practice 2   Write the following in 한글.

han.gŭl	kŭ.rŭl	nan.gan
kŭn.hak	ha.na	kŭ.nŭl

한글 is written either horizontally across the page, as in this book, or vertically, as in many South Korean newspaper. In North Korea, only the horizontal writing is practiced.

1.2 Vowel letters

Letter shapes

한글 consists of vowel and consonant letters corresponding to vowel and consonant sounds in Korean speech. All vowel letters are composed of one or more of three kinds of strokes: a long vertical stroke (ㅣ), a long horizontal stroke (ㅡ), and a short horizontal or vertical stroke (˗ or ㅣ). The short stroke was originally a round dot (•). The three basic strokes were modeled after the cosmological philosophy of heaven (•), earth (ㅡ), and human being (ㅣ).

한글 has six simple letters and two compound letters to represent eight simple vowel sounds. (We have seen that the spelling 한글 contains two of these vowel letters, ㅏ and ㅡ.)

simple letters	ㅏ	ㅓ	ㅗ	ㅜ	ㅡ	ㅣ
	a	*ŏ*	*o*	*u*	*ŭ*	*i*
compound letters	ㅐ	ㅔ				
	ae	*e*				

ㅐ is the combination of ㅏ and ㅣ, and ㅔ is the combination of ㅓ and ㅣ. In fact, when 한글 was created, ㅐ was pronounced as *ay* and ㅔ as *ŏy*. They have subsequently evolved into the simple vowels *ae* and *e*, respectively.

The short stroke is placed horizontally on a long vertical vowel stroke, as in ㅏ and ㅓ and vertically on a long horizontal stroke, as in ㅗ and ㅜ. The vowel sounds with a short stroke on the right or above a long stroke (ㅏ and ㅗ) are called "bright" vowels, whereas the vowels with a short stroke on the left or below a long stroke (ㅓ and ㅜ) are called "dark" vowels, because the former sounds are perceived as brighter or more sonorous to native speakers than the latter. The vowels represented by ㅡ and ㅣ are neutral vowels. A bright vowel and a dark vowel are not combined in a single syllable block in making a diphthong.

bright vowels	ㅏ ㅗ
dark vowels	ㅓ ㅜ
neutral vowels	ㅡ ㅣ

Of the eight vowel letters given above, five are upright or vertical whereas the remaining three are lying or horizontal. In writing a syllable block, an initial consonant letter is placed on the left side of a vertical vowel letter, as in 한 and on top of a horizontal vowel letter, as in 글.

Practice 3 The basic stroke order in 한글 orthography is left to right and top to bottom, as in Chinese characters. Practice the orders:

ㅏ: ㅣ ⇒ ㅏ	ㅓ: ㅡ ⇒ ㅓ	
ㅗ: ㅣ ⇒ ㅗ	ㅜ: ㅡ ⇒ ㅜ	
ㅐ: ㅣ ⇒ ㅏ ⇒ ㅐ	ㅔ: ㅡ ⇒ ㅓ ⇒ ㅔ	
한: ㅎ ⇒ 하 ⇒ 한	글: ㄱ ⇒ 그 ⇒ 글	

Vowel pronunciation

The qualities of Korean vowels are not the same as those of English vowels, although they can be approximated as follows.

ㅏ	a	*father, yarn* (shorter than this *a*)
ㅓ	ŏ	*awake, young* (with the root of the tongue pulled back)
ㅗ	o	*own* (without the *w*-color)
ㅜ	u	*boo, you* (shorter than this *oo* or *ou*)
―	ŭ	*houses, put* (like ㅜ but without lip-rounding)
ㅣ	i	*see* (shorter than this *ee*)
ㅐ	ae	*care*
ㅔ	e	*met, yes*

The eight simple vowels of Korean may be arranged in box form as follows.

ㅣ	―	ㅜ
ㅔ	ㅓ	ㅗ
ㅐ	ㅏ	

Each vowel is located at the approximate place where it is articulated in the mouth. For example, the vowel ㅣ *i* is produced when the top of the tongue approaches the hard palate, the vowel ㅜ *u* when the back of the tongue approaches the rear part of the soft palate, and the vowel ㅏ *a* when the space between the back of the lowered tongue and the soft palate is widened. Only ㅜ and ㅗ are pronounced with the lips rounded.

Practice 4 | Listen to and repeat after the instructor in producing the eight vowels. Notice the tongue positions for each vowel. Pay attention to the different spacings between the tongue and the palate.

The vowels ㅔ *e* and ㅐ *ae* are very similar. Although they can be distinguished by careful pronunciation when you repeat after your instructor, both of these vowels are pronounced indistinguishably by many speakers in casual speech as a sound between *e* and *ae*. However, the difference is maintained in writing, as in 게 'crab' and 개 'dog'.

Since accurate pronunciation of the eight vowels is essential in learning spoken Korean, make a special effort to keep English pronunciation from interfering with your learning of Korean vowels. Completely master the pronunciations of the eight basic vowels through intensive practice with your instructor and via tape recording.

Practice 5 | Listen to your instructor and identify the vowels being pronounced by the instructor.

(a) 가   (b) 개   (c) 거   (d) 게
(e) 고   (f) 구   (g) 그   (h) 기

Practice 6 | Listen to and pronounce each of the following pairs many times. Have your pronunciations checked by the instructor.

(a) 가, 거   (b) 거, 고   (c) 그, 거   (d) 고, 그
(e) 그, 구   (f) 구, 고   (g) 게, 거   (h) 개, 가

Practice 7 | Listen to your instructor, and write down the syllable blocks in the order you hear them.

Examples: (a) 고, 그, 거, 구   (b) 누, 노, 너, 느
               (c) 허, 흐, 호, 후   (d) 글, 걸, 갈, 굴, 골

There is a distinction between short and long vowels in many words, although this distinction is not represented in 한글 orthography. For example, when 눈 is pronounced short, it means 'eye', whereas when it is pronounced long, it means 'snow'. Similarly, a short 밤 is 'night' and a long 밤 is 'chestnut'; and a short 말 is 'horse' and a long 말 is 'language'. This short-long distinction, which is relatively strict in the speech of the older generation, has disappeared in the speech of the younger generation.

1.3 Diphthong (semivowel + vowel) letters

Diphthongs with the semivowel *y*

One additional short stroke makes each of the six single-letter vowels a diphthong with *y,* as follows. Remember that stroke order is top-to-bottom and left-to-right.

simple vowel ⇒ diphthong	stroke order
ㅏ ⇒ ㅑ *ya*	ㅣ ⇒ ㅏ ⇒ ㅑ
ㅓ ⇒ ㅕ *yŏ*	─ ⇒ = ⇒ ㅕ
ㅗ ⇒ ㅛ *yo*	ㅣ ⇒ ‖ ⇒ ㅛ
ㅜ ⇒ ㅠ *yu*	─ ⇒ ㅜ ⇒ ㅠ
ㅐ ⇒ ㅒ *yae*	ㅣ ⇒ ㅏ ⇒ ㅑ ⇒ ㅒ
ㅔ ⇒ ㅖ *ye*	─ ⇒ = ⇒ ㅕ ⇒ ㅖ

The distinction between ㅐ and ㅔ is lost in casual speech, both being pronounced as ㅔ, but is retained in writing as well as in extremely careful pronunciation.

| Practice 8 | Repeat after your instructor in pronouncing the following syllable blocks several times, and then identify in writing the ones pronounced by your instructor. |

가,   겨,   교,   규,   개,   계

| Practice 9 | Read the following syllables in the order given until you become completely fluent. Dictionary entries follow this order. |

가,   개,   갸,   걔,   거,   게,   겨,   계,
고,   교,   구,   규,   그,   기

Diphthongs with the semivowel *w* and the diphthong *ŭi*

There are six diphthongs beginning with the sound *w* (as in English *week, Washington, work*). These are graphically expressed by combining two simple vowel letters. The letters ㅗ and ㅜ are used to represent the semivowel sound *w*. There is an idiosyncratic diphthong which consists of ㅡ and ㅣ.

simple vowel	+	simple vowel	=	diphthong	
ㅗ	+	ㅏ	=	과	*wa*
ㅗ	+	ㅐ	=	괘	*wae*
ㅗ	+	ㅣ	=	괴	*we*
ㅜ	+	ㅓ	=	궈	*wŏ*
ㅜ	+	ㅔ	=	궤	*we*
ㅜ	+	ㅣ	=	귀	*wi*
ㅡ	+	ㅣ	=	의	*ŭi*

Practice 10 | Practice proper stroke order in writing the combinations
above.

Example: ㅣ → ㅗ → ㅚ → 나

The letters ㅚ and ㅔ, which used to be pronounced differently, are now pronounced identically as *we*, although the distinction is kept in writing.

Combinations of ㅗ + ㅓ, ㅗ + ㅔ, ㅜ + ㅏ, and ㅜ + ㅐ are not permitted. This is due to the so-called vowel harmony principle in Korean, which does not allow a bright vowel (ㅏ, ㅗ) to be combined with a dark vowel (ㅜ, ㅓ) within a syllable, although either may combine with the neutral vowel ㅣ, as in ㅐ, ㅔ, ㅚ and ㅟ. Thus, for example, the syllable blocks 과, 귀, 꽤, and 꿰 are acceptable, whereas 궈, 꽈, 괘, and 꿰 are not.

The diphthong ㅢ is unstable and is pronounced as *ŭ* or *ŭi* (in word-initial position not preceded by a consonant) and *i* (in non-initial position and after a consonant in initial position). For example, the word 의논 'discussion' is pronounced as *ŭ.non* or *ŭi.non* (ㅇ in the syllable block 의 is a silent or zero consonant). 흰 'white' is pronounced only as *hin* because ㅢ is preceded by a consonant, ㅎ. (In addition, the possessive particle 의 'of' is uniquely pronounced like 에 *e*.)

Practice 11 | Repeat after your instructor in pronouncing the following
syllable blocks several times, and then write down the ones
pronounced by the instructor.

화,   홰,   회,   희,   휘,   훼,   휘

Practice 12 | Read and write the following syllable blocks many times in
the order given. This is the order that Korean students
learn for dictionary and other uses.

(a)   가,   개,   갸,   걔,
(b)   거,   게,   겨,   계,
(c)   고,   과,   괘,   괴,   교,
(d)   구,   궈,   궤,   귀,   규,
(e)   그,   긔,   기

1.4 Consonant letters

Letter shapes

There are nineteen consonant letters. Consonant letters originally depicted the speech organs that produce consonant sounds: the lips, tooth, tongue, and throat. The shapes of these organs are associated with the following 5 consonant letters.

ㅁ   *m*: lips

ㄴ   *n*: tongue tip touching the gum ridge

ㅅ   *s*: tooth (for hissing sounds)

ㄱ   *k/g*: tongue back touching the soft palate

ㅇ   *ng*: throat

The remaining fourteen consonants are produced in the same general areas as the above five places of articulation. Thus, the letters representing the sounds related to the above five sounds are derived by adding extra strokes to the basic letters.

Lip sounds

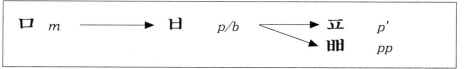

Gum-ridge (alveolar) sounds

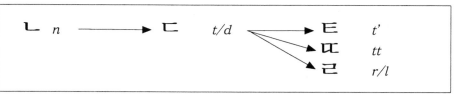

Hissing sounds (hard-palate sounds)

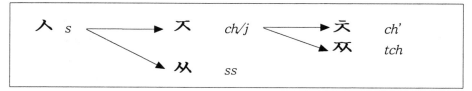

Soft-palate (velar) and throat sounds

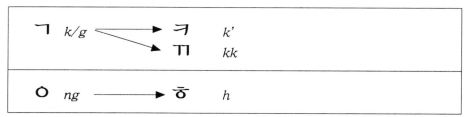

Practice 13 Write the 19 consonant letters repeatedly until you are able to remember them along with the romanized letters. In writing the letters, follow the correct stroke order, keeping the principle of left-to-right and top-to-bottom in mind.

Examples: ㄹ: ㄱ → ㄷ → ㄹ
                  ㅌ: ─ → ㄷ → ㅌ
                  ㅋ: ㄱ → ㅋ

Consonant pronunciation

Of the nineteen consonant letters given above, the sound qualities of the four
letters ㅁ, ㄴ, ㅇ, and ㅎ are essentially the same as in English: *m* (as in *map,
team*), *n* (as in *nose, moon*), *ng* (as in *song, king*), and *h* (as in *hit, hope*),
respectively. The only exception is that ㄴ is pulled to the hard-palate position
before the palatal vowel *i* or the semivowel *y,* as in 언니 and 안녕. This
pronunciation is called palatalization, in that ㄴ is assimilated to the palatal vowel
or semivowel.

The sound quality of ㄹ is very different from that of either English *l* or
English *r*, although ㄹ is romanized as *r/l*. In word-initial position, between two
vowels, or between a vowel and the consonant ㅎ, ㄹ is pronounced as a so-called
flap *r* like the Japanese or Spanish *r*. Examples: 라디오 *radio,* 나라 *nara,* and
말한다 *maranda.* In word-final position, between a vowel and a consonant, or when
adjacent to another ㄹ, it is pronounced like the so-called English light *l* that
appears before a vowel (e.g., *lung, slope*). Example: 말 *mal,* 말과 *mal.gwa,* and
빨리 *ppal.li.* In 나를 *na.rŭl,* for example, the first ㄹ in 를 is pronounced as a flap
r and the second ㄹ as a light *l*. In no situation does a so-called dark *l* (e.g.,
milk, bill) appear in Korean. This is the reason Koreans have difficulty
pronouncing English words with a dark *l* occurring in syllable-final position, and
English speakers have difficulty producing Korean light *l* when it occurs after a
vowel.

When two ㅁ's, ㄴ's, or ㄹ's occur in sequence, each ㅁ, ㄴ, or ㄹ is pronounced
distinctly, as in 감미 *kam.mi,* 반날 *pan.nal,* and 불량 *pul.lyang.*

| Practice 14 | Repeat after the instructor several times for the pronunciation
of the following words. Then pronounce them as directed.

    (a) 마음   (b) 엄마   (c) 한강   (d) 만남
    (e) 김치   (f) 노래   (g) 라일락   (h) 마을
    (i) 사람   (j) 안녕   (k) 영어   (l) 밀크

Korean has two distinctive kinds of *s*-sounds: plain ㅅ and tensed ㅆ, which is
tense in the sense that the speech organs involved become tensed for its
articulation. The tense ㅆ has the sound quality similar to the initial *s* in English
words like *sun* and *sea,* where *s* is followed by a vowel, whereas the plain ㅅ is
similar in sound quality to the *s* in words like *strong, spoil,* and *steam,* where *s*

is followed by a consonant. While English s is pronounced with the tip of the tongue approaching the gum-ridge area, the Korean ㅅ and ㅆ are produced with the top of the tongue approaching the gum-ridge and front part of the hard palate and the tongue tip touching the lower teeth. Both ㅅ and ㅆ are pronounced in the back part of the hard palate when they are followed by the palatal vowel i or semi-vowel y, as in 시, 쉬, 씨 and 샤쓰.

| Practice 15 | Pronounce the following pairs with particular attention to the plain and tense distinction, on one hand, and the palatalized and unpalatalized distinction, on the other.

Then write the words in 한글 as they are pronounced by the instructor.

(a) 사다   싸다
(b) 살   쌀
(c) 시름   씨름
(d) 시계   셔츠

The following twelve plosive consonants are contrasted with one another depending on whether they are pronounced with a puff of air (aspirated) and whether they are pronounced with muscle tension (tense) in the relevant speech organs. If neither quality is present, they are plain consonants.

Plain	Aspirated	Tense
ㅂ	ㅍ	ㅃ
ㄷ	ㅌ	ㄸ
ㅈ	ㅊ	ㅉ
ㄱ	ㅋ	ㄲ

In word-initial position in English, only the aspirated consonants corresponding exactly to the four aspirated Korean consonants occur, as in *pill, tall, church*, and *king*. In Korean, however, all plain, aspirated, and tense consonants occur in word-initial position. Thus, English speakers have no problem in pronouncing the four Korean aspirated consonants (ㅍ, ㅌ, ㅊ, ㅋ), but they need much practice to master the plain and tense sounds.

The Korean tense consonants ㅃ, ㄸ, ㅉ, and ㄲ are very similar to the underlined consonants in English words such as *speak, steam, midget,* and *skill,* respectively.

As for the plain set of plosive consonants, if you can eliminate the puff of air (aspiration) from the initial consonants in *pill, tall, church,* and *king,* you can pronounce Korean ㅂ, ㄷ, ㅈ, and ㄱ, respectively. Your instructor will tell you whether you are producing the Korean plain consonants correctly.

The plain consonants ㅂ, ㄷ, ㅈ, and ㄱ (but not ㅅ) undergo sound change in certain environments. When they are preceded and followed by voiced sounds such as vowels and nasal consonants, they are assimilated to these sounds and pronounced as the voiced sounds *b, d, j,* and *g,* respectively, as in 한번 더 *han.bŏn.dŏ,* 놀자 *nol.ja* and 한국 *han.guk.* In other environments they are voiceless, as in 밥 *pap,* 다시 *ta.si,* 질문 *chil.mun,* and 가요 *ka.yo.* In 부부 *pubu,* for example, the first 부 is articulated with a voiceless ㅂ *p* and the second 부 with a voiced ㅂ *b.*

Practice 16   Pronounce the following words with voiced and voiceless plain consonants.

ㅂ:	밥	바람	바보	공부	일본	가방
ㄷ:	달	대학	도둑	바다	어디	라디오
ㅈ:	집	질문	중국	자주	사전	어제
ㄱ:	길	교실	공책	가게	미국	불고기

Practice 17   Repeat after your instructor several times and have your pronunciations checked. Then identify, first verbally and then through spelling, the words the instructor pronounces from the following list.

1. (a) 불   (b) 풀   (c) 뿔
2. (a) 달   (b) 탈   (c) 딸
3. (a) 자다   (b) 차다   (c) 짜다
4. (a) 근   (b) 큰   (c) 끈

1.5 Syllable–block building

한글 letters are combined into syllable blocks. As has been observed, a square syllable block has one initial consonant position (C) followed by one vowel or diphthong position. In the final consonant (받침 *pat'ch'im*) position one or two consonants may occur.

    If a syllable does not have an initial consonant, the syllable block must have the letter ㅇ in the initial consonant position, as in 안 *an* or 위 *wi*. ㅇ is silent and functions as a zero consonant in the initial position of a syllable block. If the vowel letter in the syllable block contains only one or two long vertical strokes, it is written to the right of the initial consonant letter.

C	V

V = ㅏ ㅑ ㅓ ㅕ ㅣ ㅐ ㅖ ㅒ ㅖ

Examples: 나   이   해   계   따

If the vowel letter in the syllable block contains only a long horizontal stroke, the vowel letter is written below the initial consonant letter.

C
V

V = ㅗ ㅛ ㅜ ㅠ ㅡ

Examples: 드   무   토   유   쑤

If a diphthong letter contains a long horizontal stroke and a long vertical stroke, the initial consonant letter occurs in the upper left corner.

C	
V₁	V₂

$V_1 + V_2 =$ ㅘ ㅝ ㅚ ㅙ ㅞ ㅟ ㅢ

Examples: 뵈   왜   희   꿰   쉬

When a syllable has one or two final consonants (받침), they follow one of the following three models.

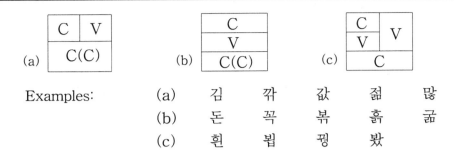

Examples: (a) 김 깎 값 젊 많
(b) 돈 꼭 볶 흙 굶
(c) 흰 뵙 꿩 봤

As final consonants (받침), the following two-letter combinations are available in addition to single consonant letters:

ㄲ, ㅆ ㄳ, ㄵ, ㄶ, ㄺ, ㄻ, ㄼ, ㄽ, ㄾ, ㄿ, ㅀ, ㅄ

In writing, the shape and size of the letters in syllable blocks should be balanced to fill the space.

Practice 18 Compose 한글 syllable blocks that correspond to the following romanized spellings.

pu.bu		*kim.ch'i*		*o.ren.ji*	
mi.guk		*ma.ra.t'on*		*kal.bi*	
talk		*k'ŏ.p'i.syop*		*ppal.lae*	
kulm.ŏ		*ŭlp'.ta*		*kang.a.ji*	
an.nyŏng.ha.se.yo				your name	

Practice 19 Pronounce the following and observe the differences between Korean and English pronunciations of the given words. Discuss in class the possible reasons for the pronunciation differences.

(a) 아메리카 (b) 캐나다 (c) 잉글랜드
(d) 이탈리아 (e) 프랑스 (f) 브라질
(g) 뉴질랜드 (h) 말레이시아 (i) 코리아

(j) 오렌지   (k) 스트레스   (l) 비타민

(m) 마스크   (n) 오스트레일리아

1.6 Summary of 한글 letters

Vowels	ㅏ ㅓ ㅗ ㅜ ㅡ ㅣ ㅐ ㅔ					
Diphthongs						
y + vowel	ㅑ	ㅕ	ㅛ	ㅠ	ㅒ	ㅖ
w + vowel	ㅘ	ㅙ	ㅚ	ㅝ	ㅞ	ㅟ
ŭ + i	ㅢ					
Consonants						
Simple	ㄱ ㄴ ㄷ ㄹ ㅁ ㅂ ㅅ ㅇ ㅈ					
Aspirated	ㅊ ㅋ ㅌ ㅍ ㅎ					
Tense	ㄲ ㄸ ㅃ ㅆ ㅉ					

1.7 Alphabetic order and the names of the letters

한글 letters are alphabetically ordered for dictionary entries, directories, word lists, and indexes (as in this book). Each letter has a name. In the following tables, boldface letters are relatively more basic than the other letters.

Vowel and diphthong letters

Order	ㅏ	ㅐ	ㅑ	ㅒ	ㅓ	ㅔ	ㅕ	ㅖ	ㅗ	ㅘ	ㅙ	ㅚ
Name	아	애	야	얘	어	에	여	예	오	와	왜	외
	a	ae	ya	yae	ŏ	e	yŏ	ye	o	wa	wae	we

Order	ㅛ	ㅜ	ㅝ	ㅞ	ㅟ	ㅠ	ㅡ	ㅢ	ㅣ
Name	요	우	워	웨	위	유	으	의	이
	yo	u	wŏ	we	wi	yu	ŭ	ŭi	i

Consonant letters

Order	ㄱ	ㄲ	ㄴ	ㄷ	ㄸ	ㄹ	ㅁ	ㅂ	ㅃ	ㅅ
Name	기역	쌍기역	니은	디귿	쌍디귿	리을	미음	비읍	쌍비읍	시옷
	ki.yŏk	ssang ki.yŏk	ni.ŭn	ti.gŭt	ssang ti.gŭt	ri.ŭl	mi.ŭm	pi.ŭp	ssang pi.ŭp	si.ot

Order	ㅆ	ㅇ	ㅈ	ㅉ	ㅊ	ㅋ	ㅌ	ㅍ	ㅎ
Name	쌍시옷	이응	지읒	쌍지읒	치읓	키읔	티읕	피읖	히읗
	ssang si.ot	i.ŭng	chi.ŭt	ssang chi.ŭt	ch'i.ŭt	k'i.ŭk	t'i.ŭt	p'i.ŭp	hi.ŭt

Notice that the name of each consonant letter begins and ends with the sound in question. Notice further that, for certain consonants, their sound quality when ending a name is not the same as when beginning a name: ㅅ (시옷 si.ot), ㅈ (지읒 chi.ŭt), ㅊ (치읓 ch'i.ŭt), ㅋ (키읔 k'i.ŭk), ㅌ (티읕 t'i.ŭt), ㅍ (피읖 p'i.ŭp), and ㅎ (히읗 hi.ŭt). This is due to the "unrelease" or "closure" of word-final consonants in Korean. For example, when 옷 is pronounced without releasing the speech organs involved for ㅅ, the outcome is ot.

As the name 이응 i.ŭng indicates, ㅇ has two functions. It has a silent or zero quality in syllable-initial position, as in 이 i. It simply fills the zero consonant position in a syllable block which begins with a vowel sound. When it occurs in syllable-final position, it has the nasal quality ng.

The term 쌍 ssang means 'twin'. This is to indicate that the same letter is doubled to represent tenseness.

2. Pronunciation Rules

The 한글 spelling convention follows the principle of spelling a lexical item (that is, word element) in one fixed way, regardless of its pronunciation changes in different combinations with other lexical items. For example, 'Korea' is pronounced *han.guk* and spelled 한국. When this word is followed by 말 'language' to mean 'the Korean language', the pronunciation of *han.guk* changes to *han.gung* 'Korea' as in *han.gung.mal* 'the Korean language' because of the assimilation of *k* to the following nasal consonant, *m*. Yet the spelling is 한국말, and not 한궁말. This is similar to the English practice of expressing past action with *-ed* despite the fact that pronunciations vary depending on the phonetic environments, as in *kicked, nibbled,* and *knitted.* Since the sound changes are predictable given relevant sound environments, the student needs a set of simple rules for pronouncing words written in 한글. The following rules are basic and essential for the beginning student. These, as well as other less general rules, will be reiterated as needed throughout this volume.

Rule 1. Resyllabification

When a syllable-final consonant is followed without pause by a vowel in the following syllable, that consonant is carried over to the following syllable to function as its initial consonant in pronunciation. The following syllable may be a part of a suffix or another word. This linking of syllable-final consonant to following syllable in pronunciation is technically called "resyllabification." For example, 한글로 does not show any linking, but 한글은 is pronounced [한그른]. In this case, the sound quality of ㄹ changes from *l* to *r* because ㄹ now appears between two vowels. Similarly, when a syllable block ends in a double consonant letter, the second consonant is carried over to the following vowel-initial syllable in pronunciation, as in 읽어요 [일거요].

Practice 20	
(a) 책을 펴세요 [채글 펴세요]	(b) 알았어요 [아라써요]
(c) 질문이 있어요	(d) 읽어 보세요
(e) 잘 들으세요	(f) 맞았어요
(g) 앉으세요	(h) 천만에요
(i) 책이 이 층에 없어요	(j) 영어를 쓰지 마세요
(k) 백화점에 갔어요	(l) 옷을 받았어요

Rule 2. Syllable-final closure (unrelease)

At the end of a word or before a consonant, all Korean consonants are pronounced with closure of the speech organs involved, that is, without releasing air. As a result, sound changes occur in consonants in word-final or pre-consonantal position. For example, 꽃은 'as for flowers' is pronounced as *kko.ch'ŭn* without any change in ㅊ because the word 꽃 'flower' is immediately followed by the vowel-initial particle 은 'as for'. However, 꽃 'flower' and 꽃도 'flower also' are pronounced [꼳] *kkot* and [꼳또] *kkot.tto*, respectively, and not as *kkoch* and *kkoch.to*. The change of ㅊ *ch* to ㄷ *t* here happens because the speech organs (the tongue and the hard palate) responsible for the articulation of the word-final and pre-consonantal ㅊ are not released. Thus, the following changes occur in the same positions.

Lips	ㅂ, ㅍ	→ ㅂ *p*
Gum ridge and hard palate	ㄷ, ㅌ, ㅅ, ㅆ, ㅈ, ㅊ →	ㄷ *t*
Soft palate	ㄱ, ㅋ, ㄲ	→ ㄱ *k*

Practice 21	(a) 잎이 [이피]	잎 [입]	잎과 [입꽈]
	(b) 같아요	같지요	
	(c) 옷을	옷	옷도
	(d) 갔어	갔다	갔지
	(e) 낮에	밤낮	낮과
	(f) 빛이	빛	빛조차
	(g) 부엌에	부엌	부엌 바닥
	(h) 낚아요	낚시	낚다가
	(i) 꽃이	꽃	꽃씨

The only consonant sounds that occur at the end of a word or before another consonant are the seven simple consonants ㅂ *p*, ㄷ *t*, ㄱ *k*, ㅁ *m*, ㄴ *n*, ㅇ *ng*, and ㄹ *l*.

Rule 3. Nasal assimilation

All plosive and fricative consonants become the corresponding nasal consonants before a nasal consonant (ㅁ, ㄴ), as indicated below. Notice that even ㅎ is included in the change.

ㅂ, ㅍ	→ ㅁ *m*
ㄷ, ㅌ, ㅅ, ㅆ, ㅈ, ㅊ, ㅎ	→ ㄴ *n*
ㄱ, ㅋ, ㄲ	→ ㅇ *ng*

Practice 22   (a) 입만 [임만]   (b) 앞문
(c) 없나요   (d) 받는다
(e) 끝나다   (f) 몇 년
(g) 있는데   (h) 일학년
(i) 낳는다   (j) 모르겠습니다
(k) 한국말로 뭐라고 합니까   (l) 여기서 끝내겠습니다

Rule 4. ㄴ to ㄹ assimilation

When ㄹ and ㄴ come together, the ㄴ sound is usually replaced by the ㄹ sound, as in 칠 년 [칠련]. When ㄹ is followed by the vowel *i* or the semivowel *y* in some compound words, another ㄹ is inserted between them, as in 물약 [물략].

Practice 23   (a) 진리   (b) 신라
(c) 전라도   (d) 달님
(e) 팔 년   (f) 서울역
(g) 길 이름

Rule 5. Tensification

When a plain plosive consonant (ㅂ, ㄷ, ㅈ, ㄱ) or the fricative consonant ㅅ is preceded by a plosive or fricative consonant, it is reinforced to become a corresponding tense consonant, as in 몇번 [멸뻔] (careful speech) or [며뻔] (casual speech), 학생 [학쌩] and 없다 [업따].

Practice 24 (a) 몇 과   (b) 식당
             (c) 학교   (d) 숙제
             (e) 꽃집   (f) 책상   ·
             (g) 몇 시간   (h) 처음 뵙겠습니다
             (i) 질문이 없습니다

Tensification also occurs in compound nouns. This and other kinds of reinforcement will be discussed later.

Practice 25 (a) 여름 방학 'summer vacation'   [여름빵악]
             (b) 길가 'roadside'   [길까]
             (c) 강가 'riverside'   [강까]
             (d) 봄비 'spring rain'   [봄삐]
             (e) 누구 거예요 'Whose is it?'   [누구 꺼예요]
             (f) 마이클 거예요 '(It is) Michael's'   [마이클 꺼예요]

Rule 6. Aspiration and ㅎ weakening

The fricative consonant ㅎ is produced in the throat, soft palate, hard palate, or lips depending on the following vowel. When it is followed or preceded by a plain plosive consonant (ㅂ, ㄷ, ㅈ, ㄱ), it merges with the consonant to produce the corresponding aspirate consonant (ㅍ *p'*, ㅌ *t'*, ㅊ *ch'*, ㅋ *k'*), as in 좋다 [조타] and 닫히다 [다치다].

ㅎ + ㅂ, ㄷ, ㅈ, ㄱ	=	ㅍ, ㅌ, ㅊ, ㅋ
ㅂ, ㄷ, ㅈ, ㄱ + ㅎ	=	ㅍ, ㅌ, ㅊ, ㅋ

Practice 26 (a) 좋고   (b) 입학
             (c) 많다   (d) 좋지 않다
             (e) 책하고   (f) 시작합시다
             (g) 어떻게   (h) 꽃하고
             (i) 대답하세요

Between two voiced sounds (vowels, nasals, or ㄹ consonants), ㅎ tends to become silent in casual speech, as in 좋아요 [조아요] and 말한다 [마란다].

Practice 27	(a) 전화	(b) 여름 방학
	(c) 사랑한다	(d) 안녕하세요
	(e) 많아요	(f) 좋았어요
	(g) 잘했어요	(h) 천천히 말해 보세요
	(i) 감사합니다	(j) 괜찮아요

Rule 7. Double consonant reduction

As indicated under rule 1, the second of the two consonants at the syllable-final position (e.g., 값, 없, 읽, 않, 덟, 앉) is carried over to the following syllable in pronunciation if this syllable does not have an initial consonant, as in 값이 [갑씨]. However, one of the two consonants becomes silent at the end of a word or before a consonant, as in 값 [갑] and 값도 [갑또]. Unlike in English where up to three consonants may occur in sequence in a syllable (e.g., _street_, _ma<u>sks</u>_), even a cluster of two consonants is not allowed in a single Korean syllable.

It is difficult to predict which of two syllable-final consonants will become silent. Normally the silent consonant is the second one, but there are exceptions.

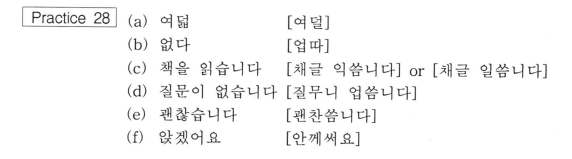

Practice 28	(a) 여덟	[여덜]
	(b) 없다	[업따]
	(c) 책을 읽습니다	[채글 익씀니다] or [채글 일씀니다]
	(d) 질문이 없습니다	[질무니 업씀니다]
	(e) 괜찮습니다	[괜찬씀니다]
	(f) 앉겠어요	[안께써요]

Rule 8. Palatalization

When a word ending in ㄷ or ㅌ is followed by a suffix beginning with the vowel _i_ or the semivowel _y_ (whether ㅎ intervenes or not), the ㄷ and ㅌ are pronounced ㅈ and ㅊ, respectively, as in 닫혀요 [다처요] and 붙이다 [부치다]. This change is technically called "palatalization" because the original gum-ridge consonants are articulated in the area of the hard palate.

Practice 29	(a) 붙어요	붙여요
	(b) 다 같아요	다 같이 가요
	(c) 밑에	밑이

Rule 9. Place assimilation

In casual speech, [ㄷ] is optionally pronounced [ㅂ] before ㅂ or ㅃ and as [ㄱ] before ㄱ or ㄲ, as in 꽃병 [꼳뼝/꼽뼝] and 갔고 [갇꼬/각꼬]. Similarly, [ㄴ] is optionally pronounced [ㅁ] before ㅂ, ㅃ, or ㅁ, and [ㅇ] before ㄱ or ㄲ, as in 한미 [한미/함미], 빗물 [빈물/빔물], and 한강 [한강/항강].

Practice 30	(a) 옷감	(b) 신문
	(c) 옷빨래	(d) 한국어
	(e) 젖병	(f) 눈꺼풀
	(g) 닫고	(h) 꽃무늬
	(i) 밭갈이	(j) 신발

Useful Classroom Expressions

Here are some basic expressions that you will hear and use frequently in the classroom context. They are not intended for you to memorize at this stage, but it is good to be familiar with them from the beginning.

1. Everyday Greetings

a. 안녕하세요?

How are you?/Hello./How do you do?

Note: In Korean, 안녕하세요?, literally meaning 'Are you in peace?' is used as a greeting at any time of the day, for example, 'Good morning', 'Good afternoon', or 'Good evening'. It can also be used for 'How are you?' or 'Nice to meet you.'

b. 안녕히 계세요.
c. 안녕히 가세요.

Good-bye (to the one staying).
Good-bye (to the one leaving).

Note: 안녕히 계세요 literally means 'Please stay in peace', and 안녕히 가세요, 'Please go in peace.'

2. Courtesies

a. 고맙습니다.
   감사합니다.
b. 미안합니다.
   죄송합니다.

Thank you.
Thank you.
I'm sorry. (to apologize)
I'm truly sorry. (to apologize to a senior or distant equal)

(늦어서) 죄송합니다.   I'm sorry (I am late).

c. 실례합니다.   Excuse me. (lit. I am committing
                                     rudeness and discourtesy.)

3. Teacher's General Instructions

(다 같이) 따라하세요.   (All together) please repeat after me.

읽어 보세요.   Please read.
칠판을 보세요.   Please look at the blackboard.
잘 들으세요.   Please listen carefully.
다시 한 번 해 보세요.   Please try it once more.
대답하세요.   Please answer.
받아 쓰세요.   Please write it down.
한국말로 하세요.   Please say it in Korean.
영어를 쓰지 마세요.   Please don't use English.
외우세요.   Please memorize it.
둘이서 해 보세요.   Please do it as a pair.
숙제 내세요.   Please hand in your homework.

책을 펴세요.　　　　　　　　Please open your book.

책을 보지 마세요.　　　　　　Please don't look at your book.

4. Teacher's Comments

좋아요.　　　　　　　　Good.

잘 했어요.　　　　　　　Well done.

아주 잘 했어요.　　　　　You did it very well.

맞았어요.　　　　　　　You are right.

틀렸어요.　　　　　　　You are wrong.

오늘은 이만 하겠어요. We will stop here today.

5. Conversational Exchanges

a. Teacher: 이름이 뭐예요?　　　What's your name? (Cannot be used to a senior)

　　Student: _____입니다.　　I'm _____.

b. Teacher: 알겠어요?　　　　　　Do you understand?

　　Student: 네, 알겠어요.　　　　Yes, I do.

　　　　　아니오, 잘 모르겠어요. No, I don't.

c. Teacher: 질문 있어요?　　　　Do you have any questions?

　　Student: 네, 질문 있어요.　　Yes, I do.

d. Teacher: 숙제에 대해서　　　Do you have any questions

　　　　　질문 있어요?　　　about the homework?

　　Student: 아니오, 질문 없어요. No, I don't.

제1과 인사

(Lesson 1: Greetings)

OBJECTIVES

CULTURE	1. Greetings with a bow
	2. Korean names
	3. Social hierarchy and terms of address
GRAMMAR	G1.1 Equational expressions:
	(Noun₁은/는) Noun₂이에요/예요. (N₁ = N₂)
	(Noun₁은/는) Noun₂(이/가) 아니에요. (N₁ ≠ N₂)
	G1.2 Omission of redundant elements
	G1.3 Comparing items: 은/는 vs. 도
	G1.4 Yes-or-no questions:
	A: N이에요/예요?
	B: 네/아니오, N이에요/예요.
	G1.5 Using a title or a name instead of "you"
TASK/FUNCTION	1. Greetings
	2. Introducing oneself
	3. Describing another person

CONVERSATION

1

(Prof. Lee and his students introduce themselves in a classroom.)

이민수 선생님　　스티브 월슨　　김영미　　마이클 정

이 선생님:　안녕하세요?

저는 이민수입니다.[G1.1]

저는 한국어 선생님이에요.

스티브:　　안녕하세요?

저는 스티브 월슨입니다.

삼학년이에요.[G1.2]

영미:　　　안녕하세요?

저는[G1.3] 김영미예요.

저는 일학년이에요.

마이클:　　마이클 정이에요.

저도[G1.3] 일학년이에요.

2

(Michael meets Sandy for the first time.)

마이클 정

샌디 왕

마이클: 처음 뵙겠습니다.
저는 마이클 정입니다.
이름이 뭐예요?

샌디: 샌디 왕이에요. 처음 뵙겠습니다.

마이클: 샌디 씨는[G1.5] 한국 사람이에요?[G1.4]

샌디: 아니오, 중국 사람이에요.[G1.4]

마이클: 아, 그래요? 저는 한국 사람이에요.

NARRATION

한국어 클래스

이민수 선생님은 한국어 선생님이에요. 한국 사람이에요. 김영미, 마이클 정, 샌디 왕, 스티브 윌슨은 학생이에요. 김영미는 한국 사람이에요. 마이클 정도 한국 사람이에요. 샌디 왕은 한국 사람이 아니에요. 중국 사람이에요. 스티브 윌슨도 한국 사람이 아니에요. 미국 사람이에요.

NEW WORDS AND EXPRESSIONS

NOUNS

미국 사람	American (person)
삼학년	junior
선생님	teacher
씨	(attached to an adult equal or younger person's name to indicate the speaker's courtesy toward the person)
영어 (G1.4)	the English language
이름	name
이학년 (G1.2)	sophomore
인사	greeting
일학년	freshman
제1과	lesson 1
중국 사람	Chinese (person)
학년	school year
학생	student
한국 사람	Korean person
한국어/한국말	the Korean language

PROPER NOUNS

김영미	Kim Young-mee
마이클 정	Michael Chung
미국	America
샌디 왕	Sandy Wang
스티브 윌슨	Steve Wilson
이민수	Lee Min-soo
중국	China
한국	Korea

LOANWORD

클래스	class

PRONOUNS

나 (G1.5)	I (plain)
뭐	what? (question word, contracted form of 무엇)
저	I (humble) (저는 한국 사람이에요.)

NUMBERS

일	1
이 (G1.2)	2
삼	3

VERB

뵙겠습니다	(뵙다)	to see (a senior)

ADJECTIVES

그래요	(그렇다)	to be so
안녕하세요	(안녕하다)	to be well (a greeting equivalent to 'Hi, how are you?')

COPULAS

아니에요	(아니다)	to not be
이에요/예요	(이다)	to be
입니다	(이다)	to be (deferential)

ADVERBS

아니오	no
처음	for the first time (also used as a noun with the meaning 'the first, the beginning')

INTERJECTION

아	ah

PARTICLES

가^(G1.1) subject particle
도 also, too
은/는 as for; topic particle
이 subject particle

SUFFIX

~님 attached to an occupational or kinship title, notes speaker's respect for the person named

---

Pronunciation

뵙겠습니다 [뵙께씀니다], [뵙껟씀니다] or [뵈께씀니다] (casual)
삼학년 [삼항년] or [사망년] (casual)
샌디 [쌘디]
안녕하세요 [안녕하세요] or [안녕아세요] (casual)
예요 [예요] or [에요] (casual)
이민수입니다 [이민수임니다] or [이민숨니다] (casual) (Note: 입니다 is pronounced as [ㅁ니다] in casual speech when the preceding word ends in a vowel.)
일학년 [일항년] or [이랑년] (casual)
저도 [저도] or [저두] (casual)
한국어 [한구거] or [항구거] (casual)

Vocabulary by Theme

Greetings
안녕하세요? How are you?
처음 뵙겠습니다. Nice to meet you.

Personal Information

이름	name	선생님	teacher
학생	student	학년	academic year
일학년	freshman	이학년	sophomore
삼학년	junior	사학년	senior

Sino-Korean Numbers

일	1	이	2
삼	3	사	4

NOTES ON NEW WORDS AND EXPRESSIONS

Conversation 1

(1) **안녕하세요?** is a greeting that asks about the other person's well-being or good health. This expression can be used at any time of the day.

The closest equivalent expression in English is 'Hi, how are you?' except that 'How are you?' is responded to with 'I'm fine.' or 'O.K.', whereas **안녕하세요?** does not demand a literal answer. The appropriate response is simply **안녕하세요?**

(2) Reference to the speaker himself/herself (first person pronouns)

Plain form	나
Humble form	저

Conversation 2

(1) 처음 뵙겠습니다 'Nice to meet you' literally means 'It is the first time I meet you (the honorable person)'. It is a humble idiomatic expression used to an adult whom one meets for the first time.

(2) The question word 뭐 'what?' is a contracted form of 무엇, which is not used much in colloquial speech: 무엇 > 무어 > 뭐.

The question word 뭐/무엇 is used for nonhuman referents, including animals, objects, abstract concepts, events and states of affairs, etc.

(3) 이름이 뭐예요? cannot be used to a senior. To a senior, 성함이 어떻게 되세요? must be used.

(4) 씨, as in 샌디 씨, 마이클 씨, 김영미 씨, denotes the speaker's courtesy toward colleagues, fellow students, co-workers, or even toward his/her students, juniors, or supervisees at work. It is not appropriate to use 씨 to speak or refer to one's seniors, teachers, or older people. 씨 should be attached to the last name plus the first name or to the first name only. Attaching 씨 to Korean last names alone is condescending.

(5) Naming a language and nationality/ethnicity

Country name	Language name country name + 어	Nationality/ethnicity country name + 사람
한국 'Korea'	한국어	한국 사람
미국 'USA'	영어	미국 사람
영국 'England'	영어	영국 사람
일본 'Japan'	일(본)어	일본 사람
중국 'China'	중국어	중국 사람
프랑스/불란서 'France'	프랑스어/불어	프랑스/불란서 사람
독일 'Germany'	독(일)어	독일 사람
스페인 'Spain'	스페인어	스페인 사람
러시아 'Russia'	러시아어	러시아 사람

Informally, people often use:
한국말 (= 한국어), 중국말 (= 중국어), 일본말 (= 일본어), and so forth.

(6) 그래요? is a semiautomatic reaction meaning 'Is that so/right?'

CULTURE

1. Greetings with a bow

In Korea, bowing shows courtesy when you greet someone unless the other party is a junior. The degree of the bow depends on such factors as the degree of politeness, seniority, and social status. To show the highest degree of politeness, you bend your head and waist about 45˚. Common courtesy to most people is shown by bending your head and waist about 15˚. In a very casual meeting with a person about your age, nodding your head would be enough. People often bow while shaking hands with one or both hands.

2. Korean names

In English, the given name comes first, and the family name follows it, as in "Steve Wilson." In Korean, however, as in many other Asian cultures, the family name comes first, and the given name follows. In 저는 김영미예요, 김 is the family name, and 영미 is the given name.

Throughout this textbook, we will follow the customs of each language in presenting names. That is, Korean names will be presented in the Korean way, e.g., 김영미, and English names will be presented in the English way, e.g., 스티브 윌슨 (Steve Wilson).

Korean family names have more significance than their English counterparts in that they represent kin that may be traced back hundreds of years. There are 274 last names reported in Korea. The five most common last names are 김, 이, 박, 최, 정. Usually romanized as Kim in English, 김 is the most common (21.7%), followed by 이, commonly spelled as Lee, Rhee, or Yi, and 박, as Park, Pak, or Bak.

3. Social hierarchy and terms of address

Western value orientations may be summarized in general as individualistic and egalitarian. Despite the fact that contemporary Koreans, especially the younger generation, have become very westernized in their behavior, traditional values of collectivism and social hierarchism still persist in the consciousness of most Koreans. This traditional culture is reflected in the Korean language, especially in the use of a wide variety of address and reference terms. Kinship terms such as 형 '(male's) older brother', and 언니 '(female's) older sister' are frequently used to address one's seniors in college, while the junior is referred to by a first name-based address, such as 영미야 and 유진아. Kinship terms like 아저씨 'uncle' and 아주머니 'aunt' are still often used by a person of any age group to address strangers between the ages of forty and sixty.

GRAMMAR

G1.1　Equational expressions：
　　　　(Noun₁은/는) Noun₂이에요/예요. (N₁ = N₂)
　　　　(Noun₁은/는) Noun₂(이/가) 아니에요. (N₁ ≠ N₂)

Examples

---

(1) 스티브 월슨: 저는 스티브 월슨이에요.
　　　　　　　　삼학년이에요.
　　김영미:　　　김영미예요.
　　　　　　　　저는 일학년이에요.
(2) 샌디 왕은 한국 사람(이) 아니에요.

Notes

1. Topic-comment structure: All the examples above have topic-comment structure. In Korean, topic-comment structure is the basic sentence type.

	Topic		Comment
	Topic	Particle	
(i)	저	는 (after vowel)	스티브 윌슨이에요.
(ii)			삼학년이에요.
(iii)	샌디 왕	은 (after consonant)	한국 사람이 아니에요.

Topic-comment structure is one of the fundamental ways of conveying ideas, where the speaker picks a person, idea, or object as the topic, and contributes the subsequent statement(s) (comments) to describing the selected item.

The most typical use of topic-comment structure is in identifying statements such as the above examples, where equational expressions ($N_1 = N_2$) are used. In (i), for example, 저 'I' is the topic, and 스티브 윌슨이에요 is the comment. In (ii), the topic is omitted, because it is redundant from the preceding context (see G1.2). In (iii), 샌디 왕 'Sandy Wang' is the topic, and 한국 사람이 아니에요 '[she] is not a Korean' is the comment.

은/는 is the topic particle. It indicates that the attached noun is the topic described by the subsequent statement.

After consonant	이민수 선생님은	한국 사람이에요.
	마이클 정은	
After vowel	저는	
	김영미는	

2. Equational expression: $N_1 = N_2$.

Polite style	(N_1은/는) N_2이에요/예요.
Deferential style	(N_1은/는) N_2입니다.

N이에요 is used when N(oun) ends in a consonant, and N예요 is used when N ends in a vowel.

		N이에요 (after a consonant)	N예요 (after a vowel)
Polite style	저는	스티브 월슨이에요.	이민수예요.
		한국어 선생님이에요.	김영미예요.
		일학년이에요.	
		한국 사람이에요.	

		N입니다 (after a consonant)	N ㅂ니다 (after a vowel)
Deferential style	저는	스티브 월슨입니다.	김영밉니다.
		한국 사람입니다.	이민숩니다.

3. Negative equational construction: $N_1 \neq N_2$

N_1은/는	N_2(이/가) 아니에요.
샌디왕은	한국 사람(이) 아니에요.
저는	스티브(가) 아니에요.

아니에요 is the negative counterpart of 이에요/예요. In conversation, the particle 이/가 after N_2 is frequently omitted.

[연습] To the given name or the year in school, add (i) 이에요 or 예요, (ii) 입니다, and (iii) 이/가 아니에요.

> 보기: 마이클: (i) 저는 마이클이에요.
> (ii) 저는 마이클입니다.
> (iii) 저는 마이클이 아니에요.

(1) 윌슨: _____.
(2) 샌디: _____.
(3) 탐: _____.
(4) 삼학년: _____.

G1.2   Omission of redundant elements

Examples

(1) 안녕하세요?	How are [you]?
(2) 스티브: 안녕하세요?	How are [you]?
저는 스티브 윌슨이에요.	I am Steve Wilson.
삼학년이에요.	[I] am a junior.
김영미: 안녕하세요?	How are [you]?
김영미예요.	[I] am Young-mee Kim.
(3) 처음 뵙겠습니다.	It is the first time [I] meet [you].
(4) 마이클: 저는 마이클 정이에요.	I am Michael Chung.
이름이 뭐예요?	What is [your] name?
샌디: 샌디 왕이에요.	[I] am Sandy Wang.

Missing elements in Korean are indicated by [ ] in the English translation.

Notes

1. In Korean, subjects are often omitted when they are obvious, as can be seen in (1) through (4) above.

2. Omissions are not limited to subjects. Any element can be omitted as long as the context makes the referent clear. In (3), for example, not only the reference to the speaker (I) but also to the listener (you) is omitted. In (4), even the reference to the possessor (your) is omitted, because it is obvious that the speaker is asking the listener's name.

[**연습** 1] Introduce yourself with your name and your year in school, as specified. Avoid redundancy as much as you can.

보기: [김영미, 일학년] <u>저는 김영미예요. 일학년이에요.</u>

(1) [스티브, 삼학년] _____. _____.
(2) [마이클, 일학년] _____. _____.
(3) [샌디, 이학년] _____. _____.

[**연습** 2] Introduce yourself with your name and your nationality/ethnicity, as specified. Avoid redundancy as much as possible.

보기: [김영미, 한국 사람] <u>저는 김영미예요. 한국 사람이에요.</u>

(1) [스티브, 미국 사람] _____. _____.
(2) [마이클, 한국 사람] _____. _____.
(3) [샌디, 중국 사람] _____. _____.

G1.3 Comparing items: 은/는 vs. 도

Examples

(1) 스티브: 저는 스티브예요. **삼학년**이에요.
영미: 저는 김영미예요. 저는 **일학년**이에요. (different)
린다: 린다예요. 저**도 일학년**이에요. (parallel)
(2) 김영미는 한국 사람이에요. 마이클 정도 한국 사람이에요.
샌디 왕은 한국 사람이 아니에요. 중국 사람이에요.

Note

The particles 은/는 and 도 are used to compare two or more items.

은/는	The items are different or contrastive.
도	The items are parallel.

[연습] Fill in the blank with either **저도** or **저는**.

> 보기: A: 저는 일학년이에요.
>
>   B: <u>저는</u> 삼학년이에요.

(1) A: 저는 선생님이에요.

    B: ＿＿ 선생님이에요.

(2) A: 저는 중국 사람이에요.

    B: ＿＿ 미국 사람이에요.

(3) A: 저는 선생님이에요.

    B: ＿＿ 학생이에요.

G1.4   Yes-or-no questions:

     A: N이에요/예요?

     B: 네/아니오, N이에요/예요.

Examples

> 이 선생님: 영미, **한국 학생**이에요?
>
> 영미: 네, **한국 학생**이에요.
>
> 이 선생님: **삼학년**이에요?
>
> 영미: **아니오, 일학년**이에요.

Notes

1. In English, a question involves special grammar. Namely, a verb (either 'do' or 'be') is put in front of the subject, as in:

Are you Korean? (compare 'You *are* Korean.')

In Korean, however, only the intonations change, and no special grammar is used, at least in the polite and intimate speech styles. The word order remains the same, and the same verbal ending is used both for questions and for statements. That is, the equational construction N이에요/예요 can be made into a question merely by changing the intonation.

2. Answering a yes-or-no question involves affirmation or denial of the content of the question. In Korean, an affirmative answer is made with 네/예, indicating that the content of the question is true, and a denial is made with 아니오, which indicates that the content of the question is false.

Content is true	네/예
Content is not true	아니오

[연습 1] Say 네 or 아니오, whichever is appropriate for the given context.

> 보기: A: 한국 사람이에요?
>   B: <u>아니오</u>, 중국 사람이에요.

(1) A: 삼학년이에요?
    B: _____, 일학년이에요.
(2) A: 미국 사람이에요?
    B: _____, 미국 사람이에요.
(3) A: 영어 선생님이에요?
    B: _____, 한국어 선생님이에요.

[**연습** 2] Make up a question that will lead to the answer given.

보기: A: <u>일학년이에요?</u>
        B: 네, 일학년이에요.

---

(1) A: _____?
    B: 아니오, 한국 사람이에요.
(2) A: _____?
    B: 네, 한국어 선생님이에요.
(3) A: _____?
    B: 아니오, 삼학년이에요.

G1.5   Using a title or a name instead of "you"

Examples

(1) 마이클:	**샌디 씨**는 한국 사람이에요?	Are *you* Korean, Sandy?
샌디:	아니오, 중국 사람이에요.	No, I am Chinese.
(2) 스티브:	**영미 씨**는 일학년이에요?	Are *you* a freshman, Young-mee?
영미:	네, 일학년이에요.	Yes, I am.
(3) 이 선생님:	**학생**은 이름이 뭐예요?	What is *your* name?
스티브:	스티브 월슨입니다.	My name is Steve Wilson.

Notes

1. English has a rich pronoun system with a full range of pronouns: I (me, my, mine), you (your, yours), he (him, his), she (her, hers), it (its), we (us, our, ours), they (them, their, theirs), and so on. Korean has personal pronouns, too, such as 저/나 'I', but the range of pronominal expressions is much narrower, than in English, and usage is very limited. In referring to the listener, which is "you" in English, pronouns are rarely used, and names and titles are used instead. In (1),

for example, Michael is speaking to Sandy, and refers to her with **샌디 씨**. That is, a name, **샌디**, instead of a pronoun, is used to refer to the listener. This is also illustrated in (2).

2. A title can be used in referring to the listener, as in (3), where **이 선생님** 'Prof. Lee' addresses one of his students as **학생** 'student'. It is very common to refer to and address a senior as **선생님**, even when the person is not a teacher. **학생** is used only by an adult to a younger person who looks like a student; it cannot be used among students.

[연습 1] Assume that you are talking to the following person. Ask about year in school and nationality/ethnicity.

> 보기: [린다] (i) 린다 씨는 일학년이에요?
>   (ii) 린다 씨는 미국 사람이에요?

(1) [마이클] _____? _____?
(2) [샌디]   _____? _____?
(3) [스티브] _____? _____?

[연습 2] Ask your partner for his/her year in school and nationality/ethnicity using his/her name instead of a pronoun.

TASK/FUNCTION

1. Greetings

> A: 안녕하세요? 처음 뵙겠습니다.
> B: (네,) 안녕하세요? 처음 뵙겠습니다.

[연습] Exchange greetings with your partner.

2. Introducing oneself

> 안녕하세요? 저는 마이클 정이에요.
> 일학년이에요. 한국 사람이에요.

[연습 1] Introduce yourself as in the example above. Include (i) **이름** (name), (ii) **학년** (year in school), **일학년, 이학년, 삼학년,** or **사학년,** and (iii) nationality/ethnicity.

[연습 2] Based on the following summary, introduce yourself as if you were the person specified.

Character	학년 (School year)	Ethnicity
(1) 스티브 윌슨	삼학년 junior	미국 사람 American
(2) 김영미	일학년 freshman	한국 사람 Korean
(3) 마이클 정	일학년 freshman	한국 사람 Korean
(4) 샌디 왕	이학년 sophomore	중국 사람 Chinese

3. Describing another person

You:	이름이 뭐예요?	← Asking name
마이클:	마이클 정이에요.	
You:	이학년이에요?	← Asking school year
마이클:	아니오, 일학년이에요.	
You:	한국 사람이에요?	← Asking ethnicity
마이클:	네, 한국 사람이에요.	

Use 이에요/예요? in order to obtain the necessary information about the other party. Having obtained the information, you can describe him or her to the rest of the class.

> 마이클 정은 일학년이에요.
> 한국 사람이에요.

[연습 1] Describe the main characters in lesson 1 in Korean.

(1) 이 선생님
(2) 스티브 윌슨
(3) 김영미
(4) 샌디 왕

[연습 2] Interview three people in the class and fill in the table, then introduce your interviewees to the rest of the class.

Name	학년 (School year)	Ethnicity
스티브 윌슨	삼학년	미국 사람

Lesson 1   Greetings

CONVERSATION

1

(Prof. Lee and his students introduce themselves in the classroom.)

Prof. Lee: Hello.
                I am Min-soo Lee.
                I'm your Korean (language) professor.
Steve: Hello.
                I'm Steve Wilson.
                I'm a junior.
Young-mee: Hi.
                I am Young-mee Kim.
                I'm a freshman.
Michael: I'm Michael Chung.
                I'm also a freshman.

2

(Michael meets Sandy for the first time.)

Michael: It's nice to meet you.
                I'm Michael Chung.
                What is your name?
Sandy: I'm Sandy Wang.
                Pleased to meet you.
Michael: Are you Korean?
Sandy: No, I'm Chinese.
Michael: Oh, is that right? I'm Korean.

제2과 대학 캠퍼스

(Lesson 2: The University Campus)

OBJECTIVES

CULTURE	1. Exchanging business cards
	2. Introducing friends or acquaintances
	3. Social hierarchy and sentence endings
GRAMMAR	G2.1 Verbs vs. adjectives
	G2.2 The structure of predicates: The polite ending ~어요/아요
	G2.3 The honorific ending ~(으)세요
	G2.4 The subject particle 이/가
	G2.5 [Place]에 있어요
	G2.6 The discourse particle 은/는 (changing the topic)
	G2.7 The conjunction 그리고
TASK/FUNCTION	1. Introducing friends
	2. Inquiring about another person's health
	3. Asking about the location of something or someone
	4. Seeking information about things and objects
	5. Making requests

CONVERSATION

1

(Linda and Sandy are eating breakfast in the school cafeteria. Steve enters the cafeteria and sees them.)

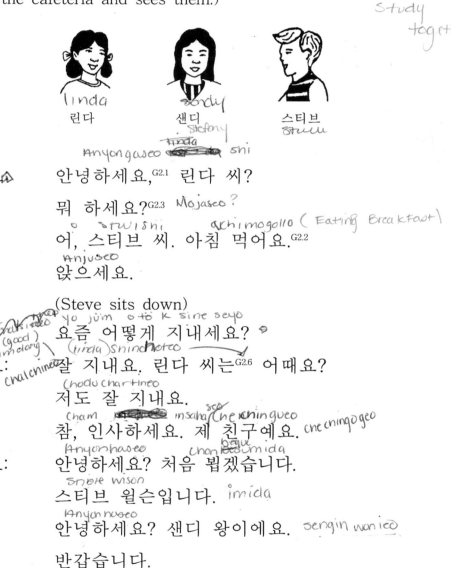

린다   샌디   스티브

스티브: 안녕하세요,[G2.1] 린다 씨?

뭐 하세요?[G2.3]

린다: 어, 스티브 씨. 아침 먹어요.[G2.2]

앉으세요.

(Steve sits down)

요즘 어떻게 지내세요?

스티브: 잘 지내요. 린다 씨는[G2.6] 어때요?

린다: 저도 잘 지내요.

참, 인사하세요. 제 친구예요.

스티브: 안녕하세요? 처음 뵙겠습니다.

스티브 월슨입니다.

샌디: 안녕하세요? 샌디 왕이에요.

반갑습니다.

2

(Young-mee is looking for the school cafeteria and runs into Linda.)

린다 영미

영미: 저어, 여기 학교 식당이[G2.4] 어디 있어요?

린다: 유니온 빌딩에 있어요.[G2.5] 일층에 있어요.

그리고[G2.7] 도서관 밑에도 있어요.

영미: 유니온 빌딩은 어디 있어요?

린다: 우체국 아세요?

영미: 네. Ne

린다: 우체국 앞에 있어요.

영미: 학교 식당 음식이 어때요? 괜찮아요?

린다: 네, 좋아요. 커피가 맛있어요.

Ne Choayo copigu Mashiseyo

우체국 유니온 빌딩

도서관

NARRATION

캠퍼스

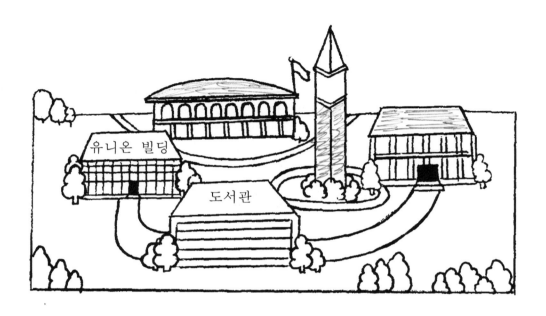

대학 캠퍼스는 참 커요. 그리고 학생이 아주 많아요. 도서관도
아주 좋아요. 학교 식당은 유니온 빌딩 안에 있어요. 음식이
싸요. 그리고 커피가 맛있어요. 유니온 빌딩 안에는 책방도 있
어요. 유니온 빌딩 뒤에는 운동장이 있어요. 운동장이 아주 넓
어요.

NEW WORDS AND EXPRESSIONS

NOUNS

가방 (G2.5)	bag
기숙사 (G2.5)	dormitory
대학	college
도서관	library
뒤	the back, behind
맛	taste
밑	the base, the bottom, below, under
시계 (G2.5)	clock, watch
식당	restaurant
아침	breakfast, morning
안	the inside
앞	the front
어디	what place? where? (question word)
옆 (G2.5)	the side, beside, next to
우산 (G2.5)	umbrella
우체국	post office
운동장	field, playground
위 (G2.5)	the upper side, the top side, above
음식	food
의자 (G2.5)	chair
제2과	Lesson 2
창문 (G2.5)	window
책 (G2.5)	book
책방	bookstore
책상 (G2.5)	desk
친구	friend
칠판 (G2.5)	blackboard
학교	school
학교 식당	school cafeteria

PROPER NOUNS

뉴욕 대학(G2.7)	New York University
린다	Linda
블루밍턴(G2.5)	Bloomington
서울대학(G2.5)	Seoul National University
아트 빌딩(G2.5)	Art Building
유니온 빌딩	Union Building
인디애나 대학(G2.5)	Indiana University

COUNTER

층	floor, layer (일층, 이층, 삼층. . .)

LOANWORDS

빌딩	building
안테나(G2.5)	antenna (electrical)
캠퍼스	campus
커피	coffee
텔레비전(G2.5)	television

PRONOUN

제	my (humble) (compare 내 my [plain])

VERBS

가요(G2.2)	(가다)	to go
공부해요(G2.2)	(공부하다)	to study
먹어요	(먹다)	to eat
숙제해요(G2.2)	(숙제하다)	to do homework
아세요	(알다)	to know
앉으세요	(앉다)	to sit (down)
알아요(G2.2)	(알다)	to know
인사하세요	(인사하다)	to greet
읽으세요(G2.3)	(읽다)	to read

있어요	(있다)	to exist
자요 (G2.2)	(자다)	to sleep
전화해요 (G2.2)	(전화하다)	to make a phone call, to telephone
지내요	(지내다)	to pass by, spend days
하세요	(하다)	to do
해요 (G2.2)	(하다)	to do

ADJECTIVES

괜찮아요	(괜찮다)	to be all right, O.K.
넓어요	(넓다)	to be spacious, wide
많아요	(많다)	to be many, much
맛있어요	(맛있다)	to be tasteful
반갑습니다	(반갑다)	to be glad, happy
싸요	(싸다)	to be cheap
어때요	(어떻다)	how is . . . ?
재미있어요 (G2.1)	(재미있다)	to be fun
좋아요	(좋다)	to be good
커요	(크다)	to be big

COPULA

| 이세요/세요 (G2.3) | (이다) | to be (honorific) |

ADVERBS

아주	very much
어떻게	how
여기	here
요즘	these days
잘	well
참	really, very

CONJUNCTION

| 그리고 | and |

INTERJECTIONS

네	yes
어	oh
저어	uh (expression of hesitation)
참	by the way

PARTICLE

에	in, at, on (indicates a static location)

SUFFIXES

~습니다	deferential ending
~어요/아요	polite ending
~(으)세요	honorific polite ending

Pronunciation

괜찮아요	[괜차나요]	앉으세요	[안즈세요]
넓어요	[널버요]	어떻게	[어떠케]
많아요	[마나요]	음악	[으막]
맛있어요	[마시써요]	전공	[전공] or [정공] (casual)
식당	[식땅]	친구	[친구] or [칭구] (casual)

Vocabulary by Theme

Common Greetings

요즘 어떻게 지내세요?	How are you doing these days?
잘 지내요.	I am fine.
반갑습니다.	It's nice to meet you.

Places on Campus

대학 캠퍼스	university campus	학교 식당	school cafeteria
도서관	library	빌딩	building
책방	bookstore	운동장	field, playground
대학	college	우체국	post office
클래스	class	기숙사	dormitory

Question Words

어디	where?
어떻게	how?
음식이 어때요?	How is the food?

Floors of a Building

일층	first floor	이층	second floor
삼층	third floor	사층	fourth floor

Positional Words

앞	front	옆	side, nearby
밑	underneath	아래	under, below, down
뒤	back, behind	안	in, inside
위	top, above, up		

Classroom (교실)

책상	desk	책	book
의자	chair	창문	window
시계	clock	문	door
가방	bag	칠판	blackboard
우산	umbrella	공책	notebook
교과서	textbook		

Commands
Positive

인사하세요.	Please greet him/her.
앉으세요.	Please sit down.
책을 펴세요.	Please open the book.
책을 덮으세요.	Please close the book.
잘 들으세요.	Please listen.
쓰세요.	Please write it.
칠판을 보세요.	Please look at the blackboard.
책을 읽으세요.	Please read the book.

Negative

영어를 쓰지 마세요.	Don't speak English.
책을 보지 마세요.	Don't look at the book.
얘기하지 마세요.	Don't talk.
먹지 마세요.	Don't eat/No food, please.

NOTES ON NEW WORDS AND EXPRESSIONS

Conversation 1

(1) A: 어떻게 지내세요?

　　B: 잘 지내요.

지내다 literally means 'to spend' or 'to pass one's time'. 어떻게 지내세요? is an expression asking about the other party's health. It is comparable to 'How are you doing/getting along?' in English. In response, the other party may say, 잘 지내요, meaning 'I'm doing fine'.

(2) 어때요? whose dictionary form is 어떻다, is an expression asking the other party's opinion, that is, 'How is ＿＿＿?' or 'How about ＿＿＿?' Note that 어떻 + ~어요 = 어때요.

음식이 어때요?	How's the food?
맛이 어때요?	How's the taste?
학교가 어때요?	How's school?
린다 씨는 어때요?	How about you, Linda?
식당이 어때요?	How's the restaurant?

(3) 참 'by the way' is an expression used when something suddenly occurs to the speaker which he or she has forgotten. In conversation 1, it has just occurred to 린다 that she needs to introduce 스티브 and 샌디 to each other.

(4) 인사하세요 is a request to greet, close to 'Say hi' in English. But actually it is more like 'Let me introduce someone to you.' 인사 literally means 'greeting'.

Conversation 2

(1) 저어 is an expression used for hesitation before the speaker says something. The hesitation draws the attention of the listener.

(2) 있어요 vs. 이에요/예요
In English, the verb 'to be' can be used for both (i) equation or identification and (ii) a statement of existence.

Equation/identification:	What **is** your major? My major **is** economics.
Existence of an entity:	The cafeteria **is** in the Union Building.

In Korean, two different verbs are used; 이다 'to be' for equation/identification, and 있다 'to exist, to stay' for existence. 이다 cannot be used for existence, and 있다 cannot be used for equation/identification.

Correct: 식당은 유니온 빌딩에 있어요.
Incorrect: 식당은 유니온 빌딩이에요.

Correct: 저는 학생이에요.
Incorrect: 저는 학생 있어요.

(3) 층 is a noun-classifier or counter used in counting layers, and is always used with numerals: e.g., 1층 'the first floor', 2층 'the second floor', 3층 'the third floor'

(4) 아세요: The dictionary form of 아세 is 알다. See Lesson 7 (ㄹ-irregular predicates).

(5) 괜찮아요 means that the situation is positive, not disturbing or displeasing. Depending on the situation, it could mean 'It's OK' or 'It's not too bad'.

Narration

(1) The dictionary form of 커요 is 크다. Note that ㅋ + ~어요 = 커요, with the deletion of the vowel 으.

CULTURE

1. Exchanging business cards

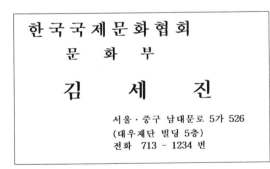

When people introduce themselves in Korea, they usually exchange business cards called 명함 (lit. name card). A business card contains an individual's full name, school affiliation or company name, and his or her position at the school or the company. It also contains the person's business address, home address, telephone and fax numbers, and more recently, e-mail or website addresses as well. Business cards are printed in both Chinese characters (한자) and 한글, and some have an English translation on the back. Business cards play an important role in developing business relationships. Recently, even high school students have begun creating stylish business cards for social reasons.

2. Introducing friends or acquaintances

In America, it is common courtesy to introduce your friends or acquaintances who are with you when you run into someone who does not know them. In Korea, however, it is not considered ill-mannered if you do not introduce your friends or acquaintances to others. Sometimes those who are accompanying you may step a few feet away so that they do not intrude on the conversation.

3. Social hierarchy and sentence endings

The Korean consciousness of the social hierarchy is mirrored in the structure and use of sentence endings. Sentence endings, which are attached to predicates (verbs and adjectives), vary to a great degree depending on whom you are speaking to (listener) and whom you are talking about (subject referent). The speaker chooses an appropriate sentence ending after considering his or her social relation to the listener and/or the subject of the sentence in terms of age, kinship, social status, and degree of intimacy.

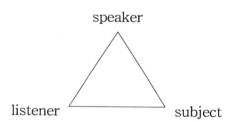

The social relation of speaker to listener is reflected in the structure and use of sentence endings. These endings are called "speech level endings." For deferential statements, ~습니다/ㅂ니다 is used; for polite statements, ~어요/아요 is used; for intimate statements, ~어/아 is used; and for plain statements, ~는다/ㄴ다/다 is used. For adult listeners, ~습니다/ㅂ니다 and ~어요/아요 are appropriate, and for child listeners, ~어/아 and ~는다/ㄴ다/다 are generally used.

The social relation of the speaker to the subject of the sentence is reflected in the presence or absence of the "honorific" marker ~(으)시/으(세). The honorific marker immediately follows the predicate stem in a grammatically correct sentence. For example, in **안녕하세요**, ~세 is the honorific marker that indicates the speaker's respect to the subject of the sentence (who in this case is the listener), and ~요 at the end is a polite marker that indicates the speaker's politeness toward the listener.

GRAMMAR

G2.1 Verbs versus adjectives

Predicate expressions in Korean can largely be classified into two groups, verbs and adjectives. Verbs typically denote actions and processes (including mental processes), whereas adjectives typically denote states (size, weight, quality, quantity, shape, appearance, perception, and emotion). The distinction is very important in Korean grammar, and this will become clearer in later lessons. Compare the verbs and adjectives that occur in this lesson.

Verbs		Adjectives	
먹어요	to eat	안녕하세요	to be well
앉으세요	to sit	괜찮아요	to be all right
아세요	to know	좋아요	to be good
인사하세요	to greet	맛있어요	to be tasteful
지내요	to spend (time)	커요	to be big, large
		많아요	to be many, much
		싸요	to be cheap, inexpensive
		넓어요	to be spacious
		반갑습니다	to be glad (used when meeting a person)
		재미있어요	to be fun

Notes

1. 있어요 'to exist, to stay' is a verb/adjective of existence. It behaves like a verb in some places and like an adjective in others.

2. The copula 이에요/예요 'to be' is, as illustrated in lesson 1 (G1.1), a special kind of adjective which expresses an equational relation, like 'to be' in English.

3. Notice that while adjectives in English need the copula 'be' in order to be used as predicates (it *is cheap*), adjectives in Korean are used directly as predicates without the copula 이에요/예요: 싸다, not 싸이다.

[연습] Based on the meaning of the predicate given, identify whether it is a verb (V) or an adjective (A).

보기: 먹어요 (V)

(1) 커요   (   )   (2) 지내요   (   )
(3) 괜찮아요   (   )   (4) 앉아요   (   )
(5) 맛있어요   (   )   (6) 넓어요   (   )
(7) 좋아요   (   )   (8) 많아요   (   )
(9) 싸요   (   )   (10) 인사해요 (   )
(11) 재미있어요   (   )

G2.2 The structure of predicates: The polite ending ~어요/아요

Examples

(1) 영미: 학교 식당이 어디 있어요?
    린다: 유니온 빌딩에 있**어요**. 일층에 있**어요**.
(2) 영미: 학교 식당 음식이 어때요?
    린다: 네, 좋아요. 커피가 맛있어요.

Notes

1. The structure of predicates consists of a stem and an ending. For dictionary entries, the meaningless ending ～다 is attached to verb and adjective stems. Examples of dictionary forms are given below:

Copula stem	Ending	Verb stem	Ending	Adjective stem	Ending
이	다	하	다	넓	다
아니	다	인사하	다	있	다
		먹	다	맛있	다
		지내	다	많	다
		알	다	괜찮	다
		앉	다	좋	다
				반갑	다
				싸	다

2. The polite ending ～어요/아요 is the most frequently used form in conversation. It has a number of variations. The lefthand column in each of the following boxes gives verbs in dictionary form; the righthand column gives verbs with the appropriate polite ending.

a. When the last vowel of the stem is either 아 or 오, ～아요 is used.

좋다	좋아요
많다	많아요
앉다	앉아요
괜찮다	괜찮아요
알다	알아요

b. All other stems take ~어요.

먹다	먹어요
있다	있어요
맛있다	맛있어요
넓다	넓어요

c. There are exceptions to the above rules.

이다	이에요/예요
아니다	아니에요
하다	해요

All verbs that contain 하다 'to do' are subject to this change.

인사하다	인사해요
공부하다	공부해요
숙제하다	숙제해요
전화하다	전화해요

d. Vowel contractions may change the ending.

가다	가요 (가 + ~아요)
지내다	지내요 (지내 + ~어요)
싸다	싸요 (싸 + ~아요)
자다	자요 (자 + ~아요)
크다	커요 (크 + ~어요)

[**연습** 1] Given the dictionary form, write the appropriate form of ~**어요/아요** ending.

보기: 먹다   <u>먹어요</u>

(1) 공부하다_____   (2) 지내다 _____
(3) 있다   _____   (4) 앉다 _____
(5) 맛있다 _____   (6) 싸다 _____
(7) 가다   _____   (8) 좋다 _____
(9) 많다   _____

[**연습** 2] Given the ~**어요/아요** form, write the dictionary form.

보기: 먹어요   <u>먹다</u>

(1) 인사해요 _____   (2) 재미있어요 _____
(3) 넓어요   _____   (4) 괜찮아요 _____
(5) 이에요/예요 _____   (6) 아니에요 _____

G2.3   The honorific ending ~(으)세요

Examples

(1) 스티브: 뭐 하**세요?**
    린다: 아침 먹어요.
(2) 린다: 요즘 어떻게 지내**세요?**
    스티브: 잘 지내요.
(3) 린다: 스티브 씨, 앉**으세요.**
          참, 인사하**세요.** 제 친구예요.

Notes

1. ~(으)세요 is an honorific form of ~어요/아요. It is a combination of the honorific marker ~(으)시 and ~어요, that is,

~(으)시 + ~어요 = ~(으)세요

~으세요 (after a consonant)		~세요 (after a vowel)	
좋	으세요	지내	세요
앉	으세요	아	세요
읽	으세요	인사하	세요

2. ~(으)세요 is used when the speaker respects the person being talked about.

(Sandy and Linda are talking about Prof. Lee.)
샌디: 이 선생님은 안녕하세요?   How's Prof. Lee?

린다: 네, 안녕하세요.   He is fine.

Prof. Lee is respected by both Sandy and Linda, so in talking about him, they use the ~(으)세요 ending.

3. When the person being talked about is an equal or an inferior, ~(으)세요 is not used.

(Linda and Sandy are talking about their mutual friend Steve.)
샌디: 스티브는 뭐 공부해요?   What does Steve study?

린다: 한국어 공부해요.   He studies Korean.

스티브 is a mutual friend, so no honorific reference is necessary, and thus the non-honorific ~어요/아요 ending is used.

4. When asking about a listener to whom you show respect, ~(으)세요 is used. In the examples (1) and (2), the first speaker is asking a question concerning the

listener. In showing respect for the listener, the ~(으)세요 ending is used. In the response, however, the statement is about the second speaker him/herself. Therefore, the non-honorific ~어요 ending is used. For another example:

샌디: 선생님, 요즘 어떻게 지내세요?   How have you been lately?
선생님: 잘 지내요.

샌디 asks a professor how he is, and uses the ~(으)세요 ending, showing her respect for the professor. In response, the professor uses the non-honorific ~어요/아요, because the statement is about himself/herself.

Note that the greeting 안녕하세요? asks about a listener's health. It conventionally takes ~(으)세요 to show respect.

5. Requesting an action typically takes ~(으)세요 to show respect for the listener, as in (3) in the examples.

Dictionary form	~어요/아요	~(으)세요
가다	가요	가세요
앉다	앉아요	앉으세요
인사하다	인사해요	인사하세요
하다	해요	하세요

[연습] Give answers that are appropriate for the contexts. Use ~어요/아요 and ~(으)세요 properly.

보기: A: 뭐 하세요?
         B: 아침 먹어요.

---

(1) The following questions are addressed to you. Answer the questions.
학생이세요? _____.
한국어 공부하세요? _____.

한국 사람이세요? _____.

일학년이세요? _____.

(2) Talking about Prof. Lee

    마이클: _____?

    린다: 네, 한국 사람이세요.

(3) 스티브: 샌디 씨, _____?

    샌디: 잘 지내요. 스티브 씨는 어떻게 지내세요?

    스티브: _____.

           뭐 공부하세요?

    샌디: _____.

G2.4   The subject particle 이/가

Examples

(1) A: 이름**이** 뭐예요?

    B: 스티브 윌슨이에요.

(2) A: 학교 식당**이** 어디 있어요?

    B: 유니온 빌딩에 있어요.

(3) 학교 식당 음식**이** 싸요. 그리고 커피**가** 맛있어요.

Notes

1. The particle **이/가** indicates that the word attached to it is the subject of the sentence, that is, what the predicate is about.

After a consonant: 이	이름이	스티브 윌슨이에요.
	음식이	싸요.
	학교 식당이	유니온 빌딩에 있어요.
After a vowel: 가	커피가	맛있어요.
	한국어가	재미있어요.

2. Key things to remember:

이/가 usually but not always marks the subject. In the following example the noun used with 이/가 (한국 사람) is not the subject.

샌디 왕은 한국 사람이 아니에요.

Note that when a noun or a pronoun functions as a topic (G1.1) or is used for comparison (G1.3), the particle 은/는 or 도 is used instead of 이/가.

(a) 영미: 유니온 빌딩은 어디 있어요?
     린다: 우체국 앞에 있어요.
(b) 린다: 스티브 씨, 요즘 어떻게 지내세요?
     스티브: 잘 지내요. 린다 씨는 어때요?
     린다: 저도 잘 지내요.

In (a), the subject 유니온 빌딩 is marked with the topic particle 은, not with the subject particle 이, because it is selected as the topic. In (b), 저 (린다) is marked with 도 because it is compared with 스티브: 린다's health is parallel to 스티브's.

[연습] Fill in the blank with the proper particle: 이/가, 은/는, 도.

보기: A: 이름이 뭐예요?
       B: 스티브 윌슨이에요.

---

(1) 린다: 스티브 씨, 요즘 어떻게 지내세요?
    스티브: 잘 지내요. 린다 씨____ 어때요?
    린다: 저____ 잘 지내요.
(2) 영미: 저어, 여기 학교 식당____ 어디 있어요?
    린다: 유니온 빌딩에 있어요.
    영미: 학교 식당 음식____ 어때요? 맛있어요?
    린다: 네, 괜찮아요. 커피____ 맛있어요.

G2.5 [Place]에 있어요

Examples

(1) A: 학교 식당이 어디 있어요?
    B: 유니온 빌딩에 **있어요**.
(2) A: 유니온 빌딩은 어디 있어요?
    B: 우체국 앞에 **있어요**.
(3) 학교 식당은 유니온 빌딩
    안에 **있어요**.
    그리고 도서관 밑에도 **있어요**.
    도서관은 아트 빌딩 (Art Building)
    옆에 **있어요**.
(4) 유니온 빌딩 뒤에는 운동장이 **있어요**.

기숙사
우체국
유니온 빌딩
아트 빌딩 도서관

Notes

1. Reference to a location of an object in Korean requires three elements:

(a) a location
(b) a locative particle 에
(c) a verb of existence 있어요

Object	Location	Locative particle	Verb of existence
학교 식당은	유니온 빌딩	에	있어요.
인디애나 대학은	블루밍턴	에	있어요.
서울대학은	서울	에	있어요.

Sometimes a reference to a location needs to be further specified with a "position" noun indicating front, back, side, inside, under, or above.

Object	Location		Locative particle	Verb of existence
	Object location	Relative position		
유니온 빌딩은	우체국	앞 (front)	에	있어요.
운동장은	유니온 빌딩	뒤 (back)	에	있어요.
도서관은	아트 빌딩	옆 (side)	에	있어요.
학교 식당은	유니온 빌딩	안 (inside)	에	있어요.
	도서관	밑 (under)	에도	있어요.
안테나는	텔레비전	위 (top, above)	에	있어요.

2. Key points to remember:

In referring to the location of an object, the locative particle 에 and the existential verb 있다/있어요, not ~이다/이에요, must be used.

In English, locations are expressed usually by prepositions such as 'on', 'above', 'in', 'under', 'below', 'beside', and 'behind', followed by an object location (e.g., a library). In Korean, locations are expressed by a sequence of an object location (e.g., 도서관), the noun indicating the relative position (e.g., 뒤 'back'), and the locative particle 에 'at', as in 도서관 뒤에 'behind the library'.

Location		Locative particle	Translation
Object location	Relative position		
도서관	앞	에	**in front of** the library
	뒤	에	**behind/in back of** the library
	옆	에	**beside/next to** the library
	위	에	**above/on top of/over** the library
	밑	에	**underneath, below, under** the library
	안	에	**in(side)** the library

In asking for the location of something, the question noun **어디** is used, like 'where' in English. Unlike in English, where question words are placed at the beginning of a sentence, however, **어디** is placed immediately before the verb **있어요**.

A: 학교 식당이 **어디** 있어요?   **Where** is the cafeteria?

B: 유니온 빌딩 안에 있어요.   It's in the Union Building.

[**연습** 1] Based on the following picture, give the location of the building named in the question.

보기: A: 유니온 빌딩이 어디 있어요?

        B: <u>기숙사 앞에 있어요.</u>

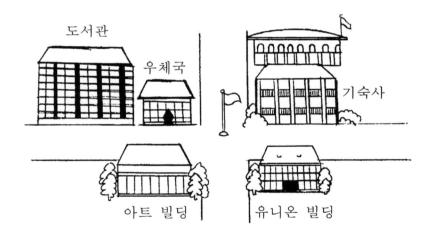

(1) A: 우체국은 어디 있어요?

     B: _____.

(2) A: 도서관은 어디 있어요?

     B: _____.

(3) A: 운동장은 어디 있어요?

     B: _____.

(4) A: 기숙사는 어디 있어요?

   B: _____ .

[연습 2] Answer the questions, based on the following picture.

> 보기: 가방이 어디 있어요?
>   <u>책상 옆에 있어요.</u>

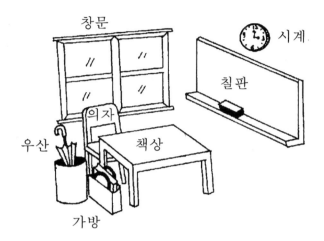

(1) 책상은 어디 있어요?

_____ .

(2) 칠판은 어디 있어요?

<u>시계 밑에 있어요</u> .

(3) 의자는 어디 있어요?

_____ .

(4) 우산은 어디 있어요?

_____ .

(5) 창문은 어디 있어요?

_____ .

(6) 시계는 어디 있어요?

<u>칠판 위에 있어요</u> .

G2.6 The discourse particle 은/는 (changing the topic)

Examples

(1) 린다: 스티브 씨, 요즘 어떻게 지내세요?

      스티브: 잘 지내요. 린다 씨는 어때요?

      린다: 저도 잘 지내요.

(2) 영미: 저어, 여기 학교 식당이 어디 있어요?

      린다: 유니온 빌딩에 있어요.

      영미: 유니온 빌딩은 어디 있어요?

      린다: 아트 빌딩 앞에 있어요.

(3) 학교 식당은 유니온 빌딩 안에 있어요.

      유니온 빌딩 안에는 책방도 있어요.

Notes

1. Recall from lesson 1 (G1.3) that the particle 은/는 is used to mark a topic. This use can be extended to shifting the topic from one item to another so that the speaker signals that he or she is now going onto something different.

In (1), after 스티브 tells about his health in response to 린다's question, he turns to 린다's health. This shift of topic is signaled by the topic particle 는 that is attached to 린다 씨 in 스티브's question.

In (2), 영미 and 린다 initially talk about the location of 학교 식당. 영미 wants to know about the location of the Union Building mentioned in 린다's response. Again, this shift of topic is signaled by the topic particle 은 attached to 유니온 빌딩 in 영미's second question.

2. In some cases discourse particles such as 은/는 and 도 can be added even after another particle such as 에, as in (3). However, it should be noted that such particles cannot be added to 이/가.

[연습 1] Using the word in brackets, change the topic.

> 보기: A: 학교 식당이 어디 있어요?
>   B: 유니온 빌딩에 있어요.
>   A: [유니온 빌딩] 유니온 빌딩은 어디 있어요?
>   B: 아트 빌딩 앞에 있어요.

(1) A: 여기 도서관 어디 있어요?
     B: 우체국 옆에 있어요.
     A: [기숙사] _____?
     B: 운동장 뒤에 있어요.
(2) A: 유니온 빌딩 안에 학교 식당이 있어요?
     B: 네, 1층에 있어요.
     A: 책방도 1층에 있어요?
     B: [책방] 아니오, _____.

G2.7   The conjunction 그리고

Examples

> (1) 영미: 여기 학교 식당이 어디 있어요?
>   린다: 유니온 빌딩 안에 있어요.
>   **그리고** 도서관 밑에도 있어요.
> (2) 뉴욕 대학은 커요. **그리고** 학생이 많아요.
> (3) 학교 식당은 싸요. **그리고** 커피가 맛있어요.

Note

그리고 is a conjunction that means 'and'.

[**연습** 1] Using **그리고**, add more content to the given message.

> 보기: 뉴욕 대학은 아주 커요.
> → <u>뉴욕 대학은 아주 커요. 그리고 학생이 아주 많아요.</u>

(1) 학교 식당 음식이 참 싸요.

→ _____.

(2) 유니온 빌딩에는 학교 식당이 있어요.

→ _____.

(3) 저는 한국어 공부해요.

→ _____.

[**연습** 2] Using the expression '. . . **어때요?**', talk to your partner about the given items. Give two attributes for each item.

> 보기: 학교 식당 음식
> A: 학교 식당 음식 어때요?
> B: 아주 맛있어요. 그리고 싸요.

(1) your school

A: _____.

B: _____.

(2) your roommate/friend

A: _____.

B: _____.

(3) the city you live in

A: _____.

B: _____.

(4) your class

A: _____.

B: _____.

TASK/FUNCTION

1. Introducing friends

> 린다: 스티브 씨, 인사하세요.
>   제 친구예요.
> 스티브: 안녕하세요? 처음 뵙겠습니다.
>   스티브 윌슨입니다.
> 샌디: 안녕하세요? 샌디 왕이에요.

Steps
(a) Get someone ready by calling him or her by name or title: 스티브 씨!
(b) Initiate the introduction: 인사하세요.
(c) Identify the other person, giving your relation to the person:

제 룸메이트예요.   (룸메이트 'roommate')

제 친구예요.

제 남자 친구예요   (남자 'man', 남자 친구 'boyfriend')

제 여자 친구예요.   (여자 'woman', 여자 친구 'girlfriend')

Note that 인사하세요 cannot be used if the first person is senior to the other person, because it is the junior who needs to do the greeting first.

Responding to an introduction

(a) Greeting: 안녕하세요?
                       (처음 뵙겠습니다)
(b) Identifying yourself: 스티브 윌슨입니다/이에요.

You may add 처음 뵙겠습니다 between (i) and (ii), which means that it is your first meeting with the other person.

[**연습**] Role play: Imagine that you're introducing your boyfriend/girlfriend and roommate to each other. Make a dialogue.

2. Inquiring about another person's health

린다:	스티브 씨, 안녕하세요?
	요즘 어떻게 지내세요?
스티브:	잘 지내요. 린다 씨는 어때요?
린다:	저는 조금 바빠요. (바빠요 to be busy) I am a bit busy.

Possible responses:

바빠요.	I'm busy.
그저 그래요.	Just so-so.
괜찮아요.	I'm all right. *or* Not too bad.
좋아요.	I'm fine.

[**연습**] Pair off and exchange greetings, using some of the expressions above.

3. Asking about the location of something or someone

You can use the same pattern for asking about and giving the location of people as for an object or place.

(1) A: 마이클 어디 있어요?	Where's Michael?
B: 집에 있어요. (집 home, house)	He's at home.
(2) A: 샌디 어디 있어요?	Where's Sandy?
B: 교실 안에 있어요. (교실 classroom)	She's in the classroom.

Practice asking about and giving locations, exploring all the possible spatial positions, that is, **위, 밑, 옆, 앞, 뒤,** and **안**.

[**연습** 1] Ask and give the location of places on your campus.

보기: [학교 식당]   A: 학교 식당이 어디 있어요?
                 B: 학교 식당은 유니온 빌딩 안에 있어요.

(1) [도서관] _____.
(2) [기숙사] _____.
(3) [책방] _____.
(4) [운동장] _____.
(5) [우체국] _____.

[**연습** 2] Answer the questions by specifying the relative position of the person in question with respect to the one given in [   ].

보기: 린다는 어디 있어요?
      [영미] 영미 앞에 있어요.

(1) 샌디는 어디 있어요?
    [스티브] _____.
(2) 마이클은 어디 있어요?
    [스티브] _____.

(3) 영미는 어디 있어요?

[스티브] _____.

(4) 스티브는 어디 있어요?

[마이클] _____.

(5) 학생들은 어디 있어요?

[교실] _____.

4. Seeking information about things and objects

(1) A: 이게 뭐예요?

B: 학교 지도예요. (지도 a map) It is a campus map.

(2) A: 이름이 뭐예요?

B: 샌디 왕이에요.

(3) 스티브: 린다 씨, 뭐 하세요?

린다: 아, 스티브 씨. 아침 먹어요.

(4) 영미: 유니온 빌딩 안에 뭐가 있어요?

린다: 학교 식당이 있어요. 그리고 책방도 있어요.

When you are looking for information about things, objects, concepts, or situations (events or states of affairs), the question word 뭐 is used followed by an appropriate verb or adjective.

Asking about the identity of a thing, object, or concept: Noun이/가 뭐예요?

이게 뭐예요?   What is this?

(이게 is a contraction of "이것 'this [thing]' + subject particle 이.")

이름이 뭐예요?   What is your/the name?

전화 번호가 뭐예요?   What is your/the phone number?

(전화 telephone, 번호 number)

Asking about an action or activity: 뭐 해요/하세요?

Asking about the existence of an object: [Place]에 뭐가 있어요?

[연습 1] Make up a question that leads to the given answer.

보기: A: <u>뭐 해요?</u>
　　　B: 아침 먹어요.

(1) A: _____?
　　 B: 스티브 월슨이에요.
(2) A: _____?
　　 B: 유니온 빌딩 안에 책방이 있어요.
(3) A: _____?
　　 B: 한국어 공부해요.

[연습 2] Make up an answer that is appropriate for the given question.

(1) A: 친구 이름이 뭐예요?
　　 B: _____.
(2) A: 교실 안에 뭐가 있어요?
　　 B: _____.
(3) A: 전화 번호가 뭐예요?
　　 B: _____.

5. Making requests

When you ask someone to do something, the verb designating the requested action refers to the listener as the subject. In a polite request, then, you need to show respect for the subject (listener). Use the ~(으)세요 ending.

Study some of the instructions or requests used in the classroom.

Instructions

책을 펴세요

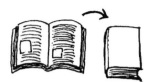

책을 덮으세요

칠판을 보세요

따라하세요

쓰세요

읽으세요

잘 들으세요

Requests that can be used by students

다시 한 번 말씀해 주세요.	Please say that again.
크게 말씀해 주세요.	Please speak louder.
천천히 말씀해 주세요.	Please speak slowly.

[**연습** 1] Follow the instructions.

(1) 책을 읽으세요.
(2) 따라 하세요.

(3) 책을 펴세요.

(4) 칠판에 쓰세요.

[**연습** 2] Make a request appropriate to the situation.

(1) [You cannot hear the teacher's voice clearly.]

_____.

(2) [You did not hear what the teacher said.]

_____.

(3) [You cannot follow the teacher's explanation because it is too fast.]

_____.

Lesson 2 The University Campus

CONVERSATION

1

(Linda and Sandy are eating breakfast in the school cafeteria. Steve enters the cafeteria and sees them.)

Steve: Hi, Linda.
      What are you doing?
Linda: Oh, hi, Steve. I'm eating breakfast.
      Please sit down.
      (Steve sits down.)
      How are you doing these days?
Steve: Fine. How about you?
Linda: By the way, let me introduce my friend.
Steve: Hi. It's nice to meet you.
      I'm Steve Wilson.
Sandy: Hello. I'm Sandy Wang. It's nice to meet you, too.

2

(Young-mee is looking for the school cafeteria and runs into Linda.)

Young-mee: Excuse me, where is the cafeteria?
Linda: It's in the Union Building, on the first floor.
      And it is in the basement of the library, too.
Young-mee: Where is the Union Building?
Linda: Do you know the Post Office?
Young-mee: Yes.
Linda: The Union Building is in front of the Post Office.
Young-mee: How's the food at the cafeteria? Is it okay?
Linda: Yes, it's good. The coffee is delicious.

제3과 한국어 수업

(Lesson 3: Korean Language Class)

OBJECTIVES

CULTURE	1. Korean collectivism: 우리 집, 우리 나라, 우리 반, 우리 학교
	2. Extending family terms to friends and acquaintances
	3. *T'aegŭkki*, the Korean national flag
GRAMMAR	G3.1　Use of 있다/없다 to express possession
	G3.2　Expressing possessive relations: N₁ (possessor) N₂ (possessed)
	G3.3　Alternative questions
	G3.4　은/는, 도, and 만
	G3.5　Joining nouns: N₁하고 N₂ 'N₁ and N₂'
	G3.6　The object particle 을/를
	G3.7　Omission of particles
TASK/FUNCTION	1. Inquiring about a person's hometown and family
	2. Talking about someone's major (전공)
	3. Describing people

CONVERSATION

1

(Prof. Lee moves around the classroom, checking whether the students brought their things for Korean class.)

이 선생님   영미   스티브

이 선생님: *yong mi tada jaseyo*
              영미, 한국어 사전[G3.7] 있어요?[G3.1]

영미: *Ani, o   chingo po ooilo*
              아니오, 지금 없어요. 집에 있어요.

이 선생님: (Pointing to a dictionary on the desk)

              그럼, 이건 누구 사전이에요?[G3.2]
              wrum igun   yogum   san iyeyo

영미: 스티브 거예요.
              Steve   u yeyo.

이 선생님: (Finding Steve with no Korean textbook in hand)

              스티브, 한국어 책[G3.7] 어디 있어요?

스티브: 가방 안에 있어요.

              (The bell rings)
이 선생님: *uni mun ima ga be-seyo*
              오늘은 이만 하겠어요.
              Chil mun iseyo (any questions)
              질문 있어요?

영미: *Ne chill mun isey*
              네, 질문 있어요. 오늘 숙제 있어요?

이 선생님: *Ne onul sute nun songba yasip monguyo*
              네, 오늘 숙제는 3과 연습 문제예요.
              monje Nal ieyo.
              내일까지 내세요.

2

(Linda is sitting in her seat, and Sandy comes in and takes her seat.)

린다   샌디

린다: (Looking at Sandy's backpack)

샌디 씨, 가방이 참 예뻐요.

샌디: 네, 내 동생 거예요.

린다: 아, 동생 있으세요?

여동생이에요, 남동생이에요?[G3.3]

샌디: 여동생이에요.

린다 씨도 동생 있으세요?

린다: 아니오, 없어요. 언니만[G3.4] 있어요.

샌디: 언니는 어디 계세요?

린다: 보스톤에 있어요.

샌디: 부모님도 보스톤에 계세요?

린다: 아니오, 우리 아버지, 어머니는 시카고에 계세요.

NARRATION

내 친구 샌디

샌디는 내 클래스메이트예요. 경제학을 공부해요.
샌디는 중국 사람이에요. 집이 홍콩이에요. 홍콩에
아버지하고[G3.5] 어머니하고 오빠가 계세요. 샌디 오빠
는 대학원생이에요. 정치학을[G3.6] 공부해요. 샌디는
여동생도 있어요. 샌디 여동생은 고등 학생이에요. 샌디하고
샌디 동생은 사이가 참 좋아요.

NEW WORDS AND EXPRESSIONS

NOUNS

거	thing (contracted form of 것)
경제학	economics
고등 학생	high school student
남동생	younger brother
내일	tomorrow (also used as an adverb)
누나 (G3.4)	the older sister of a male
대통령 (G3.2)	president (of a country)
대학원생	graduate student
동생	younger sibling
부모님	parents
사이	relationship
사전	dictionary
수도 (G3.2)	capital
수업	class
숙제	homework, assignment
시간 (G3.1)	time (duration)
아버지	father
어머니	mother
언니	the older sister of a female
여동생	younger sister
연습 문제	exercises
오늘	today
오빠	the older brother of a female
은행 (G3.4)	bank
정치학	political science
제3과	lesson 3
질문	question
집	home, house
형	older brother of a male

PROPER NOUNS

보스톤	Boston
시카고	Chicago
영국(G3.2)	England
하와이(G3.1)	Hawaii
홍콩	Hong Kong

LOANWORDS

뉴스(G3.2)	news
룸메이트(G3.5)	roommate
클래스메이트	classmate

PRONOUNS

내	my (plain) (compare 제 [humble])
누가(G3.5)	who? (as subject; from 누구 + particle 가)
누구	who?
우리	we, us, our
이거	this (thing) (contracted form of 이것)

VERBS

계세요	(계시다)	to exist, stay (honorific)
내세요	(내다)	to turn in, hand in
마셔요(G3.6)	(마시다)	to drink
만나요(G3.6)	(만나다)	to meet
봐요(G3.6)	(보다)	to watch

ADJECTIVES

나빠요(G3.1)	(나쁘다)	to be bad *좋아요*
맛없어요	(맛없다)	to be tasteless *맛있어요*
바빠요(G3.1)	(바쁘다)	to be busy *안바빠요*
비싸요(G3.1)	(비싸다)	to be expensive *싸요*
없어요	(없다)	to not exist, have, own *있어요*

예뻐요	(예쁘다)	to be pretty, beautiful	안 어l뻐요
작아요	(작다)	to be small	커요
재미없어요	(재미없다)	to be no fun, to be uninteresting	재미있어요
적어요	(적다)	to be not plentiful	많아요
좁아요	(좁다)	to be narrow	넓어요

ADVERBS

또 (G3.5)	and, also, too
이만	this much, this only
좀 (G3.1)	a little, please
지금	now (also used as a noun)

CONJUNCTION

| 그럼 | (if so) then |

INTERJECTION

| 네 | I see |

PARTICLES

까지	until, by (a time)
만	only
의 (G3.2)	. . . 's, of (possessive particle)
하고	and (joins nouns; colloquial form)

Pronunciation

대통령	[대통녕]	없어요	[업써요]
맛없다	[마덥따]	역사	[역싸]
숙제	[숙쩨]	연습 문제	[연습문제]
스티브 거	[스티브꺼]		

Vocabulary by Theme

Time Expressions

아침	morning	지금	now
어제	yesterday	어제 아침	yesterday morning
오늘	today	오늘 아침	this morning
내일	tomorrow	내일 아침	tomorrow morning

Schools and Students

초등 학교	elementary school	초등 학생	elementary school student
중학교	middle school	중학생	junior high school student
고등 학교	high school	고등 학생	high school student
대학교	college, university	대학생	college student
대학원	graduate school	대학원생	graduate student

Family (가족)

부모님	parents	오빠	older brother of a female
아버지	father	언니	older sister of a female
어머니	mother	누나	older sister of a male
		형	older brother of a male
		여동생	younger sister
		남동생	younger brother

Question Words

누구	someone, who (누구세요? 'Who is it?')
누구(의)	whose (누구 사전이에요? 'Whose dictionary is it?')
누가	someone, who (as subject) (누가 공부해요? 'Who is studying?' 누가 전화해요? 'Who is making a call?' 누가 집에 있어요? 'Who is at home?'
어디	where

NOTES ON NEW WORDS AND EXPRESSIONS

Conversation 1

(1) 없어요/없다 'to not exist, have' is the antonym of 있어요/있다 'to exist, have'.

(2) 집 may refer to either a house (the building) or a home.

(3) 이건 is the contracted form of 이거 (from 이것) + topic marker ㄴ (from 은/는).

(4) When 누구 'who?' is attached to the subject particle 가, 누가 should be used instead of 누구가.

(5) 거 is the contracted form of 것. In general, 거 is used in colloquial speech, and 것 is used in writing and in formal situations.

(6) 이만하겠어요 literally means 'we'll do only this much', and is used when the speaker ends a certain activity. It is often used by teachers who are ending classes.

(7) Referring to days:

어제	오늘	내일
yesterday	today	tomorrow

Conversation 2

(1) 계시다 is the honorific word for 있다. It is used when the subject is a respected person, e.g., a teacher, a parent, a grandparent, and so on.

(2) Family terms in Korean: In English, siblings are referred to depending on their gender (brother, sister), regardless of one's own gender. In Korean, proper references for siblings depend on both the gender of the sibling and of the self, as well as their relative ages. 동생 'younger sibling', however, can be used to refer to either a male (남동생) or a female (여동생).

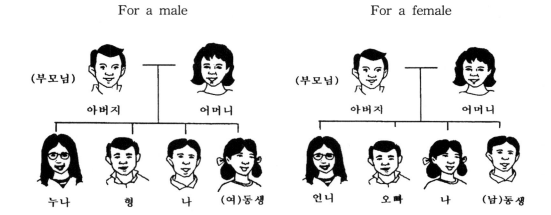

| For a male | For a female |

Narration

(1) 집이/은 N이에요/예요 is an expression indicating residence. It may indicate either a hometown or a local residence, and does not refer to a specific location but to a general area. In order to refer to a specific location, N에 있어요 should be used.

우리 집이/은 시카고예요.   My hometown is Chicago.

우리 집이/은 워싱턴 애비뉴에   My house is on Washington Avenue.
있어요.

(2) School terms:

School		Student	
초등 학교	elementary school	초등 학생	elementary school student
중학교	middle school	중학생	junior high school student
고등 학교	high school	고등 학생	high school student
대학교	college	대학생	college student
대학원	graduate school	대학원생	graduate student

Note: 초등 학교 used to be called 국민 학교.

(3) **사이가 좋아요** means that two or more people are on good terms.

(4) Some property concepts that are opposites:

좋아요(좋다)	to be good	↔	나빠요(나쁘다)	to be bad
맛있어요(맛있다)	to be tasteful	↔	맛없어요(맛없다)	to be tasteless
커요(크다)	to be big, large	↔	작아요(작다)	to be small, little
많아요(많다)	to be plentiful	↔	적어요(적다)	to be scarce
싸요(싸다)	to be cheap	↔	비싸요(비싸다)	to be expensive
넓어요(넓다)	to be spacious	↔	좁아요(좁다)	to be narrow
재미있어요(재미있다)	to be fun	↔	재미없어요(재미없다)	to be no fun

CULTURE

1. Korean collectivism: 우리 집, 우리 나라, 우리 반, 우리 학교

Certain objects, people, or concepts do not necessarily belong to one individual, but to a group of people, such as a nation, school, family, house, classes, etc. In Korean, the possessor of these items frequently reflects this 'group possession' in speech, referring to them with a plural possessive pronoun 우리 (or its humble form 저희) 'we/us/our', opposed to the singular 나 (or its humble form 저) 'I/my/mine'. This is frequently the case even when the speaker may be speaking of only one person or him- or herself, as in 우리 아내 'my wife'. Compare English and Korean.

English	Korean
my/our country	우리 (or 저희) 나라
my/our house	우리 (or 저희) 집
my/our family	우리 (or 저희) 가족
my/our father/mother	우리 (or 저희) 아버지/어머니
my/our class	우리 (or 저희) 반
my/our school	우리 (or 저희) 학교

2. Extending family terms to friends and acquaintances

In Korean, some family terms are often extended in referring to social relations. Most generally, elderly men are called 할아버지, which originally means 'grandpa', and elderly women are called 할머니, which means 'grandma'. 아저씨 'uncle' now can informally refer to any male adult between roughly forty and sixty, and likewise 아주머니 'aunt' to any female adult of similar age, when you do not know a title or name.

Among members of a similar age group, senior members are called and referred to by kinship terms for siblings. A junior female member calls/refers to a senior female member as 언니 and a senior male member as 오빠. Some female members feel reluctant to use 오빠 and prefer the term 형. A junior male member calls/refers to a senior female member as 누나 and a senior male member as 형.

Parents of your friends are often addressed as 아버님 (honorific form of 아버지) and 어머니 or 어머님 (honorific form of 어머니).

At a restaurant or a store, customers may refer to the server as 언니/누나. The owner or employee of the store may refer to a female customer as 언니/누나 in order to sell an item.

3. *T'aegŭkki*, the Korean national flag

The *T'aegŭkki* was first flown on August 22, 1882, by a Korean emissary to Japan, Pak Young-hyo. It was officially declared the national flag of the Republic of Korea on October 15, 1949. The flag has a white background with a *t'aegŭk* 'the Great Absolute', the two lobed *yin-yang* (in Korean, *ŭm-yang*) symbol, in the center, flanked by four of the Eight Trigrams from the *Book of Changes*. The *t'aegŭk* symbolizes the philosophy of the dualism of the universe—the balance and harmony in nature of opposite forces and elements which are in perpetual motion. It represents the ultimate source of all existence and the basis of all values. The upper red lobe stands for *yang*: positive, masculine, active, constructive, light, heat, and dignity, whereas the lower blue lobe stands for *ŭm*: negative, feminine, passive, destructive, dark, cold, and hope. As for the black trigrams in each corner, the three solid bars of the upper left corner represent heaven, spring, east, and benevolence; the upper right bars, moon, winter, north, and wisdom; the lower right bars, earth, summer, west, and righteousness; and the lower left bars, sun, autumn, south, and etiquette. The flag as a whole symbolizes the ideal of the Korean people developing forever in harmony with the universe.

GRAMMAR

G3.1 Use of 있다/없다 to express possession

Examples

(1) 샌디:　　　린다 씨, 동생 **있어요?**

　　　린다:　　　아니오, **없어요.** 언니만 **있어요.**

(2) 이 선생님: 영미, 한국어 사전 **있어요?**

　　　영미:　　　아니오, 지금 **없어요.** 집에 **있어요.**

(3) A: 오늘 시간 좀 **있으세요?**　　　Do you have some (spare) time today?

　　　B: 아니오, 오늘은 좀 바빠요.　　　No, I am a bit busy today.

　　　A: 내일은 어때요?　　　How about tomorrow?

　　　B: 내일은 시간 있어요.　　　I have time tomorrow.

(4) 이 선생님: 질문 **있어요?**　　　Do you have any questions?/ Is there a question?

　　　린다:　　　네, **있어요.**　　　Yes, I do/There is.

　　　　　　오늘 숙제 **있어요?**　　　Do we have homework today?/ Is there homework today?

　　　이 선생님: 네, 오늘 숙제는　　　Yes, today's homework is

　　　　　　3과 연습 문제예요.　　　the exercises in lesson 3.

Notes

있다 refers to either the existence or the possession of an object or person. In honorific forms, the two different words are used as follows.

	Existence	Possession
Non-honorific	있어요	
Honorific	계세요	있으세요

부모님은 하와이에 계세요.   My parents are in Hawaii.

선생님, 시간이 있으세요?   Do you have a minute, professor?

[연습] Make a dialogue using the words in brackets.

> 보기: [한국어 책]
>   A: 한국어 책 있어요?
>   B: 아니오, 없어요.

(1) [사전]

A: _____?

B: 네, _____.

(2) [동생]

A: _____?

B: 아니오, _____.

(3) [시간]

A: 내일 _____?

B: 아니오, _____.

G3.2 Expressing possessive relations:
N₁ (possessor) N₂ (possessed)

Examples

(1) 이 선생님: 이거 **누구 사전**이에요?

영미: **스티브 거**예요.

(2) 이 선생님: 마이클, 이거   Michael, is this your book?

마이클 책이에요?

마이클: 네, **제 거**예요.   Yes, it's mine.

(3) 린다: 샌디 씨, 가방이 참 예뻐요.   Sandy, (your) backpack
is pretty.

샌디: **제 동생 거**예요.   It's my younger sibling's.

(4) 샌디: 부모님도 보스톤에   Are (your) parents also in

계세요?   Boston?

린다: 아니오, **우리 아버지,**   No, my father and mother

어머니는 시카고에 계세요. are in Chicago.

Notes

1. Possession involves two parts, the possessor and the possessed. The most common way of expressing the possessive relation is to place the possessor and the possessed side by side.

Possessor	Possessed	
마이클	책	Michael's book
샌디	가방	Sandy's bag/backpack
우리	아버지, 어머니	my (our) father and mother
학생	이름	the student's name

2. The possessive particle 의 (usually pronounced [에]), comparable to the English preposition 'of', may be used sometimes, but usually not in conversation, except for

limited contexts, mostly when both the possessor and the possessed refer to abstract concepts.

미국의 대통령	the president of the United States of America
영국의 수도	the capital of England
오늘의 뉴스	the news of the day

3. The possessive pronouns 내, 제, and 누구(의) are formed by combining the regular pronoun with the particle 의. Sometimes contractions occur.

	I	my
Possessive	나	내 (나 + 의)
Humble	저	제 (저 + 의)

누구 is used for 'who' and 'whose'. In writing, the possessive particle 의 may be used (as in 누구의 책).

Question word	who	whose
	누구	누구(의)

4. When the possessed object is obvious from the preceding context, 거/것, which literally means 'thing', can substitute for it.

| A: 이거 누구 책이에요? | Whose book is this? |
| B: 스티브 거예요. | (It's) Steve's. |

When 거 is combined with possessive pronouns, it creates the equivalent of English 'mine, ours, yours, his, hers, and theirs'.

내	my (plain)	+ 거 = 내 거	mine (lit. my thing)
제	my (humble)	+ 거 = 제 거	mine (lit. my thing)
우리	we/us	+ 거 = 우리 거	ours (lit. our thing)

[**연습** 1] Using the given item, say 'It's my _____.' in both (i) the plain form and (ii) the humble form.

> 보기: 가방   (i) <u>내 가방이에요.</u>
>   (ii) <u>제 가방이에요.</u>

(1) 책   _____.

            _____.

(2) 사전   _____.

            _____.

(3) 동생   _____.

            _____.

(4) 친구   _____.

            _____.

(5) 클래스메이트 _____.

            _____.

[**연습** 2] Complete the dialogue using 거.

> 보기: A: 누구 가방이에요?
>   B: [마이클] <u>마이클 거예요.</u>

(1) A: 이거 누구 책이에요?

    B: [스티브] _____.

(2) A: 이거 누구 사전이에요?

    B: [나] _____.

(3) 린다: [가방] _____?

    샌디: 동생 거예요.

G3.3   Alternative questions

Examples

(1)	린다:	샌디 씨, 동생 있어요?	Sandy, do you have a younger sibling?
	샌디:	네, 있어요.	Yes, I do.
	린다:	**남동생이에요, 여동생이에요?**	Is your younger sibling male or female?
	샌디:	여동생이에요.	
(2)	스티브:	**샌디 씨는 한국 사람이에요, 중국 사람이에요?**	
	영미:	중국 사람이에요.	
(3)	선생님:	**스티브는 일학년이에요, 이학년이에요?**	
	스티브:	삼학년이에요.	

Note

Alternative questions are used to ask someone to choose one from the given choices.

[**연습**] Make up an alternative question.

> 보기: 마이클: <u>샌디 씨는 일학년이에요, 삼학년이에요?</u>
>   샌디: 일학년이에요.

(1) 마이클: ___미국 사람이에요, 한국 사람이에요___?
    샌디: 미국 사람이에요.
(2) 샌디: ___학생이에요, 선생님이에요___?
    스티브: 학생이에요.
(3) 린다: 부모님은___홍콩에 계세요___?
    샌디: 홍콩에 계세요.

(4) 영미: 집이 _시카고에요, 뉴욕이에요_ ?

린다: 시카고예요.

(5) 샌디: _스티브 씨는 한국어 공부해요_ ? 영어 공부해요

스티브: 한국어 공부해요.

G3.4 은/는, 도, and 만

Examples

(1) 샌디: 린다 씨, 동생 있어요?

린다: 아니오, 없어요.

샌디: 오빠는 있어요?

린다: 오빠도 없어요. 언니만 있어요.   I only have an older sister.

(2) 샌디: 린다 씨, 집이 어디예요?

린다: 시카고예요.

시카고에 아버지, 어머니가 계세요.

샌디: 언니도 시카고에 계세요?

린다: 아니오, 언니는 보스톤에 있어요.

시카고에는 부모님만 계세요.

Notes

As discussed in lesson 1 (G1.3), the particles 는 and 도 are used to compare items, 는 when the two items compared are different, and 도 when the two items are parallel. The particle 만 is a marker of exclusivity. In the last sentence in (1), for example, 린다 has only an older sister (언니), and no other sibling.

[연습] Write a description using the given information.

보기: [스티브 윌슨 (3학년), 김영미 (1학년), 마이클 정 (1학년)]

김영미는 1학년이에요. 마이클 정도 1학년이에요.

스티브 윌슨은 3학년이에요. 스티브 윌슨만 1학년이 아니에요.

(1) [한국어 클래스: 김영미 (한국 사람), 마이클 정 (한국 사람),
    샌디 왕 (중국 사람)]_____.

(2) [Language lab: 린다 한 (한국어 학생), 샌디 정 (한국어 학생),
    스스끼 요꼬 (중국어 학생)]

_____.

(3) [유니온 빌딩: 식당 (1층), 책방 (1층), 은행 (2층)]

_____.

(4) [마이클 has: no older brother, no older sister, but only a younger
    brother] _____.

(5) [스티브's family: 부모님, 여동생, 누나 are all in Boston. Only Steve
    is in New York.]

_____.

G3.5 Joining nouns: N_1하고 N_2 'N_1 and N_2'

Examples

> (1) 샌디는 집이 홍콩이에요. 홍콩에 부모님**하고** 오빠가 있어요.
> (2) 샌디**하고** 샌디 동생은 사이가 좋아요.
> (3) 스티브**하고** 마이클은 룸메이트예요.

Notes

The particle 하고, like 'and' in English, is attached to a noun expression and joins it to another noun expression. This particle is usually used in colloquial speech and informal writing.

[**연습**] Complete the dialogue using the words given.

> 보기: 린다: 스티브 씨, 뉴욕에 누가 있어요?
>
>   스티브: [남동생, 누나] 남동생하고 누나가 있어요.

(1) 영미: 유니온 빌딩 안에 뭐가 있어요?

린다: [식당, 책방] _____.

(2) 샌디: [마이클, 민호, 룸메이트] _____?

영미: 아니오, 민호는 마이클 동생이에요.

(3) 린다: 홍콩에 누가 계세요?

샌디: [아버지, 어머니, 오빠] _____.

G3.6   The object particle 을/를

Examples

(1) 린다가 아침을 먹어요.

(2) 영미가 텔레비전을 봐요.

(3) 샌디가 커피를 마셔요.

(4) 스티브가 친구를 만나요.

Notes

1. The particle 을/를 marks the object of the verb.

After a consonant: 을	아침을	먹어요.
	텔레비전을	봐요.
After a vowel: 를	친구를	만나요.
	커피를	마셔요.

2. The basic sentence patterns: N이/가 N을/를 ~어요/아요

Subject	Object	Verb
린다가	아침을	먹어요.
영미가	텔레비전을	봐요.
샌디가	커피를	마셔요.
스티브가	친구를	만나요.

In the above examples, the subjects designate the actors, the ones who do the action, and the objects designate the things that the actors do something to.

[연습] Fill in the blank with the proper particle, 은/는, 도, 이/가, or 을/를.

> 보기: 스티브는 일학년이에요. 한국어를 공부해요.
>   샌디도 일학년이에요. 샌디는 경제학을 공부해요.

(1) 스티브<u>는</u> 한국어<u>를</u> 공부해요.
    린다<u>도</u> 한국어<u>를</u> 공부해요.
(2) 린다<u>는</u> 샌디____ 만나요.
(3) 린다____ 아침____ 먹어요.
    샌디____ 커피____ 마셔요.
    학교 식당은 커피____ 싸요.

G3.7 Omission of particles

Examples

> (1) 이 선생님: 영미, **한국어 사전** 있어요?
>   영미: 아니오, 없어요.
>   [in reporting]   영미는 한국어 사전**이** 없어요.

(2) 이 선생님: 스티브, **한국어 책** 어디 있어요?
    스티브: 가방 안에 있어요.
    [in reporting] 스티브는 한국어 책**이** 가방 안에 있어요.
(3) 스티브: 린다 씨, **뭐** 하세요?
    린다: **아침** 먹어요.
    [in reporting] 린다는 아침을 먹어요.
(4) 영미: 샌디 씨, **뭐** 공부하세요?
    샌디: **경제학** 공부해요.
    [in reporting] 샌디는 경제학을 공부해요.

Notes

1. We have learned that nominals (nouns, pronouns, numerals, etc.) may be marked with a particle, e.g., **이/가** for subjects (G2.4) and **을/를** for objects (G3.6). In conversation, however, nominals frequently are not marked with any particle at all.

2. When the purpose is to report who does what to whom and when, where, and how in precise terms, the particle usually is needed.

3. In conversation, a particle is necessary when the speaker wants to focus on a specific element the speaker assumes the listener is not thinking of.

영미: 저어, 여기 학교 식당**이** 어디 있어요?
린다: 유니온 빌딩에 있어요.

샌디: 누가 한국어를 공부해요?
마이클: 영미**가** 공부해요.

[**연습** 1] Based on the given report, complete the dialogues.

보기: [Report: 샌디는 경제학을 공부해요.]
        영미: 샌디 씨는 뭐 공부하세요?
        샌디: 경제학 공부해요.

(1) [Report: 샌디는 오빠가 있어요. 정치학을 공부해요.]
  린다: 샌디 씨 _____?
  샌디: 네, 있어요. 홍콩에 있어요.
  린다: 오빠는 뭐 공부하세요?
  샌디: _____.

(2) [Report: 린다가 커피를 마셔요. 커피가 맛있어요.]
  스티브: 린다 씨, 뭐 하세요?
  린다: _____.
  스티브: _____?
  린다: 네, 맛있어요.

(3) [Report: 영미는 지금 사전이 없어요. 집에 있어요.]
  스티브: 영미 씨 _____?
  영미: 지금 없어요. 집에 있어요.
  스티브: 이건 누구 사전이에요?
  영미: 마이클 거예요.

[**연습** 2] Write a report based on the dialogue given.

보기: 영미: 샌디 씨는 뭐 공부하세요?
       샌디: 경제학 공부해요.
       [Report: 샌디는 경제학을 공부해요.]

---

(1) 스티브: 린다 씨, 뭐 하세요?
   린다: 아침 먹어요.
   [Report: _____.]
(2) 린다: 스티브 씨는 아침에 뭐 하세요?
   스티브: 커피 마셔요. 린다 씨는 뭐 하세요?
   린다: 저는 주스 마셔요.
   [Report: _____.]
(3) 마이클: 샌디 씨 오빠 있어요?
   샌디: 네 있어요.

마이클: 언니도 있어요?

샌디: 네, 언니도 있어요.

[Report: _____.]

[**연습** 3] Interview your partner regarding the items below and report to the class about your partner.

(1) major   (2) about younger siblings
(3) about older siblings   (4) Korean dictionary

TASK/FUNCTION

1. Inquiring about a person's hometown and family

스티브: 샌디 씨는 집이 어디예요?

샌디: 홍콩이에요.

스티브: 홍콩에 부모님이 계세요?

샌디: 네. 아버지, 어머니하고 또 오빠도 있어요.

        스티브 씨는 집이 어디예요?

스티브: 우리 집은 보스톤이에요.

        보스톤에 아버지 어머니하고, 누나, 형이 있어요.

샌디: 동생은 없어요?

스티브: 없어요.

Set patterns

(1) Asking about and describing someone's hometown:

A: (N는) 집이 어디예요?

B: (우리 집은) [Place]~이에요/예요.

(2) Asking about family members: Do you have _____?

> A: _____있어요?
> B: 네, 있어요; 아니오, 없어요.

(3) Describing where family members live:

> Use the honorific verb **계세요** for parents, grandparents, and older siblings.
> A: 부모님은 어디 계세요?
> B: [Place]에 계세요.

> A: _____은 어디 있어요?
> B: [Place]에 있어요.

> A: [Place]에 누가 있어요?
> B: _____이/가 있어요; _____이/가 계세요.

[**연습**] Ask your partner about his or her hometown and family.

2. Talking about someone's major (전공)

> 스티브: 샌디 씨는 뭐 공부하세요/전공하세요? (전공하다 to major in)
> 샌디: 경제학 공부해요/전공해요. 스티브 씨는 전공이 뭐예요?
> 스티브: 저는 음악 전공이에요.

There are three ways to ask and respond about someone's major:

> Generally asking what he/she studies:
> A: 뭐 공부해요/공부하세요?   What do you study?
> B: _____공부해요.

> Specifically asking what he/she majors in:
> A: 뭐 전공해요/전공하세요?   What do you major in?
> B: _____ 전공해요.

Using an equational expression:

A: 전공이 뭐예요?   What is your major?

B: 음악 (전공) 이에요.

Some majors:

Humanities	Social Sciences	Natural Sciences	Engineering	Arts	Professional Schools
동양학 Asian Studies	경제학 Economics	물리학 Physics	기계 공학 Mech. Engr.	음악 Music	건축학 Architecture
언어학 Linguistics	교육학 Education	생물학 Biology	전기 공학 Electric. Engr.	피아노 Piano	법학 Law
인류학 Anthropology	사회학 Sociology	수학 Mathematics	컴퓨터 공학 Computer Science	미술 Art	약학 Pharmacology
영문학 English Literature	심리학 Psychology	화학 Chemistry	화공학 Chem. Engr.	디자인 Design	의학 Medicine
역사학 History	정치학 Political Science	천문학 Astronomy	토목 공학 Civil Engr.	조각 Sculpture	경영학 Management

[**연습**] Answer each question, based on the content of the main text in this lesson and the model dialogue above.

(1) 샌디는 전공이 뭐예요?
(2) 샌디 오빠는 뭐 전공해요?
(3) 스티브는 뭐 공부해요?
(4) Say what your major is in the three ways discussed above.

3. Describing people

[**연습** 1] Describe each of the people below based on the information given.

> 보기: 샌디 왕은 집이 홍콩이에요. 샌디 왕은 중국 사람이에요.
>   그리고 경제학을 공부해요. 샌디 왕은 한국어 학생이에요.
>   지금 2학년이에요.

Name	Year	Nationality/Ethnicity	Major	Status/Relationship	Hometown
샌디 왕	2학년	중국 사람	경제학	한국어 학생/린다 친구	홍콩
스티브 윌슨	3학년	미국 사람	음악	마이클 룸메이트	보스톤
마이클 정	1학년	한국 사람	컴퓨터	한국어 학생	뉴욕
스스끼 요꼬	4학년	일본 사람	동양학	스티브 윌슨 친구	도쿄
린다 한	1학년	한국 사람	생물학	마이클 여자 친구	시카고

[연습 2] First interview your classmates and fill in the chart below, then report the information to the class based on the example (보기) given in [연습 1].

Name	Year	Nationality/ Ethnicity	Major	Status/Relation	Home- town

Lesson 3 Korean Language Class

CONVERSATION

1

(Prof. Lee moves around the classroom, checking whether the students brought their things for Korean class.)

Prof. Lee:	Young-mee, do you have your Korean dictionary?
Young-mee:	No, I don't. It's at home.
Prof. Lee:	(Pointing to a dictionary on the desk)
	Then whose dictionary is this?
Young-mee:	It's Steve's.
Prof. Lee:	(Finding Steve with no Korean textbook in hand)
	Steve, where is your Korean textbook?
Steve:	It's in the bag.
	(The bell rings.)
Prof. Lee:	That's all for today. Do you have any questions?
Young-mee:	Yes, I have a question. Do we have homework today?
Prof. Lee:	Yes, today's homework is the exercises in lesson 3.
	Please turn it in by tomorrow.

2

(Linda is sitting in her seat, and Sandy comes in and takes her seat.)

Linda:	(Looking at Sandy's backpack)
	Sandy, your backpack is so pretty.
Sandy:	Thanks, it's my younger sibling's.
Linda:	Oh, do you have a younger sibling?
	A younger sister or a younger brother?
Sandy:	A younger sister. Do you have any younger siblings?
Linda:	No, I don't. I only have an older sister.
Sandy:	Where does your sister live?
Linda:	She's in Boston.
Sandy:	Are your parents also in Boston?
Linda:	No, my mom and dad are in Chicago.

제4과 학교에서

(Lesson 4: At School)

OBJECTIVES

CULTURE	1. Asking where others are going
	2. 안녕히 가세요 vs. 잘 가
GRAMMAR	G4.1 The locative particles 에 and 에서
	G4.2 Numbers
	G4.3 Noun counters
	G4.4 [Time]에
	G4.5 Irregular verbs in -ㄷ: 듣다
	G4.6 Changing the topic of conversation: 그런데
	G4.7 ~(으)러 ([Place]에) 가요
	G4.8 The basic sentence pattern
	N이/가 N에서 (N을/를) ~어요/아요.
TASK/FUNCTION	1. Asking and telling about destination and purpose
	2. Asking and telling time
	3. Asking and telling about quantity; counting
	4. More greetings; saying good-bye
	5. Asking reasons: 왜 'why?'

CONVERSATION

1

(Steve runs into Jenny on campus on his way to Korean class.)

제니

스티브

제니: 스티브 씨, 어디 가세요?

스티브: 한국어 수업에 가요.G4.1

제니: 한국어 수업은 어디서 해요?

스티브: 이스트 홀에서 해요.

제니: 교실이 몇 층G4.3이에요?

스티브: 2층이에요.

제니: 학생이 많아요?

스티브: 좀 많아요. 스무G4.2 명이에요.

            참, 지금 몇 시예요?

제니: 열두 시 사십오 분이에요.

스티브: 아이구, 오늘 한 시에G4.4 한국어 시험이 있어요.

제니: 그럼, 빨리 가세요.

            안녕히 가세요.

스티브: 네, 안녕히 가세요.

2

(Jenny runs into Michael on campus.)

제니

마이클

제니: 마이클 씨, 안녕하세요?

마이클: 어, 제니 씨, 오래간만이에요.

            요즘 어떻게 지내세요?

제니: 잘 지내요.

            마이클 씨는 어때요?

마이클: 저는 좀 바빠요.

제니: 왜요?

마이클: 이번 학기에 다섯 과목을 들어요.[G4.5]

            그런데, 제니 씨 어디 가세요?[G4.6]

제니: 도서관에 가요.

            마이클 씨는 어디 가세요?

마이클: 저는 선물 사러 백화점에 가요.[G4.7]

            내일이 여자 친구 생일이에요.

NARRATION

한국어 공부

안녕하세요? 제 이름은 스티브예요. 지금 뉴욕 대학에서 한국어를 공부해요.[G4.8] 한국어 공부가 재미있어요. 저는 한국어 연습하러 매일 랩에 가요. 오늘은 랩에서 4과를 연습해요. 4과에 단어가 아주 많아요. 한국어 수업은 오후 1시에 있어요. 학생은 스무 명이에요. 남학생이 열두 명, 여학생이 여덟 명이에요. 한국어 선생님은 이민수 선생님이세요.

NEW WORDS AND EXPRESSIONS

NOUNS

과목	subject, course 과목
교실	classroom
남학생	male student
단어	word, vocabulary
반 (G4.4)	half
방 (G4.3)	room
백화점	department store
생일	birthday
선물	present, gift 선물
수업	class
숫자 (G4.2)	number, numeral 숫자
시험	test, exam 시험
어제 (G4.4)	yesterday
여자	woman
여자 친구	girlfriend
여학생	female student
연습	exercise, practice 연습
오래간만	for the first time in a while
오후	afternoon 오후
옷 (G4.7)	clothes
옷가게 (G4.7)	clothing store
인구 (G4.2)	(human) population
점심 (G4.7)	lunch 점심
제4과	lesson 4
학기	semester, academic term

PROPER NOUN

이스트 홀	East Hall

COUNTERS

개 (G4.3)	items
과	lesson (in order), number of lessons
과목	academic subjects/courses
권 (G4.3)	volumes
년 (G4.3)	years
달 (G4.3)	months
마리 (G4.3)	animals
명	persons
병 (G4.3)	bottles
분	minutes
시	the hour, o'clock (point in time)
시간 (G4.3)	hours (duration)
원 (G4.2)	won (Korean currency)
월 (G4.3)	month (1월 January, 2월 February)
일 (G4.3)	date (days of the month)
잔 (G4.3)	glasses, cups
장 (G4.3)	sheets

LOANWORDS

달러 (G4.2)	dollar (= 불) (U.S. currency)
랩	lab
카페 (G4.7)	cafe
테이프 (G4.8)	audiotape
햄버거 (G4.3)	hamburger

NUMBERS

사십	forty (Sino-Korean)
스무	twenty (always occurs with a counter)
여덟	eight
열두	twelve (always occurs with a counter)

| 오 | five (Sino-Korean) |
| 한 | one (always occurs with a counter) |

VERBS

가르치세요[G4.8]	(가르치다)	to teach
들어요	(듣다)	to listen, to take a course
사러	(사다)	to buy
연습하러	(연습하다)	to practice

ADVERBS

매일	every day
빨리	fast, quickly
안녕히	peacefully, safely
왜	why?

PRE-NOUNS

| 몇 | how many? what? (question word before a counter) |
| 이번 | this time |

CONJUNCTION

| 그런데 | by the way, but then |

INTERJECTION

| 아이구 | Oh my! My goodness! |

PARTICLES

| 에 | in/at . . . (static location), to [a place] (destination), at [a point of time] |
| 에서 | in/at . . . (location of action) |

SUFFIX
~(으)러   in order to (the purpose of going/coming)

Pronunciation

다섯 과목 [다섣꽈목], [다석꽈목] 열두 시   [열뚜시]
많아요   [마나요]   오래간만이에요 [오래감마니에요]
몇 시   [멷씨], [며씨]   학기   [학끼]
십육   [심뉵]   한국어   [한구거], [항구거]

Vocabulary by Theme

Greetings
오래간만이에요   I have not seen you for a long time.
잘 있었니?   How have you been? (to a child or a
                          junior)

Farewells
안녕히 가세요.   Good-bye. (to an adult who is leaving)
안녕히 계세요.   Good-bye. (to an adult who is staying)

Places in Town
백화점	department store	옷가게	clothing store
미장원	beauty shop	카페	cafe
우체국	post office	극장	movie theatre
은행	bank	이발소	barber shop

Numbers
Note that the number 0 is read as **영** or **공**. For telephone numbers 0 is read as **공**, and in other cases it is read as **영**. The telephone number 258-5037 is **이오팔 오공삼칠**.

Counting People

한 명	one person	두 명	two people
세 명	three people	네 명	four people
다섯 명	five people	여섯 명	six people
일곱 명	seven people	여덟 명	eight people
아홉 명	nine people	열 명	ten people
열한 명	eleven people	열두 명	twelve people
스무 명	twenty people		

Counting Courses

한 과목	one course	두 과목	two courses
세 과목	three courses	네 과목	four courses
다섯 과목	five courses	몇 과목?	how many courses?

Time Expressions

한 시	one o'clock	두 시	two o'clock
세 시	three o'clock	네 시	four o'clock
다섯 시	five o'clock	여섯 시	six o'clock
일곱 시	even o'clock	여덟 시	eight o'clock
아홉 시	nine o'clock	열 시	ten o'clock
열한 시	eleven o'clock	열두 시	twelve o'clock

오 분	five minutes	십 분	ten minutes
십오 분	fifteen minutes	이십 분	twenty minutes
이십오 분	twenty-five minutes	삼십 분	thirty minutes
삼십오 분	thirty-five minutes	사십 분	forty minutes
사십오 분	forty-five minutes	오십 분	fifty minutes
오십오 분	fifty-five minutes		

오전	A.M.	어제 오전	yesterday morning
		오늘 오전	this morning
		내일 오전	tomorrow morning

오후	P.M.	어제 오후	yesterday afternoon
		오늘 오후	this afternoon
		내일 오후	tomorrow afternoon
매일	every day	매일 아침	every morning

Question Words

몇 명?	how many people?
몇 시	what time (hour)?
몇 분	what time (minute)?
몇 시간	how many hours?
몇 과목	how many courses?
몇 층	what floor?
몇 년	what year?
몇 월	what month?
며칠	what day of the month? (오늘은 며칠이에요?)

NOTES ON NEW WORDS AND EXPRESSIONS

Conversation 1

(1) 몇 'how many?' is a question word for quantity. It is almost always followed by a counter.

(2) As in 교실이 몇 층이에요? and 2층이에요, the copula 이다 can be used to ask or tell about the location of places.

극장이 어디예요?
도서관이 어디예요?
은행이 어디예요?

(3) 좀 literally means 'a little' or 'a bit'. It is the contracted form of 조금.

(4) 아이구 is an exclamatory expression that is used when someone is in trouble or the speaker sees someone rather unexpectedly. In the conversation above,

스티브 realizes that he is in trouble because he has only fifteen minutes to reach Korean class for his exam.

If you meet someone unexpectedly, you can say,

아이구, 이게 누구예요? 'Oh my goodness, who is this?'

(5) 안녕히 가세요, literally meaning 'Go well/in peace', is a greeting used when two people leave each other in a neutral place. If the place belongs to one of the parties, the one staying in his/her territory says 안녕히 가세요, and the person leaving says 안녕히 계세요 'Stay in peace'.

Conversation 2

(1) 오래간만이에요 is an expression used when two people meet after a long while. The expression literally means 'it has been a long time in-between'. In more idiomatic English, it is equivalent to 'it's been a long while', or more colloquially, 'Long time no see'.

(2) [Course/subject]을 들어요: 듣다/들어요 means 'to listen'. To listen to a course/subject means 'take a course'.

이번 학기에 다섯 과목을 들어요. I am taking five courses this semester.
이번 학기에 한국어를 들어요.   I am taking Korean this semester.

CULTURE

1. Asking where others are going

In English-speaking countries, it is considered impolite to ask where another person is going. In Korea, however, it is not considered rude to ask 어디 가세요 'Where are you going?' It is considered part of a greeting and not necessarily prying. If one does not want to reveal where he/she is going, he/she can simply say, 네 'yes', or 네, 어디 좀 가요 'Yeah, I am going somewhere'.

2. 안녕히 가세요 vs. 잘 가

Koreans' respect for age is reflected in greetings and leave-takings. 안녕하세요 is used only for adults and 안녕, 잘 있었니, or 잘 있었어 for children or close friends. 안녕히 가세요 or 안녕히 계세요 'Good-bye' is used for adults in leave-taking, whereas 잘 가, 잘 있어, or 안녕 is appropriate for children or close friends.

GRAMMAR

G4.1 The locative particles 에 and 에서

Examples

Static location
(1) 영미: 여기 학교 식당이 어디 있어요?
    린다: 유니온 빌딩에 있어요.
(2) 린다: 샌디 씨 언니는 어디 계세요?
    샌디: 보스톤에 있어요.
(3) 선생님: 스티브, 한국어 책 어디에 있어요?
    스티브: 가방 안에 있어요.

Destination/goal

(4) 스티브: 영미 씨 어디 가세요?

영미: 도서관에 가요.

스티브 씨는 어디 가세요?

스티브: 백화점에 가요.

Dynamic location

(5) A: 한국어 수업 어디(에)서 해요?

B: 이스트 홀에서 해요.

A: 몇 층에서 해요?

B: 2층에서 해요.

(6) A: 생일 선물 어디(에)서 사요?

B: 백화점에서 사요.

Notes

1. Recall from lesson 2 (G2.5) that the locative particle 에 is used to indicate where an object exists ([place]에 있어요), as in (1)–(3). What is indicated is a static location and the simple existence of an object.

2. The particle 에 is also used to indicate destination or goal, typically for directional verbs such as 가다 'to go' and 오다 'to come' ([place]에 가요/와요), as in (4); the object or person in question ends up being in that location.

3. A different particle, 에서, is used to indicate the location of activity. It refers to a dynamic location, because the action or activity takes place in that location.

[연습 1] Answer each question according to the picture.

보기: A: 어디(에)서 공부해요?

B: 도서관에서 공부해요.

(1)　영미:　지금 어디 가요?

　　　스티브: _____.

(2)　영미:　한국어 수업은 어디서 해요?

　　　스티브: _____.

(3)　영미:　한국어 교실은 어디 있어요?

　　　스티브: _____.

(4)　영미:　어디(에)서 연습하세요?

　　　스티브: _____.

(5)　영미:　랩은 어디 있어요?

　　　스티브: _____.

이스트 홀

LAB

[**연습** 2] Use the following questions in a conversation, as in the example.

보기:　스티브: 샌디 씨, 어디서 공부해요?
샌디:　　저는 도서관에서 공부해요.
스티브 씨는 어디서 공부해요?
스티브: 저는 집에서 공부해요.

(1) 어디서 공부해요?

_____.

(2) 어디서 점심 먹어요?

_____.

(3) 어디서 커피 마셔요?

_____.

(4) 어디서 한국어 연습해요?

_____.

G4.2 Numbers

Korean uses two sets of numbers, native Korean numbers and Sino-Korean numbers.

Arabic numerals	Sino-Korean	Native Korean	Native Korean before counters
1	일	하나	한
2	이	둘	두
3	삼	셋	세
4	사	넷	네
5	오	다섯	다섯
6	육	여섯	여섯
7	칠	일곱	일곱
8	팔	여덟	여덟
9	구	아홉	아홉
10	십	열	열
11	십일	열하나	열한
12	십이	열둘	열두
13	십삼	열셋	열세
14	십사	열넷	열네
15	십오	열다섯	열다섯
16	십육 [심뉴]	열여섯	열여섯
17	십칠	열일곱	열일곱
18	십팔	열여덟	열여덟
19	십구	열아홉	열아홉
20	이십	스물	스무
30	삼십	서른	서른
40	사십	마흔	마흔
50	오십	쉰	쉰
60	육십	예순	예순
70	칠십	일흔	일흔
80	팔십	여든	여든
90	구십	아흔	아흔
100	백		
1,000	천		
10,000	만		

Notes

1. Some native Korean numbers have two forms, depending on whether they are followed by a counter or used in isolation.

하나 → 한 (명) 둘 → 두 (명) 셋 → 세 (명) 넷 → 네 (명)

스물 → 스무 (명)

2. For multiples of 100, 1,000, 10,000, and more, only Sino-Korean numbers are used.

100	백	200	이백
1,000	천	2,000	이천
10,000	만	20,000	이만
100,000	십만	200,000	이십만
1,000,000	백만	2,000,000	이백만
10,000,000	천만	20,000,000	이천만
100,000,000	억	200,000,000	이억
1,000,000,000	십억	2,000,000,000	이십억
10,000,000,000	백억	20,000,000,000	이백억
100,000,000,000	천억	200,000,000,000	이천억
1,000,000,000,000	조	2,000,000,000,000	이조

1달러는 1200원이에요.	One dollar is (equivalent to) 1200 won.
서울 인구는 천이백만이에요.	The population of Seoul is 12 million.
미국 인구는 2억 오천만이에요.	The population of the U.S. is 250 million.
한국 인구는 4천 오백만이에요.	The population of Korea is 45 million.

G4.3   Noun counters

Examples

(1) 제니: 한국어 클래스가 몇 **층**에 있어요?
스티브: 이층에 있어요.
제니: 학생이 많아요?
스티브: 스무 **명**이에요.

(2) 제니: 마이클 씨, 이번 학기에 수업 몇 **과목** 들으세요?
마이클: 다섯 **과목** 들어요.
제니 씨는 몇 **과목** 들으세요?
제니: 저는 세 **과목** 들어요.

(3) 저는 지금 뉴욕 대학에서 한국어를 공부해요.
한국어는 참 재미있어요.
오늘은 사 **과**를 공부해요.

Notes

1. When you count, you must use different counters. Nouns are classified into many groups depending on shape or kind. As indicated in G4.2, the following five native Korean numbers have slightly different forms when used with counters: 하나 → 한, 둘 → 두, 셋 → 세, 넷 → 네, 스물 → 스무. There is no change in 스물 in 스물한 **명**, 스물두 **명**, and so on.

Counter	Kinds of things counted	Counting
층	layers	일층, 이층, 삼층, . . . 십층 . . . 이십층
명/사람	people	한 명, 두 명, 세 명, . . . 열 명 . . . 스무 명
마리	animals	한 마리, 두 마리, 세 마리, . . . 열 마리
시간	hours (duration)	한 시간, 두 시간, 세 시간, 네 시간
시	hour (point in time)	한 시, 두 시, 세 시, 네 시, . . . 열두 시

Counter	Kinds of things counted	Counting
분	minutes	일 분, 이 분, 삼 분, . . . 십 분, . . . 육십 분
분	honored persons	한 분, 두 분, 세 분
과목	academic subjects/courses	한 과목, 두 과목, 세 과목, . . . 열 과목
과	lessons (in order)	일 과, 이 과, 삼 과, 사 과, . . . 십 과
과	number of lessons	한 과, 두 과, 세 과, 네 과, 다섯 과
개	items	한 개, 두 개, 세 개, 네 개, 다섯 개
권	volumes	한 권, 두 권, 세 권, 네 권, 다섯 권
장	sheets	한 장, 두 장, 세 장, 네 장, 다섯 장
병	bottles	한 병, 두 병, 세 병, 네 병, 다섯 병
잔	cups, glasses	한 잔, 두 잔, 세 잔, 네 잔, 다섯 잔

2. In counting people or ordering food, counters may be omitted, as in **오빠 하나** and **햄버거 둘**.

3. Some counters take Sino-Korean numbers, and others take native numbers. For example, 2층 is read as **이층** (with a Sino-Korean number) while 20명 is read as **스무 명** (with a native Korean number).

With Sino-Korean number		With native Korean number	
학년	school year	명/사람	people
층	layer, story	개	items
과	lesson	과	lessons
년	years	과목	courses
월/일	month/date	달	months

With Sino-Korean number	With native Korean number	
분	minutes	시	the hour
달라 (= 불)	dollars	시간	hours
원	won	마리	animals
마일	miles	병	bottles
		잔	glasses, cups
		장	sheets

Some counters can be used with Sino-Korean numbers in higher numbers; for example, 20명 may be read as **이십 명** as well as **스무 명**.

4. **몇** is the question word for quantity, and almost always is followed by a counter.

몇 층, 몇 명/사람, 몇 마리, 몇 시, 몇 분, 몇 시간, 몇 과목, 몇 과, 몇 권, 몇 장, 몇 병, 몇 잔, 몇 월, 며칠 (from the earlier form 몇 일)

5. Word order in counting is noun + (particle +) number + counter. See the table below.

Noun	(Particle)	Number	Counter
오빠	(가)	두	명
방	(이)	세	개
수업	(을)	네	과목
개	(가)	한	마리
창문	(이)	다섯	개

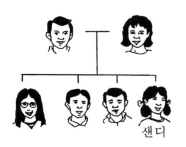
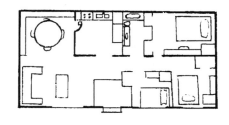

샌디는 오빠가 두 명 있어요.   우리 집에는 방이 세 개 있어요.

[연습] Answer each question in Korean, using the proper counter.

보기: How many courses are you taking this semester?
        이번 학기에 (수업을) 다섯 과목 들어요.

(1) How many students are there in the Korean class?
(2) What year are you in at school?
(3) What lesson are we studying now?
(4) How many lessons are there in the Korean textbook?
(5) On which floor is the Korean-language classroom?
(6) How many (bed)rooms do you have in your place?

G4.4   [Time]에

Examples

(1) A: 한국어 수업은 **몇 시에** 있어요?
    B: **1시에** 있어요.

(2) A: 아침 **몇 시에** 먹어요?
   B: **8시 반에** 먹어요.

(3) A: 아침에 학교에 **몇 시에** 와요?
   B: **9시 15분에** 와요.

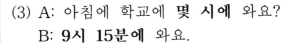

Notes

1. The particle 에 is also used to specify a time reference. However, 오늘 and 어제 cannot occur with 에.

2. 시 occurs with native Korean numbers, and 분 occurs with Sino-Korean numbers.

12시   50분
열두 시   오십 분

Native Korean   Sino-Korean
numbers   numbers

[연습] Answer the following questions according to your own schedule.

(1) 한국어 수업은 몇 시에 있어요?

_____.

(2) 몇 시에 아침을 먹어요?

_____.

(3) 몇 시에 자요?

_____.

G4.5 Irregular verbs in ㅡㄷ: 듣다

Examples

(1) 선생님:	잘 들으세요.		Listen carefully.
(2) A:	랩에서 뭐 해요?		What do you do in the lab?
B:	한국말을 들어요.		I listen to Korean.
(3) A:	이번 학기에 뭐 들어요?		What are you taking this semester?
B:	경제학 들어요.		I am taking economics.

Notes

While most verb stems do not change, some verbs are subject to variation depending on the following sound. These verbs are called irregular verbs. For example, the verb 듣다 has ㄷ at the end of the stem, and this ㄷ changes to ㄹ when followed by a vowel, as shown below.

들 + 어요 → 들어요
들 + 으세요 → 들으세요

G4.6 Changing the topic of conversation: 그런데

Examples

(1) 마이클: 영미 씨, 요즘 어떻게 지내세요?
영미: 잘 지내요. 마이클 씨는 어때요?
마이클: 저는 좀 바빠요.
그런데, 영미 씨 어디 가세요?
영미: 도서관에 가요.
(2) 제니: 스티브 씨, 어디 가세요?
스티브: 한국어 수업에 가요.

제니: 한국어 수업 재미있어요?
스티브: 네, 재미있어요.
　　　그런데, 제니 씨는 이번 학기에 몇 과목 들어요?
제니: 세 과목 들어요. 스티브 씨는 몇 과목 들어요?
스티브: 저는 다섯 과목 들어요.

Notes

그런데 is used when the speaker shifts from one topic to another. In (1), **영미** and **마이클** are talking about their health, then **마이클** turns the topic to where **영미** is going. In (2), **스티브** changes the subject of the conversation from Korean class to how many courses he and **제니** are taking.

[**연습**] Complete the dialogue using 그런데.

보기: 제니: 스티브 씨는 이번 학기 몇 과목 들어요?
　　　스티브: 다섯 과목 들어요.
　　　　　<u>그런데, 제니 씨 어디 가세요?</u>
　　　제니: 도서관에 가요.

(1) 제니: 한국어 수업 재미 있어요?
　　마이클:네, 재미있어요.
　　　_____?
　　제니: 세 과목 들어요.
(2) 샌디: 린다 씨, 동생 있어요?
　　린다: 아니오, 없어요.
　　　_____?
　　샌디: 홍콩이에요. 홍콩에 아버지, 어머니하고 오빠가 계세요.
(3) 영미: 학교 식당 음식이 어때요?
　　린다: 괜찮아요. 커피가 맛있어요.
　　　_____?
　　영미: 1학년이에요.

G4.7 ~(으)러 ([Place]에) 가요

Examples

(1) A: 어디 가세요?
    B: 공부하러 도서관에 가요.
(2) A: 어디 가세요?
    B: 생일 선물 사러 백화점에 가요.

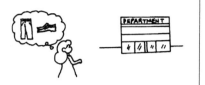

Notes

~(으)러 is used with directional verbs (가다, 오다) to indicate the purpose of going or coming.

점심 먹으러 식당에 가요.　　친구 만나러 카페에 가요.

옷 사러 옷가게에 가요.

[연습 1] Make a list of places and write what you would do there. Then describe why you are going to those places.

보기:	[place]	[what you do there]	
	도서관 —	공부해요 →	공부하러 도서관에 가요.

(1) _____ — _____ → _____.

(2) _____ — _____ → _____.

(3) _____ — _____ → _____.

(4) _____ — _____ → _____.

(5) _____ — _____ → _____.

[**연습** 2] Describe where the person in the picture usually goes and why.

보기: 공부하러 도서관에 가요.

(1) _____

(2) _____

(3) _____

(4) _____

G4.8　The basic sentence pattern
N이/가 N에서 (N을/를) ~어요/아요.

Examples

(1) 린다가 식당에서 햄버거를 먹어요.

(2) 샌디가 랩에서 한국어 테이프를 들어요.

(3) 이 선생님이 교실에서 한국어를 가르치세요.

Notes

The basic word order of Korean is different from that of English. Korean is a subject-object-verb language, whereas English is a subject-verb-object language. For example, the word order of the sentence 'Young-mee studies Korean in the classroom' is as follows:

영미가	교실에서	한국어를	공부해요.
Young-mee	in the classroom	Korean	study.

The word order is flexible as long as the predicate is placed at the end.

　교실에서 영미가 한국어를 공부해요.
　한국어를 영미가 교실에서 공부해요.

영미가 한국어를 교실에서 공부해요.
교실에서 한국어를 영미가 공부해요.
한국어를 교실에서 영미가 공부해요.

[**연습**] Look at the pictures and say who is doing what and where.

보기: <u>스티브</u>가 교실에서 공부해요.

(1) _____ (2) _____

마이클

영미

(3) _____ (4) _____

제니

린다

TASK/FUNCTION

1. Asking and telling about destination and purpose

(1) A: 어디 가세요?
  B: 도서관에 가요.
(2) A: 도서관에 뭐 하러 가세요?
  B: 공부하러 가요.
(3) A: 어디 가세요?
  B: 공부하러 도서관에 가요.

[연습] Practice as in the example.

보기: (1) A: 어디 가세요?
      You: [도서관] 공부하러 도서관에 가요.
    (2) A: 어디 가세요?
      You: [선물 사러] 선물 사러 백화점에 가요.

(1) A: 어디 가세요?
  You: [학교 식당] _____

(2) A: 어디 가세요?
  You: [옷가게] _____

(3) A: 어디 가세요?
  You: [점심 먹으러] _____

2. Asking and telling time

지금 몇 시예요?
__시 __분이에요.

(1) A: 지금 몇 시예요?
 B: 10시 24분 (열 시 이십사 분)이에요.

(2) A: 지금 몇 시예요?
 B: 8시 반이에요.

(3) A: 지금 몇 시예요?
 B: 9시 10분 전 이에요.

Recall that in referring to time, hours take native Korean numbers, and minutes and seconds take Sino-Korean numbers, as in (1).

In (2), notice that 30 분 can also be stated as 반, which means 'half': 6시 30분 = 6시 반.

[연습] Based on the given context, create a dialogue with your partner.

보기: What time is your Korean class?
A: 한국어 수업이 몇 시에 있어요?
B: 1시에 있어요.

(1) What time do you come to school?
(2) What time do you eat breakfast?
(3) What time is it now?
(4) What time do you go to bed?

3. Asking and telling about quantity; counting

(1) A: 한국어 반이 몇 층이에요?
B: 2층이에요.
(2) A: 몇 학년이에요?
B: 일학년이에요.
(3) A: 한국어 반 학생이 몇 명이에요?
B: 스무 명이에요.
(4) A: 오늘은 몇 과 공부해요?
B: 삼 과 공부해요.
(5) A: 이번 학기에 몇 과목 들어요?
B: 두 과목 들어요.

If one wants to ask for an unspecified number, the question word 몇 is used. Practice the following questions.

이번 주에는 몇 과 공부해요?
한국어 수업은 몇 시에 해요?
지금 몇 시예요?
이번 학기에 몇 과목 들어요?

[연습 1] Count the given items aloud.

보기: [your fingers] 하나, 둘, 셋, 넷, 다섯, 여섯, . . . (열 개예요)

(1) number of students in class
(2) floors in the building

(3) number of windows in the classroom

(4) number of lessons in your Korean textbook

(5) school years from first grade to twelfth grade

[연습 2] Make up a question that is appropriate for the response.

보기: A: 한국 학생이 몇 명이에요?
　　　　B: 스무 명이에요.

(1) A: _____

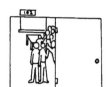

　　 B: 삼층에 있어요.

(2) A: _____

　　 B: 15명이에요.

(3) A: _____

　　 B: 4과를 공부해요.

(4) A: _____

　　 B: 이학년이에요.

4. More greetings; saying good-bye

(1) Greetings after a long separation

When two people meet after a long while, they ask after each other's well-being. They also indicate that a lot of time has passed since their last encounter by saying **오래간만이에요**.

린다:　　안녕하세요? 스티브 씨, 오래간만이에요.
　　　　요즘 어떻게 지내세요?
스티브: 아, 안녕하세요, 린다 씨? 잘 지내요. 린다 씨는 어때요?
린다:　　저도 잘 지내요.

(2) Remember that, in saying good-bye, location must be taken into account.

    B is leaving, A is in the office.
      A: 안녕히 가세요.
      B: 안녕히 계세요.

    A and B are saying good-bye on the street.
      A: 안녕히 가세요.
      B: 안녕히 가세요.

[연습] Exchange greetings with your partner that are appropriate for the given context.

(1) General greeting
(2) Introducing two of your friends to each other.
(3) Meeting someone after a long while.
(4) You are departing from your partner's place.
(5) You are seeing your partner off.

5. Asking reasons: 왜 'why?'

(1) A: 안녕하세요? 요즘 어떻게 지내세요?
     B: 좀 바빠요.
     A: 왜요?
     B: 이번 학기에 다섯 과목을 들어요.
(2) A: 왜 한국어를 공부하세요?
     B: 한국 친구가 많아요.

[연습] Make up dialogues with your partner that are appropriate for the given context.

보기: 마이클 is busy because he is taking five courses this semester.

영미: 마이클 씨, 요즘 어떻게 지내세요?

마이클: 좀 바빠요.

영미: 왜요?

마이클: 이번 학기에 다섯 과목을 들어요.

(1) The school cafeteria is usually not a favorite place for lunch. But **린다** likes to have lunch at the school cafeteria because the coffee is good.

영미: 린다 씨는 점심 어디서 먹어요?

린다: _____.

영미: _____. Any particular reason?

린다: _____.

(2) Michael is going to the Health Center.

영미: 마이클 씨, 어디 가세요?

마이클: _____.

영미: _____. What's the matter?

마이클: _____.

(3) Interview three of your classmates and find out why they are studying.

(4) **영미**, a Korean-American, is curious when she finds **스티브**, a non-Korean, studying Korean.

영미: 스티브 씨, 뭐 공부하세요?

스티브: _____.

영미: _____.

Why are you studying Korean?

스티브: _____.

Options

재미있어요.	It's fun.
쉬워요.	It's easy.
한국 친구가 많아요.	I have many Korean friends.
여자 친구가 한국 사람이에요.	My girlfriend is Korean.
한국이 좋아요.	I like Korea.
제 전공이 한국 문학/역사예요.	My major is Korean literature/history.

Lesson 4 At School

CONVERSATION

1

(Steve runs into Jenny on campus on his way to Korean class.)

Jenny:	Steve, where are you going?
Steve:	I'm going to my Korean class.
Jenny:	Where do you have Korean class?
Steve:	In East Hall.
Jenny:	Which floor is your classroom on?
Steve:	On the second floor.
Jenny:	Are there many students?
Steve:	Quite a few. There are twenty. By the way, what time is it now?
Jenny:	It's 12:45.
Steve:	Goodness, I have a Korean test at 1:00 today.
Jenny:	Then, hurry.
	Bye.
Steve:	Bye.

2

(Jenny runs into Michael on campus.)

Jenny:	Hi, Michael!
Michael:	Oh, long time no see, Jenny.
	How are you doing these days?
Jenny:	Fine.
	How about you, Michael?
Michael:	I'm a little busy.
Jenny:	Why?
Michael:	I'm taking five courses this semester.
	By the way, where are you going?
Jenny:	I'm going to the library.
	Where are you going, Michael?
Michael:	I'm going to a department store to buy a gift.
	Tomorrow is my girlfriend's birthday.

제5과 나의 하루

(Lesson 5: My Day)

OBJECTIVES

CULTURE	1. Talking about where someone lives 2. Housing
GRAMMAR	G5.1 [Place A]에서 [Place B]까지 'from place A to place B' G5.2 Vowel contraction G5.3 N(으)로 'by means of N' G5.4 The conjunction 그래서 G5.5 은요/는요? 'What about . . . ?' G5.6 The negative adverb 안 G5.7 Past events: ~었어요/았어요 G5.8 N (person) 하고 (같이) ~어요/아요 G5.9 Irregular predicates in -ㅂ
TASK/FUNCTION	1. Talking about how long something takes 2. Asking about someone's residence 3. Talking about daily activities 4. Coming and going

CONVERSATION

1

(Michael and Jenny chat after class.)

마이클

제니

마이클: 제니 씨, 집에서 학교까지[G5.1] 얼마나 걸려요?[G5.2]

제니: 좀 멀어요.

           버스로[G5.3] 한 시간쯤 걸려요.

           마이클 씨는 집이 어디예요?

마이클: 저는 기숙사에 살아요.

           걸어서 10분 걸려요.

제니: 마이클 씨, 수업이 몇 시에 있어요?

마이클: 9시에 있어요.

           그래서[G5.4] 기숙사에서 아침 8시 40분에 나와요.

제니: 학교에 매일 와요?

마이클: 네, 매일 와요. 제니 씨는요?[G5.5]

제니: 저는 매일 안[G5.6] 와요.

           월요일, 수요일, 금요일 세 번만 와요.

2

(Young-mee and Michael talk about their daily activities.)

영미

마이클

영미:　　　마이클 씨, 어제 오후에 뭐 했어요[G5.7]?

마이클:　　린다하고 테니스 쳤어요.[G5.8] 영미 씨는 뭐 했어요?

영미:　　　저는 수영했어요.

마이클:　　어디서요?

영미:　　　학교 수영장에서 했어요.

　　　　　　그런데 저녁에는 보통 뭐 해요?

마이클:　　도서관에서 공부해요.

영미:　　　그럼 저녁은 몇 시에 먹어요?

마이클:　　6시 반쯤 먹어요.

영미:　　　혼자 먹어요?

마이클:　　아니오, 린다하고 같이 먹어요.

NARRATION
마이클의 하루

나는 날마다 아침 7시쯤 일어나요. 그리고, 8시에 아침을 먹어요. 수업은 9시에 있어요. 기숙사에서 학교까지는 가까워요.[G5.9] 그래서 걸어서 와요. 오후에는 수업이 없어요. 그래서, 오후에는 린다하고 테니스를 쳐요. 린다는 내 여자 친구예요. 린다도 한국어 수업을 들어요. 6시쯤 린다하고 같이 기숙사 식당에서 저녁을 먹어요. 그리고 저녁에는 도서관에서 공부를 해요. 저는 보통 11시 반쯤 자요.

NEW WORDS AND EXPRESSIONS

NOUNS

겨울 (G5.9)	winter
금요일	Friday
기차 (G5.3)	train
날씨 (G5.9)	the weather
목요일 (G5.4)	Thursday
비행기 (G5.3)	airplane
수영장	swimming pool
수요일	Wednesday
여름 (G5.9)	summer
월요일	Monday
자전거 (G5.3)	bicycle
저녁	evening; supper, dinner
제5과	lesson 5
지하철 (G5.3)	subway
차 (G5.3)	car, automobile
토요일 (G5.8)	Saturday
하루	day
화요일 (G5.4)	Tuesday

PROPER NOUNS

뉴욕 (G5.1)	New York
엘에이 (G5.1)	Los Angeles

COUNTER

번	a number of times (세 번 'three times')

LOANWORDS

마일 (G5.1)	mile
버스	bus

볼펜(G5.3)	ballpoint pen
주스(G5.2)	juice
테니스	tennis
트럭(G5.3)	truck
파티(G5.4)	party

VERBS

걸려요	(걸리다)	to take (time)
걸어서	(걷다)	to walk
기다려요(G5.2)	(기다리다)	to wait
나와요	(나오다)	to come out
몰라요(G5.6)	(모르다)	to not know, be unaware of
배워요(G5.2)	(배우다)	to learn
살아요	(살다)	to live
수영했어요	(수영하다)	to swim
쓰세요(G5.2) 써요	(쓰다)	to write
와요	(오다)	to come
일어나요	(일어나다)	to get up
일해요(G5.6)	(일하다)	to work
줘요(G5.2)	(주다)	to give
쳤어요	(치다)	to play (a game or a musical instrument)

ADJECTIVES

가까워요	(가깝다)	to be close, near
더워요(G5.9)	(덥다)	to be hot
멀어요	(멀다)	to be far, distant
쉬워요(G5.9)	(쉽다)	to be easy
어려워요(G5.9)	(어렵다)	to be difficult
추워요(G5.9)	(춥다)	to be cold

ADVERBS

같이	together
날마다	every day
보통	usually, ordinarily; commonly
안	not
얼마나	how much? (question word of degree or quantity)
조금 (G5.5)	a little
혼자	alone

CONJUNCTION

그래서	so

PARTICLES

까지	up to (a location)
(으)로	by means of
하고 (같이)	(along) with

SUFFIX

~쯤	about, around

Pronunciation

같이	[가치]	멀어요	[머러요]
걸어서	[거러서]	살아요	[사라요]
기숙사	[기숙싸]	월요일	[워료일]

Vocabulary by Theme

Counting Minutes and Hours

일 분	one minute	이 분	two minutes
삼 분	three minutes	십 분	ten minutes

삼십 분	thirty minutes	반 시간	half an hour
한 시간	one hour	한 시간 반	one and a half hours
두 시간	two hours	두 시간 반	two and a half hours
세 시간	three hours		

Days of the Week

월요일	Monday	화요일	Tuesday
수요일	Wednesday	목요일	Thursday
금요일	Friday	토요일	Saturday
일요일	Sunday		

Expressions of Frequency

한 번	once	두 번	twice
세 번	three times	네 번	four times
다섯 번	five times	여섯 번	six times
매일, 날마다	every day	매주	every week
매달	every month	매일 아침	every morning
매일 저녁	every evening	가끔	once in a while
보통	usually	자주	frequently, often

Transportation

| 차 | 자전거 | 버스 | 비행기 |

| 지하철/전철 | 기차 | 트럭 |

| 걸어서 | on foot, (by) walking | 뛰어서 | (by) running |
| 운전해서 | (by) driving | | |

Question Words

얼마나	how long/how much?	얼마나 걸려요?
몇	how many?	몇 시간 걸려요?

Meals

아침 먹다	to eat breakfast
점심 먹다	to eat lunch
저녁 먹다	to eat dinner

Time Expressions

아침	morning	오늘 아침	this morning
저녁	evening	오늘 저녁	this evening
밤	night	오늘 밤	tonight
낮	daytime		

Seasons

봄	spring	이번 봄	this spring
여름	summer	이번 여름	this summer
가을	autumn	이번 가을	this autumn
겨울	winter	이번 겨울	this winter

Places

수영장	swimming pool	랩	lab
캠퍼스	campus	식당	dining hall
책방	bookstore	아파트	apartment
도서관	library	은행	bank
기숙사	dormitory	집	house
교실	classroom	학교 밖	off campus

Everyday Activities

일어나다	to get up	쉬다	to rest
샤워하다	to take a shower	운동하다	to do exercise

아침 먹다	to have breakfast	저녁 먹다	to eat dinner
수업에 가다	to go to class	텔레비전 보다	to watch TV
점심 먹다	to eat lunch	숙제하다	to do homework
랩에 가다	to go to the lab	자다	to go to bed
공부하다	to study		

NOTES ON NEW WORDS AND EXPRESSIONS

Conversation 1

(1) 쯤 is an expression of approximate quantity and quality, best translated as 'around' or 'about'. It is always attached to a noun of time or a number.

(2) 집이 어디예요/어디세요? literally means 'Where is your house?' This question can be used to ask about a permanent residence or hometown, as was the case in lesson 3, or about a current residence. In asking about a current residence, you may also use 어디 살아요/사세요? 'Where do you live?'

> 집이 어디예요?
> ~에 살아요(?) vs. ~에서 살아요(?)

(3) As in ~에 살아요(?) and ~에서 살아요(?), 살다 'to live' may take either the static locative particle 에 or the dynamic locative particle 에서. The difference in meaning is very subtle and hardly noticeable.

학교 아파트에(서) 살아요.   (아파트 'apartment', 학교 아파트 'campus housing')

학교 밖에(서) 살아요.   (학교 밖 'off-campus')

(4) As in 걸어서, ~어서/~아서 is attached to verbs like 걷다 'walk' 뛰다 'run', or 운전하다 'drive' to express means of motion.

(5) Korean calendars start with Monday, not Sunday. Also, most people work half-days on Saturday.

Conversation 2

(1) 어디서요 consists of 어디서 + the polite marker 요. 요 can be attached to a phrase when the main predicate is omitted.

CULTURE

1. Talking about where someone lives

In Korea, you identify your residence by specifying the name of the district you live in. In Seoul, the districts end in ~동, ~로, or ~대문.

- ~동 is the smallest administrative district unit in Korea: 압구정동, 청담동, 사당동, 연희동, 신림동, 명동.

- ~로 is a major street: 종로, 을지로, 퇴계로, 세종로, 신문로.

- ~대문 or ~문 refers to the old gates to the inner city: 동대문 (East Gate), 서대문 (West Gate), 남대문 (South Gate), 광화문, 서소문, 자하문, and so on.

A: 집이 어디예요? or 댁이 어디세요?
B: 안국동이에요/종로예요/서대문이에요.

If you live in an apartment, you can be more specific about your residence by adding the name of the apartment complex after the area name.

A: 어디 사세요?
B: 압구정동 한양아파트에 살아요.

2. Housing

Housing in Korea can be one of the
following: 아파트, 단독주택, 하숙집,
오피스텔.

아파트 refers to high-rise apartment
buildings, which are very common
nowadays. 아파트 are usually named
after the construction companies that
build them, as in 현대아파트, 한양아파트, 주공아파트, 삼익아파트. A quarter of
South Korea's population resides in Seoul, and the majority of them live in 아파트.

단독주택 refers to single-unit houses
(단독 'single', 주택 'housing').

하숙집 is a boarding house. This kind
of housing is popular around colleges.
Many college students from provincial
areas who attend school in Seoul live in
하숙집.

오피스텔 is derived from 오피스 'office' and 호텔 'hotel' and refers to rooms in
high-rise buildings that are a combination of office and apartment. This is similar
to the American studio apartment, and is popular among young professionals.

GRAMMAR

> ## G5.1 [Place A]에서 [Place B]까지
> ### 'from place A to place B'

Examples

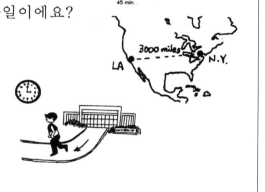

(1) A: 집**에서** 학교**까지** 멀어요?
     B: 네, 멀어요.
(2) A: 엘에이**에서** 뉴욕**까지** 몇 마일이에요?
     B: 3,000 마일이에요.

[Starting point]**에서**:
(3) A: 학교**에서** 몇 시에 나와요?
     B: 3시에 나와요.

[Ending point]**까지**:
(4) A: 어디**까지** 가세요?
     B: 뉴욕**까지** 가요.

[**연습**] Make up a question and answer to tell whether the two given places are far or near, as in the example.

> 보기: [교실, 도서관] <u>교실에서 도서관까지 멀어요?</u>
>   <u>네, 멀어요.</u>

(1) [교실, 식당]   _____?
                     네, _____.
(2) [학교, 기숙사]   _____?
                     아니오, _____.

(3) [기숙사, 수영장] _____?

네, _____.

(4) [집, 백화점]   _____?

아니오, _____.

(5) [교실, 랩]   _____?

네, _____.

G5.2 Vowel contraction

Examples

(1) A: 몇시에 **일어나요**?

B: 7시쯤 **일어나요**.

(2) A: 요즘 어떻게 **지내요**?

B: 좀 **바빠요**.

(3) 영미: 오후에 뭐 **하세요**?

마이클: 테니스 **쳐요**.

(4) 스티브: 저녁에 뭐 **하세요**?

제니: 텔레비전 **봐요**.

그런데, 스티브 씨 뭐 **배우세요**?

스티브: 한국어 **배워요**.

(5) 마이클: 제니 씨, 집에서 학교까지 멀어요?

제니: 아니오, **가까워요**.

걸어서 10분 **걸려요**.

Notes

When two vowels meet in verb/adjective conjugation, vowel contraction frequently occurs.

1. Two identical vowels (아 + 아) become a single vowel.

가	+	아요	→	가요
자	+	아요	→	자요
만나	+	아요	→	만나요
싸	+	아요	→	싸요
비싸	+	아요	→	비싸요
사	+	아요	→	사요

2. 애 causes the following 어 to be dropped.

지내	+	어요	→	지내요
내	+	어요	→	내요

3. The sequence 이 + 어 is contracted to 여.

기다리	+	어요	→	기다려요
걸리	+	어요	→	걸려요
마시	+	어요	→	마셔요
치	+	어요	→	쳐요
가르치	+	어요	→	가르쳐요

The honorific 시 + 어, however, is contracted to 세 instead of 셔.

안녕하시	+	어요	→	안녕하세요
계시	+	어요	→	계세요

4. The following combinations may be contracted to diphthongs.

우	+	어	→	워
오	+	아	→	와

The contraction is *optional* when the preceding syllable begins with a consonant.

주	+	어요	→	줘요 (주어요 is also allowed.)
보	+	아요	→	봐요 (보아요 is also allowed.)

The contraction is *obligatory* when there is no consonant.

오	+	아요	→	와요
배우	+	어요	→	배워요

5. Verbs and adjectives whose stems end in 으 lose the 으 before another vowel.

크다	+	어요	→	커요
쓰다	+	어요	→	써요

[연습 1] Add the polite ending ~어요/아요 to each predicate.

보기: 학교에 (가다). → 학교에 <u>가요.</u>

(1) 오렌지 주스를 (마시다). _____.
(2) 텔레비전을 (보다). _____.
(3) 선생님이 교실에 (계시다). _____.
(4) 오늘 식당에서 친구를 (만나다). _____.
(5) 내일 동생이 (오다). _____.

(6) 운동장에서 테니스를 (치다). _____.

(7) 언니 생일에 선물을 (주다). _____.

(8) 오빠가 은행에서 (일하다). _____.

(9) 이 가방이 아주 (비싸다). _____.

[연습 2] Give the polite ending for each 으 adjective.

> 보기: 캠퍼스가 (크다) → 캠퍼스가 <u>커요.</u>

(1) 가방이 (예쁘다) _____.

(2) 학생이 (바쁘다) _____.

(3) 수영장이 (나쁘다) _____.

G5.3 N(으)로 'by means of N'

Examples

Transportation

(1) A: 학교에 걸어(서) 가요?

　 B: 아니오, 차로 가요.

(2) A: 학교에 어떻게 가요?

　 B: 자전거로 가요.

(3) A: 학교에 차로 가요?

　 B: 저 차 없어요. 버스로 가요.

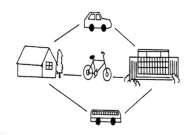

Instrument

(4) 한국어로 말하세요.　　　　Speak in Korean.

(5) 볼펜으로 쓰세요.　　　　　Write with a ballpoint pen.

irregulars: 걸어서 doesn't need 로
지하철(로) 가요

Notes

1. Means of transportation are expressed with the particle (으)로. 으로 is used after a noun ending in a consonant (except ㄹ), and 로 is used after a noun ending in a vowel.

버스로	'by bus'	차로	'by car'
비행기로	'by airplane'	트럭으로	'by truck'
지하철로	'by subway'		

2. Means of transportation can also be indicated by the verbal expression 타고 'riding':

> A: 학교에 뭐 **타고** 와요?
> B: 버스 **타고** 와요.

기차로	=	기차(를) 타고	자전거로	=	자전거(를) 타고
버스로	=	버스(를) 타고	지하철로	=	지하철(을) 타고
비행기로	=	비행기(를) 타고	차로	=	차(를) 타고

3. The particle (으)로 is also used to indicate an instrument by means of which an action is performed.

[**연습** 1] How do you come to school?

> 보기: A: 학교에 어떻게 와요?
>   B: [bicycle] <u>자전거로 와요.</u>

(1) [bus] _____.

(2) [walking] _____.

(3) [subway] _____.

(4) [car] _____.

[**연습** 2] What kind of action do you perform with the given instrument?

> 보기: [볼펜] 볼펜으로 숙제를 하세요.

(1) [영어] _____.
(2) [한국어 책] _____.
(3) [라디오] _____.

G5.4 The conjunction 그래서

Examples

> (1) 수업이 9시에 있어요. 집에서 학교까지 걸어서 10분 걸려요.
>   **그래서** 8시 40분에 집에서 나와요.
> (2) 오후에는 수업이 없어요. **그래서** 린다하고 테니스 쳐요.

Note

그래서 'so, therefore' indicates a cause-and-effect relation between two sentences.

[**연습**] Connect the following sentences using **그래서**.

(1) 학교가 가까워요. 걸어서 가요.

   _____.

(2) 화요일, 목요일에는 수업이 없어요. 학교에 안 와요.

   _____.

(3) 오늘이 제 생일이에요. 생일 파티를 해요.

   _____.

G5.5 은요/는요? 'What about . . . ?'

Examples

(1) 제니: 마이클 씨는 학교에 매일 와요?
    마이클: 네, 매일 와요. 제니 씨**는요?**
    제니: 저는 월요일, 수요일, 금요일만 와요.
(2) 영미: 마이클 씨, 아침은 몇 시에 먹어요?
    마이클: 8시에 먹어요.
    영미: 저녁**은요?**
    마이클: 저녁은 6시 반쯤 먹어요.
(3) 마이클: 제니 씨, 우체국이 유니온 빌딩에서 멀어요?
    제니: 아니오, 가까워요. 걸어서 5분쯤 걸려요.
    마이클: 도서관에서**는요?**
    제니: 도서관에서는 조금 멀어요. 15분쯤 걸려요.

Notes

1. 은요/는요? best translated as 'What about. . . ?' or 'How about. . . ?' is used to request the listener to focus on a different item.

2. The topic marker 은/는 can be attached not only to a noun, as in examples (1) and (2), but also to other phrases, such as 도서관에서는 and 저녁에는.

[연습] Using 은요/는요? complete the dialogues.

보기: 마이클: 제니 씨, 집에서 학교까지 가까워요?
      제니: 아니오, 좀 멀어요. <u>마이클 씨는요?</u>
      마이클: 저는 가까워요.

(1) 영미: 마이클 씨, 점심은 몇 시에 먹어요?
　　마이클: 12시쯤 먹어요.
　　영미: ＿＿＿＿＿＿＿＿＿＿＿＿？
　　마이클: 저녁은 6시 반쯤 먹어요.
(2) 제니: 스티브 씨, 한국어 수업은 어디서 해요?
　　스티브: 이스트 홀에서 해요.
　　제니: ＿＿＿＿＿＿＿＿＿＿＿＿？
　　스티브: 경제학 수업은 아트빌딩에서 해요
(3) 영미: 저어, 여기 학교식당은 어디 있어요?
　　린다: 1층에 있어요.
　　영미: ＿＿＿＿＿＿＿＿＿＿＿？
　　린다: 책방도 1층에 있어요.
(4) 제니: 마이클 씨, 요즘 바빠요?
　　마이클: 네, 조금 바빠요. ＿＿＿＿＿＿＿＿＿？
　　제니: 네, 저도 바빠요.

G5.6 The negative adverb 안

Examples

(1) 제니: 마이클 씨는 학교에 매일 와요?
　　마이클: 네, 매일 와요. 제니 씨는요?
　　제니: 저는 매일 **안** 와요. 화요일, 목요일에는 수업이 **없어요**.
　　　　　그래서 화요일하고 목요일에는 **안** 와요.
(2) 샌디: 린다 씨는 아침 몇 시에 먹어요?
　　린다: 저는 보통 아침 **안** 먹어요.
(3) 마이클: 영미 씨, 수영장 가세요?
　　영미: 아니오, 도서관에 가요. 오늘은 수영 **안** 해요.
(4) 린다: 우체국 알아요?
　　영미: 아니오, **몰라요**.

Notes

1. Negation of a predicate in general is made by putting the negative adverb **안** immediately before the predicate, as in examples (1) and (2):

Positive	Negative
가요	안 가요
먹어요	안 먹어요
와요	안 와요

2. Negation of noun + **하다** verbs 'do [noun]' is usually made by putting **안** between the noun and the verb **하다**, that is, [noun] **안 하다**, as in example (3).

Positive ([noun]**하다**)	Negative ([noun] **안 하다**)
공부해요	공부 안 해요
연습해요	연습 안 해요
전화해요	전화 안 해요
일해요	일 안 해요

3. Some verbs and adjectives have a special negative counterpart. For these predicates, the regular negative construction with **안** is not used.

Positive	Negative
있다/있어요	없다/없어요
N이다/이에요	N(이/가) 아니다/아니에요
알다/알아요	모르다/몰라요

[**연습**] Give a negative answer to the question.

> 보기: A: 학교에 매일 가요?
>   B: 아니오, <u>화요일, 목요일에는 안 가요.</u>

(1) A: 아침 매일 먹어요?

B: 아니오, 보통 아침을 ＿＿＿＿＿＿＿＿.

(2) A: 학교에 가요?

B: 아니오, 오늘 수업이 ＿＿＿＿＿＿＿＿. 그래서 ＿＿＿＿＿.

(3) A: 오늘도 수영해요?

B: 아니오. 내일 한국어 시험이 있어요.

그래서 오늘은 수영 ＿＿＿＿＿＿＿＿.

(4) 린다: 스티브 씨, 영미 알아요?

스티브: 아니오, ＿＿＿＿＿＿＿＿.

G5.7 Past events: ～였어요/았어요

Examples

(1) 샌디: 어제 숙제 많**았어요?**

린다: 네, 좀 많**았어요.**

(2) A: 오늘 아침 몇 시에 먹**었어요?**

B: 8시에 먹**었어요.**

(3) A: 스티브 어디 있어요?

B: 학교에 **갔어요.**

(4) 샌디: 린다 씨, 어제 오후에 뭐 **했어요?**

린다: 테니스 **쳤어요.**

Notes

1. ～였/～았/～ㅆ indicates that the event described has already taken place.

2. Selecting the correct past tense form among the three variants follows the same principle as for choosing between 어요 and 아요 (G2.2): ～았 after a stem ending in 아 or 오, and ～었 elsewhere. ～ㅆ is used when vowel contractions occur (G5.2) as in 갔어요 (from 가았어요). The final ending after ～였/～았/～ㅆ is always ～어요, not ～아요 (e.g., 좋았어요, 먹었어요).

Dictionary form	~어요/아요	~었어요/았어요
많다	많아요	많았어요
좋다	좋아요	좋았어요
오다	와요	왔어요
모르다	몰라요	몰랐어요
먹다	먹어요	먹었어요
배우다	배워요	배웠어요
가다	가요	갔어요
자다	자요	잤어요
만나다	만나요	만났어요
지내다	지내요	지냈어요
공부하다	공부해요	공부했어요
수영하다	수영해요	수영했어요
숙제하다	숙제해요	숙제했어요
이다	이에요/예요	이었어요/였어요
아니다	아니에요	아니었어요

3. 모르다 belongs to the class of 르-final predicates. In these 르 loses its vowel, and the ㄹ doubles when it is followed by a vowel.

> 모르 + ~어요/아요 → 몰라요
> 모르 + ~었어요/았어요 → 몰랐어요

4. Verbs and adjectives whose stems end in 으 have the following forms.

> 쓰다 → 써요, 썼어요
> 크다 → 커요, 컸어요

바쁘다 → 바빠요, 바빴어요
예쁘다 → 예뻐요, 예뻤어요

[연습] Give the proper form of the past tense.

> 보기: A: 어제 오후에 뭐 했어요?
>   B: <u>수영했어요</u> (수영하다).

(1) A: 어제 뭐 했어요?
    B: 도서관에서 _____ (공부하다).
(2) A: 지난 주말에 뭐 했어요?
    B: 친구를 _____ (만나다).
(3) A: 오늘 아침 몇 시에 _____ (먹다)?
    B: 7시 반에 _____ (먹다).

G5.8 N (person) 하고 (같이) ~어요/아요

Examples

> N하고 'with N'
> (1) A: 스티브 지금 뭐 해요?
>   B: 제인**하고** 전화해요.
>
>
> 제인   스티브
>
> N하고 (같이) '(together) with N'
> (2) A: 스티브 지금 뭐 해요?
>   B: 샌디**하고 (같이)** 공부해요.
> (3) 영미: 마이클 씨, 오후에 뭐 해요?
>   마이클: 린다**하고 (같이)** 수영해요.
> (4) 영미: 마이클 씨, 토요일에 뭐 해요?
>   마이클: 동생**하고 (같이)** 테니스 쳐요.
>
>

Notes

The use of N하고 (같이) is parallel to English '(together) with N'. A reciprocal verb such as 전화하다 'to make a phone call' does not allow 같이 'together'. In describing joint activities, 같이 is optional, as in examples (2), (3), (4).

We have already learned the different uses of 하고 'and' (joining two nouns) in G3.5, as in 부모님하고 오빠 and 사전하고 볼펜.

[연습] Describe the following pictures, using ~하고 or ~하고 같이.

보기: 린다가 마이클하고 (같이) 테니스 쳐요.

린다
마이클

(1)

제인   스티브

_____.

(2)

제인   마이클

_____.

(3)

스티브   마이클

_____.

G5.9 Irregular predicates in -ㅂ

Examples

(1) 마이클: 제니 씨, 집이 멀어요?
제니: 아니오, **가까워요**.
(2) 영미: 한국어 시험 **어려워요**?
스티브: 아니오, 조금 **쉬워요**.

Notes

Some predicates whose stem ends in ㅂ are subject to variation in the stem form. When the following suffix begins with a vowel, ㅂ becomes either 우 or 오. That is, ㅂ → 우 before a vowel: **가깝다: 가깝 + 어요 → 가까워요; 가깝 + 으세요 → 가까우세요 (우 + 으 = 우)**. For monosyllabic irregular verbs in -ㅂ, such as **돕다** 'to help', **곱다** 'to be pretty', ㅂ is changed to **오: 도와요** and **고와요**.

Dictionary form	Translation	~어요
가깝다	close, near	가까워요
춥다	cold	추워요
덥다	hot	더워요
쉽다	easy	쉬워요
어렵다	difficult	어려워요

Compare the regular verb 좁다, which becomes 좁아요.

All irregular predicates in -ㅂ must be contracted.

가깝 + 아요 → 가까우 + 어요 → 가까워요
irregular verb   contraction

[연습] Fill in the blank with the proper form of the given predicate.

> 보기:　한국어는 <u>쉬워요.</u> (쉽다)

(1) A: 한국은 날씨가 어때요?

　　B: 여름에는 _____. (덥다) 겨울에는 조금 _____. (춥다)

(2) A: 집에서 학교까지 멀어요?

　　B: 아니오, _____. (가깝다)

(3) A: 한국어 재미있어요?

　　B: 네, 재미있어요. 그런데 조금 _____. (어렵다)

TASK/FUNCTION

1. Talking about how long something takes

(1) A: 집에서 학교까지 얼마나 걸려요?

　　B: (i)　걸어서 30분 걸려요.

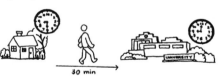

　　　 (ii)　차로 5분 걸려요.

　　　 (iii) 자전거로 15분 걸려요.

　　　 (iv) 버스로 10분 걸려요.

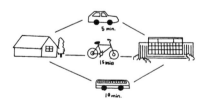

(2)   A: 엘이이에서 뉴욕까지 비행기로
         몇 시간 걸려요?
      B: 6시간 걸려요.

[Time] 걸리다 specifies how long (how much time) some action or activity takes.

[연습] How long does it take to go from your place to school?

보기: A: 집에서 학교까지 얼마나 걸려요?
        B: [by subway, 50 minutes] <u>지하철로 오십 분 걸려요.</u>

(1) [by car, 20 minutes] _____.
(2) [by bicycle, 1 hour] _____.
(3) [by bus, 45 minutes] _____.
(4) [on foot, 5 minutes] _____.

2. Asking about someone's residence

Where do you live? Do you live on campus or off campus? Do you live in an apartment or a house? Is it near or far from school? See the culture notes regarding residence types in Korea.

(1) 제니: 마이클 씨는 집이 어디예요?
     마이클: 저는 (학교) 기숙사에 살아요.
             제니 씨는 어디 살아요?
     제니: 저는 학교 밖에 살아요.
     마이클: 집이에요, 아파트예요?
     제니: 아파트예요.

마이클: 집이 멀어요?

제니: 아니오, 가까워요. 걸어서 10분 걸려요.

(2) 영미: 제인 씨는 집이 어디예요?

제인: 우리 집은 방배동이에요.

영미 씨 집은 어디예요?

영미: 저는 압구정동에 살아요.

[연습] Ask your friend the following questions.

(1) 집이 어디예요? 어디 살아요? _____.

(2) 집이에요, 아파트예요? _____.

(3) 집이 학교에서 가까워요/멀어요? _____.

3. Talking about daily activities

The following is Steve's daily schedule for this semester.

	월요일	화요일	수요일	목요일	금요일
9시					
10시	음악 350 숀버그홀 135	컴퓨터 110 웨스트홀 327	음악 350 숀버그홀 135	컴퓨터 110 웨스트홀 327	음악 350 숀버그홀 135
11시					
12시	점심	점심	점심	점심	점심
1시	한국어 101 이스트홀 203	한국어 101 이스트홀 203	한국어 101 이스트홀 203	한국어 101 이스트홀 203	한국어 101 이스트홀 203
2시					
3시					
4시		생물학 120 무어홀 446	한국어 랩 이스트홀 07	생물학 120 무어홀 446	

(1) 스티브는 매일 학교에 와요? _____.
(2) 한국어 수업은 언제 있어요? _____.
　　　한국어 수업은 어디서 해요? _____.
(3) 수요일 10시 수업은 뭐예요? _____.
(4) 화요일, 목요일은 몇 시에 학교에 와요?_____.
(5) 랩은 언제 들어요?_____.
　　　랩은 어디서 해요? _____.
(6) 점심은 언제 먹어요? _____.
(7) 스티브는 이번 학기에 몇 과목 들어요? 뭐 들어요?

_____.

[연습] (1) Make your own timetable, and describe your daily schedule.
　　　　(2) The following is Michael's daily schedule.

7시	일어나다	
8시	아침을 먹다	
8시 40분	기숙사에서 나오다	
8시 50분	학교에 오다	걸어서
9시	한국어 수업	월, 화, 수 목, 금
3시	테니스 치다	린다하고
6시 반	저녁을 먹다	기숙사 식당
7시	공부하다	도서관
10시	집에 가다	
11시	자다	

(1) 마이클은 몇 시에 일어나요? _____.
(2) 마이클은 어디서 아침을 먹어요? 집에서 먹어요, 학교에서 먹어요?

_____.
(3) 집에서 학교까지 얼마나 걸려요? _____.

(4) 학교에 어떻게 가요? _____.

(5) 한국어 수업은 몇 시에 있어요? _____.

(6) 한국어 수업은 매일 있어요? _____.

(7) 오후에는 뭐 해요? _____.

(8) 마이클은 어디서 저녁을 먹어요? _____.

(9) 저녁에는 뭐해요? _____.

(10) 마이클은 몇 시간 공부해요? _____.

(11) 마이클은 몇 시간 자요? _____.

4. Coming and going

The same motion may be described differently depending on whether the movement is toward or away from the speaker.

Away from speaker	Toward speaker
[Place]에 가다	[Place]에 오다
[Place]에서 나가다	[Place]에서 나오다
[Place]에 들어가다 to go in	[Place]에 들어오다 to come in

(1) General motion: **가다/오다**

> (1) Both speakers are at the destination (school), and actions move toward both speakers.
>
> A: 학교에 매일 와요?
>
> B: 네, 매일 와요.

(2) Neither speaker is at the destination, and actions move away from both speakers.

A: 어디 가세요?

B: 학교에 가요.

　　학교에 가세요?

A: 아니오, 집에 가요.

(3) In telephone conversation: A is at school and B is at home.

A: 오늘 학교 안 오세요?

B: 오늘 수업이 없어요.

　　그래서 안 가요.

(2) Entering and leaving a place

Entering: . . . 에 들어가다 'to go in'/들어오다 'to come in'

(1) Both speakers are outside the building.

　A: 들어가세요.

　B: 먼저 들어가세요.　　You go in first.

(2) A is inside and B is outside.

　A: 안 들어오세요?　　Aren't you coming in?

　B: 지금 들어가요.　　I am going in now.

Leaving: . . . 에서 나가다 'to go out'/나오다 'to come out'
(3) Both speakers are outside the point of origin (home).

    A: 몇 시에 집에서 나오세요?
    B: 8시 반에 나와요.

(4) Both A and B are inside the school, about to leave.
    A: 학교에서 몇 시에 나가세요.
    B: 3시에 나가요.

(5) A is outside and B is inside.
    A: 안 나와요?   Aren't you coming out?
    B: 지금 나가요.   I am going out now.

[연습] Fill in the blank with a verb that is appropriate to the given situation. Change the verb form appropriately.

가다, 오다, 나가다, 나오다, 들어가다, 들어오다

보기: [학교에서]
     린다: 영미 씨 기숙사에서 몇 시에 <u>나와요?</u>
     영미: 8시 반에 <u>나와요.</u>

(1) [기숙사에서]
    제니: 마이클 씨, 오늘 몇 시에 ＿＿＿＿＿＿＿?
    마이클: 8시 40분에 나가요.

(2) [Sandy has not yet arrived at Linda's birthday party. Linda calls
Sandy.]

린다: 샌디 씨, 왜 안 _____?

샌디: 지금 _____.

(3) [Steve is a new student. Young-mee is already in the classroom, but
Steve is still outside.]

영미: 스티브 씨, 빨리 _____.

(4) [Steve and Jenny are talking outside East Hall.]

스티브: 제니 씨, 지금 몇 시예요?

제니: 12시 55분이에요.

스티브: 아이구, 1시에 한국어 시험이 있어요.

제니: 그래요? 그럼 빨리 _____.

(5) [Sandy and Young-mee are talking about Linda's birthday party, which
is tonight.]

샌디: 영미 씨, 오늘 린다 생일 파티에 _____?

영미: 네, 샌디 씨도 _____?

샌디: 아니오, 숙제가 너무 많아요. 그래서 안 _____.

Lesson 5 My Day

CONVERSATION

1

(Michael and Jenny chat after class.)

Michael:	Jenny, how long does it take to get to school from your home?
Jenny:	It's a little far.
	It takes about an hour by bus.
	Where's your home, Michael?
Michael:	I live in the dorm.
	It takes 10 minutes to walk (to school).
Jenny:	What time do you have your class?
Michael:	I have a class at 9.
	So I leave the dorm at 8:40.
Jenny:	Do you come to school every day?
Michael:	Yes, every day. How about you?
Jenny:	I don't come every day.
	I come only three times, on Mondays, Wednesdays, and Fridays.

2

(Young-mee and Michael talk about their daily activities.)

Young-mee:	Michael, what did you do yesterday afternoon?
Michael:	I played tennis with Linda. What did you do, Young-mee?
Young-mee:	I swam.
Michael:	Where?
Young-mee:	At the school swimming pool.
	By the way, what do you usually do in the evening?
Michael:	I study at the library.
Young-mee:	Then what time do you eat dinner?
Michael:	Around 6:30.
Young-mee:	Do you eat alone?
Michael:	No, I eat with Linda.

제6과 주말

(Lesson 6: The Weekend)

OBJECTIVES

CULTURE	1. Writing dates: 2000년 10월 28일
	2. 달력 'calendar'
	3. 돌 and 환갑
GRAMMAR	G6.1 무슨 'what (kind of) N' and 어느 'which N'
	G6.2 Goal or source: N한테/께 or N한테서; [Place]에 or [Place]에서
	G6.3 Probability: ~(으)ㄹ 거예요
	G6.4 Noun(이)나
	G6.5 Negation: 안 and 못
	G6.6 Negative questions
TASK/FUNCTION	1. Talking about weekend plans: 주말에 뭐 할 거예요?
	2. Giving and receiving; making and receiving phone calls; sending and receiving letters
	3. Dates, days, and schedules
	4. Talking about likes and dislikes
	5. Organizing a birthday party

CONVERSATION

1

(Linda and Steve see each other on Monday and talk about the past weekend.)

스티브

린다

스티브: 린다 씨, 지난 주말에 뭐 했어요?

린다: 생일 파티 했어요.

          토요일이 제 생일이었어요.

스티브: 아, 그래요? 몰랐어요. 축하해요.

린다: 고마워요.

스티브: 재미있었어요?

린다: 네, 재미있었어요. 그리고 선물도 많이 받았어요.

스티브: 무슨^{G6.1} 선물 받았어요?

린다: 꽃하고 책하고 옷을 받았어요.

스티브: 꽃은 누구한테서^{G6.2} 받았어요?

린다: 마이클한테서 받았어요.

          스티브 씨 생일은 언제예요?

스티브: 제 생일은 6월 27일이에요.

          유월 이십칠일이에요

2

(Linda and Steve talk about their weekend plans.)

린다   스티브

린다: 스티브 씨, 이번 주말에 뭐 할 거예요[G6.3]?

스티브: 친구하고 영화 볼 거예요.[G6.3]

린다: 무슨 영화 볼 거예요?

스티브: 찰리 채플린 영화를 볼 거예요.

린다: 어느[G6.1] 극장에서[G6.2] 해요?

스티브: 브로드웨이 극장에서 해요.

　　　　　린다 씨는 뭐 할 거예요?

린다: 저는 그냥 집에 있을 거예요.

　　　　　보스톤에 언니가 있어요.

　　　　　그래서 오래간만에 언니한테[G6.2] 전화나[G6.4] 할

　　　　　거예요.

스티브: 언니한테 전화 자주 안 하세요?[G6.6]

린다: 네, 자주 못[G6.5] 해요.

　　　　　스티브 씨는 부모님께 전화 자주 하세요?

스티브: 아니오, 자주 못 해요. 가끔 해요.

NARRATION

주말

지난 토요일은 린다 생일이었어요. 그래서, 린다 아파트에서 생일 파티를 했어요. 린다는 꽃을 좋아해요. 그래서 나는 린다 에게 생일 카드하고 꽃을 주었어요.

    다음 주말에는 린다하고 보스톤에 놀러 갈 거예요. 린다 언 니가 보스톤에 있어요. 린다 언니는 대학교 4학년이에요. 지금 생물학을 전공해요. 내년에 졸업해요. 그리고 아마 대학원에 갈 거예요.

린다 씨에게,

린다 씨
생일을 축하해요.

2000년 10월 28일
마이클

NEW WORDS AND EXPRESSIONS

NOUNS

극장	movie theater
꽃	flower
나라(G6.1)	country
남자 친구(G6.1)	boyfriend
내년	next year
대학원	graduate school
물(G6.4)	water
생물학	biology
영화	movie
제6과	lesson 6
주말	weekend

PROPER NOUNS

디즈니(G6.1)	Disney
브로드웨이	Broadway
시어즈(G6.1)	Sears (department store)
찰리 채플린	Charlie Chaplin

LOANWORDS

라디오(G6.2)	radio
카드	card
피자(G6.4)	pizza

VERBS

놀러	(놀다)	to play, enjoy oneself, go out
받았어요	(받다)	to receive
볼 거예요	(보다)	to see, watch, look at (영화 볼 거예요.)
시장 보러(G6.1)	(시장 보다)	to go grocery shopping
얘기해요(G6.2)	(얘기하다)	to talk

여행해요(G6.3)	(여행하다)	to travel
전공해요	(전공하다)	to major in
졸업해요	(졸업하다)	to graduate
좋아해요	(좋아하다)	to like, be fond of
주었어요	(주다)	to give
축하해요	(축하하다)	to congratulate 추카해요

ADJECTIVES

| 고마워요 | (고맙다) | to be thankful, grateful |
| 머리가 아프다(G6.5) | | to have a headache |

ADVERBS

가끔	once in a while, sometimes
그냥	just, without any special reason
많이	much, many (antonym - 조금)
못	cannot (before a verb)
아마	probably, perhaps
언제	when? (question word)
자주	often, frequently

PRE-NOUNS

다음	next, following
무슨	what?, what kind of? (question word)
어느	which? (question word)
지난	last (time expression)

PARTICLES

께	to (a person; honorific form of 에게, 한테)
에게	to (a person; usually used in writing)
(이)나	just
한테	to (a person or an animal; colloquial form)
한테서	from (a person or an animal; colloquial form)

Pronunciation

10월	[시월]	못해요	[모태요]
십육 일	[심뉴길]	있었어요	[이써써요]
6월	[유월]	좋아해요	[조아해요], [조아애요]
꽃은	[꼬츤], [꼬슨]	축하해요	[추카해요], [추카애요]
꽃을	[꼬츨], [꼬슬]	책하고	[채카고]
꽃하고	[꼬타고]	~(으)ㄹ 거예요	[(으)ㄹ꺼예요]

Vocabulary by Theme

Months of the Year

일월	January	이월	February
삼월	March	사월	April
오월	May	유월	June
칠월	July	팔월	August
구월	September	시월	October
십일월	November	십이월	December

Days of the Month

일 일	the first	이 일	the second
삼 일	the third	사 일	the fourth
오 일	the fifth	육 일	the sixth
칠 일	the seventh	팔 일	the eighth
구 일	the ninth	십 일	the tenth
십일 일	the eleventh	십이 일	the twelfth
십삼 일	the thirteenth	십사 일	the fourteenth
십오 일	the fifteenth	십육 일	the sixteenth
십칠 일	the seventeenth	십팔 일	the eighteenth
십구 일	the nineteenth	이십 일	the twentieth

삼십 일	the thirtieth	삼십일 일	the thirty-first
며칠?	what day of the month?		

Dates

Sino-Korean numbers are used for years. Note that, in Korean, dates are expressed in the order year-month-day.

천구백칠십 년 시월 구 일	October 9, 1970
천구백사십오 년 팔월 십오 일	August 15, 1945
천구백오십 년 유월 이십오 일	June 25, 1950
천구백구십구 년 구월 일 일	September 1, 1999
오늘은 며칠이에요?	What day of the month is it today?
오늘은 2000년 12월 29일이에요.	Today is December 29, 2000.

Time Expressions: Days, Weeks, Months, and Years

지난		이번		다음	
지난 주	last week	이번 주	this week	다음 주	next week
지난 주말	last weekend	이번 주말	this weekend	다음 주말	next weekend
지난 일요일	last Sunday	이번 일요일	this Sunday	다음 일요일	next Sunday
지난 월요일	last Monday	이번 월요일	this Monday	다음 월요일	next Monday
지난 화요일	last Tuesday	이번 화요일	this Tuesday	다음 화요일	next Tuesday
지난 수요일	last Wednesday	이번 수요일	this Wednesday	다음 수요일	next Wednesday
지난 목요일	last Thursday	이번 목요일	this Thursday	다음 목요일	next Thursday
지난 금요일	last Friday	이번 금요일	this Friday	다음 금요일	next Friday
지난 토요일	last Saturday	이번 토요일	this Saturday	다음 토요일	next Saturday
지난 달	last month	이(번) 달	this month	다음 달	next month
작년	last year	올해	this year	내년	next year

Question Words

무슨	what?, what kind of?	어느	which?
언제	when?	어디	where?
무엇	what?	뭐	what? (colloquial)
누구	who?	누가	who? (as subject)

| 어떻게 | how?, in what way? | 얼마나 | how long (time)?/ |
| 왜 | why? | | how much? |

Leisure Activities

수영하다	to go swimming	텔레비전 보다	to watch television
골프 치다	to play golf	테니스 치다	to play tennis
영화 보다	to see a movie	풋볼 시합 보다	to watch a football game

Skills

| 잘 해요 | good, skillful at | 못 해요 | bad, unskillful at |
| 잘 못 해요 | not that good | | |

NOTES ON NEW WORDS AND EXPRESSIONS

Conversation 1

(1) **고마워요** means 'thank you' or 'I am grateful'. **고맙습니다** is used to a senior person.

(2) **받다** is a regular verb, unlike **듣다**. Compare the forms below.

Dictionary form	~아요/어요	~(으)세요	~았/었어요	~(으)ㄹ 거예요
받다	받아요	받으세요	받았어요	받을 거예요
듣다	들어요	들으세요	들었어요	들을 거예요

Conversation 2

(1) **전화(를) 하다** could mean either 'to make a phone call' or 'to be on the phone'. There is another expression **전화(를) 걸다** which means only 'to make a phone call'.

(2) 께 is the honorific counterpart of 한테. It is used for a highly respected senior, for example, a parent, a grandparent, or a teacher.

Narration

(1) 아마 'probably' is often used with ~(으)ㄹ 거예요. It never occurs with ~어요/아요.

CULTURE

1. Writing dates: 2000년 10월 28일

In Korean, dates are written from the largest unit to the smallest, that is, year first, followed by month and day. Thus, October 28, 2000, is read in Korean as 2000년 (이천.년) 10월 (시.월) 28일 (이십.팔.일). Similarly, in identifying a person's academic status, the university is named first, the major or department next, and the school year last, as in 뉴욕 대학(교) 생물학과 4학년 'a senior in the department of biology at New York University'. Addresses are also written from largest unit to smallest with the person's name at the end.

2. 달력 'calendar'

Koreans reckon days according to both the solar and lunar calendars. The solar calendar is called 양(Yang)력 and the lunar calendar 음(Yin)력. Most national holidays are observed based on the solar calendar. However, New Year's Day (설날) is celebrated according to both calendars, while the Moon Festival (추석) is observed on August 15th of the lunar calendar and usually falls in September.

3. 돌 and 환갑

A person's first birthday is called 돌, and the sixtieth birthday is 환갑. 돌 is considered very important because of the high infant mortality rate in the past. The child is dressed in new traditional Korean clothes. A male child wears the traditional headgear of the unmarried youth, and the female often wears makeup.

The child is seated before a table of various foods and objects such as rice, cakes, thread, books, notebooks, pencils, and money, which have been given by well-wishers. The child is urged to pick up one object from the table, as it is believed the one selected foretells the child's

future. If the child picks up a pencil or a book, he/she is destined to be a scholar. If he/she picks up money or rice, he/she will be wealthy; cakes or other food, a government official. If the child picks up the thread, it is believed he/she will live a long life.

환갑 has also been considered especially important, for this is the day when one has completed the zodiacal cycle five times. Even more important is the fact that in the past, before the advent of modern medicine, few people lived to be sixty. 환갑 is a time of great celebration. Children honor their parents with a large feast and much merrymaking. With the parents seated at the main table, sons and daughters, in order by age, bow and offer wine to their parents. After the direct descendants have performed this ritual, other relatives pay their respects in the same manner.

GRAMMAR

G6.1   무슨 'what (kind of) N' and 어느 'which N'

Examples

무슨:
(1) A: 생일에 **무슨** 선물을 받았어요?
    B: 꽃을 받았어요.
(2) A: (Pointing to a book) 이거 **무슨** 책이에요?
    B: 한국어 책이에요.
(3) A: 지난 주말에 뭐 했어요?
    B: 영화 봤어요.
    A: **무슨** 영화 봤어요?
    B: 찰리 채플린 영화 봤어요.

어느:
(4) A: 찰리 채플린 영화 **어느** 극장에서 해요?
    B: 브로드웨이 극장에서 해요.
(5) A: 이 선생님은 **어느** 나라 사람이에요?
    B: 한국 사람이에요.

Notes

1. 무슨 means 'what' or 'what kind of'. It always precedes a noun.

무슨 영화	'what movie'		무슨 선물	'what present'
무슨 책	'what book'		무슨 사전	'dictionary'
무슨 과목	'what subject'		무슨 빌딩	'what building'

2. 어느 is a question word that is used in asking about a choice among a set of limited candidates available, like 'which' in English. Both 무슨 and 어느 always precede a noun.

[**연습** 1] Interview your classmates using the following questions.

(1) 어느 은행에 가세요?

(2) 시장 보러 보통 어느 마켓에 가세요?

(3) 선물 사러 보통 어느 백화점에 가세요?

(4) 점심 먹으러 어느 식당에 가세요?

(5) 무슨 영화 좋아하세요?

[**연습** 2] Make up questions that are appropriate for the responses.

> 보기: A: 지난 주말에 뭐 했어요?
> B: 친구하고 영화 봤어요.
> A: <u>무슨 영화 봤어요?</u>
> B: 디즈니 영화 봤어요.
> A: <u>어느 극장에서 봤어요?</u>
> B: 브로드웨이 극장에서 봤어요.

(1) A: 어디 가세요?

   B: 이번 토요일이 남자 친구 생일이에요.

          그래서 생일 선물 사러 백화점에 가요.

   A: _____?

   B: 시어즈 백화점에요.

(2) 스티브: 영미 씨, 이번 학기에 _____?

   영미: 한국어하고 경제학 수업을 들어요.

   스티브: 한국어 수업은 _____?

          In which building is the Korean class?

   영미: 이스트 홀에서 해요.

(3) [린다 is taking 영미 around campus.]

   영미: _____?

          What building is this?

   린다: 이건 유니온 빌딩이에요.

영미: 학교 식당 _____?

    In which building is the school cafeteria?

린다: 유니온 빌딩 안에 있어요.

G6.2 Goal or source: 한테/께 or N한테서; [Place]에 or [Place]에서

(에게)

Examples

[Person]**한테/께** to a person

(1) 영미: 린다 씨, 언니**한테** 전화 자주 하세요?

    린다: 아니오, 자주 안 해요.

           영미 씨는 부모님**께** 전화 자주 하세요?

    영미: 네, 자주 해요.

(2) 어제는 린다 생일이었어요.

    그래서 린다**한테** 꽃하고 카드를 주었어요.

(3) 린다는 지난 주말에 언니**한테** 갔어요.

[Place]**에** to a place

(4) 제니: 마이클 씨, 학교**에** 몇 시에 왔어요?

    마이클: 9시에 왔어요.

(5) 스티브: 샌디 씨, 홍콩**에** 자주 전화하세요?

    샌디: 네, 자주 해요.

(6) 영미: 마이클 씨, 린다 어디 갔어요?

    마이클: 보스톤**에** 언니한테 갔어요.

[Person]**한테서** from a person

(7) 샌디: 린다 씨, 생일 선물 많이 받았어요?

    린다: 꽃하고 책을 받았어요.

    샌디: 꽃은 누구**한테서** 받았어요?

    린다: 마이클**한테서** 꽃을 받았어요.

(8) 스티브: 마이클, 린다**한테서** 전화 왔어요.

마이클: 네, 고마워요.

(9) 영미: 린다 씨, 생일 축하해요.

린다: 고마워요. 그런데, 어떻게 알았어요?

영미: 마이클**한테서** 들었어요.

[Place]**에서** from a place

(10) 제니: 마이클 씨, 집**에서** 보통 몇 시에 나와요?

마이클: 8시 40분에 나와요.

(11) 스티브: 마이클, 학교**에서** 전화왔어요.

마이클: 누구예요?

스티브: 이 선생님이세요.

Notes

1. When the recipient is a respected senior, for example, **부모님, 선생님,** and so on, the honorific particle **께** should be used instead of **한테**, as in (1).

2. The particle **도** is added after **한테** or **한테서** to indicate 'also, too'.

제인: 영미 씨, 마이클 씨**한테** 전화했어요?

영미: 네.

제인: 린다 씨**한테도** 전화했어요?

영미: 린다 씨**한테도** 어제 전화했어요.

린다: 마이클**한테서** 전화 왔어요?

스티브: 네, 왔어요.

린다: 영미**한테서도** 왔어요?

스티브: 네, 영미**한테서도** 왔어요.

[**연습** 1] Describe who is doing what to whom in the given picture.

보기: 메리가 제임스한테 얘기해요.

메리   제임스

(1)   (2)   (3)

영미   린다   스티브   영미   린다   이 선생님

(1) _____.
(2) _____.
(3) _____.

[**연습** 2] Fill in the blank with the proper particle, choosing from the box.

에, 에서, 한테, 한테서, 께

(1) 린다가 마이클 _____ 전화를 했어요.
(2) 영미는 생일에 스티브 _____ 꽃을 받았어요.
(3) 샌디는 엘에이 _____ 전화했어요. (Sandy called L.A.)
(4) 마이클은 영미 _____ 생일 선물을 줬어요.
(5) 어제 친구 _____ 전화가 왔어요.
(6) 라디오 _____ 뉴스를 들었어요.
(7) 스티브는 부모님 _____ 전화했어요.

G6.3 Probability: ~(으)ㄹ 거예요

Examples

(1) 린다: 영미 씨, 이번 주말에 뭐 **할 거예요**?

    영미: 친구하고 영화 **볼 거예요**.

          린다 씨는 뭐 **할 거예요**?

    린다: 저는 그냥 집에 있을 **거예요**.

(2) 샌디: 마이클 씨, 이번 방학에 뭐 **할 거예요**?

    마이클: 린다하고 보스톤에 **갈 거예요**.

            샌디 씨는 뭐 **할 거예요**?

    샌디: 홍콩에서 오빠가 와요. 오빠하고 여행**할 거예요**.

(3) 마이클: 샌디 씨, 오늘 린다 생일 파티에 **올 거예요**?

    샌디: 네, **갈 거예요**. 그런데, 사람들이 많이 와요?

    마이클: 린다는 친구가 많아요. 그래서 많이 **올 거예요**.

Notes

~(으)ㄹ 거예요 is an expression of probability. It marks a situation the speaker thinks is likely to happen and often expresses the speaker's or the listener's intention or plan. However, a scheduled event is often expressed in the present tense.

Probable future

다음 목요일에 시험이 있을 거예요.   There will [probably] be an exam next Thursday.

Intention or plan

다음 목요일에 저는 영화를 볼 거예요.   I intend to see a movie next Thursday.

다음 목요일에 뭐 하실 거예요?   What do you plan to do next Thursday?

Definite future

다음 목요일에 시험이 있어요.   There is an exam next Thursday.
내일이 제 생일이에요.   Tomorrow is my birthday.

Dictionary form	~어요/아요	~(으)ㄹ 거예요
놀다	놀아요	놀 거예요
듣다	들어요	들을 거예요
걷다	걸어요	걸을 거예요
춥다	추워요	추울 거예요
어렵다	어려워요	어려울 거예요

[연습] Complete the following sentences appropriately with the given predicates, using ~어요/아요, ~었어요/았어요, or ~(으)ㄹ 거예요.

```
보기:   A: 이번 주말에 뭐 할 거예요 (하다)?
        B: 친구하고 영화볼 거예요 (영화보다).
```

(1) 샌디: 린다 씨, 지난 주말에 뭐 _____ (하다)?
    린다: 생일파티 _____ (하다).
           토요일이 제 생일 _____ (이다).
    샌디: 아, 그랬어요? _____ (축하하다).
    린다: _____ (고맙다).
           샌디 씨 생일은 언제 _____ (이다)?
    샌디: 6월 27일 _____ (이다).
(2) 다음 주말에는 린다하고 보스톤에 _____ (가다).
    보스톤에 린다 언니가 _____ (있다).
    린다 언니는 지금 대학교 4학년 _____ (이다).
    내년에 아마 대학원에 _____ (가다).

(3) 마이클: 스티브 씨, 린다 생일파티에 _____ (오다)?

　　스티브: 아니오, 저녁에 친구를 _____ (만나다).

(4) 영미:　린다 씨, 이번 학기에 뭐 _____ (듣다)?

　　린다:　한국어하고 생물학을 _____ (듣다).

G6.4   Noun(이)나

used when reluctant to do something

Examples

(1) 린다:　　스티브 씨, 이번 주말에 뭐 할 거예요?

　　스티브:　친구하고 영화 볼 거예요.

　　　　　　린다 씨는 주말에 뭐 할 거예요?

　　린다:　　저는 그냥 집에 있을 거예요.

　　　　　　오래간만에 언니한테 전화**나** 할 거예요.

(2) 스티브:　영미 씨, 린다 생일 선물 뭐 줄 거예요?

　　영미:　　저는 그냥 카드**나** 줄 거예요.

　　　　　　스티브 씨는요?

　　스티브:　저도 그냥 책**이나** 줄 거예요.

(3) 제니:　　마이클 씨, 점심에 뭐 먹을 거예요?

　　마이클:　피자**나** 먹을 거예요

(4) 제니:　　마이클 씨, 우리 영화**나** 보러 가요.

　　마이클:　좋아요.

Notes

1. **(이)나** 'just' or 'or something', indicates that the chosen item may not be the best possible one for the given situation, and is just one of many possible alternatives.

2. **(이)나** is often used in making a mild suggestion, as in (4); it indicates that the item suggested is not absolute or definite. The speaker is only suggesting one out of many possible options.

3. 이나 is used when the noun ends in a consonant, and 나 is used when the noun ends in a vowel.

[연습] Complete the dialogues using (이)나.

보기: 마이클: 오늘 저녁에 집에서 뭐 할 거예요?
　　　　제니:　 <u>텔레비전이나 볼 거예요.</u>

---

(1) 영미:　 오늘 점심에 뭐 먹을 거예요?
　　 마이클: ＿＿＿＿＿＿＿＿＿＿＿＿＿＿＿.
(2) 제니:　 스티브 씨, 이번 주말에 뭐 할 거예요?
　　 스티브: ＿＿＿＿＿＿＿＿＿＿＿＿＿＿＿.
(3) 스티브: 영미 씨, 주스 줘요?
　　 영미:　 아니오, 괜찮아요. ＿＿＿＿＿＿ 주세요.
　　　　　　저는 물이 좋아요.
(4) 스티브: 린다 씨, 생일에 마이클 씨하고 같이 뭐 할 거예요?
　　 린다:　 요즘 바빠요.
　　　　　　그래서 그냥 집에서 ＿＿＿＿＿＿＿＿＿＿＿＿＿＿.
　　　　　　스티브 씨도 저녁 먹으러 오세요.

G6.5   Negation: 안 and 못

Examples

---

(1) 영미:	린다 씨, 언니한테 전화 자주 하세요?	Linda, do you call your older sister often?
린다:	아니오, 자주 **못** 해요.	No, I cannot call often.

(2) 마이클: 샌디 씨, 린다 생일 파티에
　　　　　　갈 거예요?
　　샌디:　내일 시험이 있어요.
　　　　　　그래서 **못** 갈 거예요.

(3) (Steve did not come to school today. Jenny calls him to find out why.)

제니:	스티브 씨, 왜 학교 **안** 왔어요?	Steve, why didn't you come to school?
스티브:	머리가 아파요.	I have a headache (lit. my head hurts).
	그래서 **못** 갔어요.	And so I could not go.

(4) 선생님: 숙제 다 했어요?
　　스티브: 아니오, **못** 했어요.

Notes

못 'unable, cannot' is used when external circumstances prevent a person from doing something. In contrast, **안** is used for general negation. In (4), in English you can say "I didn't do my homework because I was sick," but in Korean, you have to say **숙제 못 했어요** (not **안 했어요**). Also note that **못** occurs only with a subject with its own volition.

[**연습**] Fill in the blank with either **안** or **못**, depending on the context.

> 보기:　마이클: 샌디 씨, 린다 생일파티에 갈 거예요?
> 　　　　샌디:　내일 시험이 있어요. 그래서, 못 갈 거예요.

(1) 영미:　스티브 씨, 찰리 채플린 영화 봤어요?
　　스티브: 아니오, 저는 코메디를 ＿＿ 좋아해요. 그래서 ＿＿ 봤어요.

(2) 마이클: 스티브, 한국어 숙제 다 했어요?
　　스티브: 아니오, 어려워요. 그래서, ＿＿ 했어요.

(3) 제니:　마이클 씨, 오늘도 테니스 쳤어요?
　　마이클: 아니오, 오늘은 한 시에 시험이 있었어요.
　　　　　　그래서 ＿＿ 쳤어요.

(4) 제니: 스티브 씨, 오늘 한국어 수업 ___ 가세요?
   스티브: 네. 오늘 이 선생님이 ___ 오셨어요. 그래서 수업이 없어요.
(5) 린다: 영미 씨, 요즘 영화 많이 봤어요?
   영미: 아니오, 요즘 좀 바빠요. 그래서 영화를 ___ 봐요.

G6.6   Negative questions

Examples

(1) 스티브: 린다 씨, 주말에 뭐 했어요?
   린다: 오래간만에 언니한테 전화했어요.
   스티브: 언니한테 전화 자주 **안 하세요**?
   린다: **네, 자주 못 해요**. (agree)
(2) 스티브: 영미 씨, 찰리 채플린 영화 보러 같이 가요.
   영미: 스티브 씨, 찰리 채플린 영화 **안 봤어요**?
   스티브: **네, 안 봤어요**. (agree)
(3) 스티브: 린다 씨, 선물 뭐 받았어요?
   린다: 책하고 옷을 받았어요.
   스티브: 꽃은 **안 받았어요**?
   린다: **아니오, 꽃도 받았어요**. (disagree)
(4) 제니: 마이클 씨, 학교에 매일 와요?
   마이클: 네, 매일 와요. 제니 씨는 **매일 안 와요**?
   제니: **아니오, 저도 매일 와요**. (disagree)

Notes

In English, yes and no mean positive and negative realization of the events or states of affairs at issue, respectively, regardless of whether the question is asked positively or negatively. In Korean, however, 네/아니오 refers to whether the content of the question is true or false (the responder agrees or disagrees with it), respectively. Therefore, when a question is asked negatively, 네 means that the content of the question is true (or the speaker agrees with it), as in (1) and (2), and **아니오** means that the content of the question is false (or the speaker does not agree with it), as in (3) and (4).

English: A: Aren't you coming?
                  B: No (I'm not coming).

Korean: A: 안 와요?   Aren't you coming?
                  B: 네, (안 와요). Yes (I'm not coming).

[**연습**] Write **네** or **아니오** based on the context.

보기: 마이클: 제니 씨, 집에서 학교까지 안 가까워요?
        제니: <u>아니오</u>, 가까워요.

---

(1) 제니: 마이클 씨, 오늘 한국어 수업 안 가세요?
    마이클: _____, 안 가요.
(2) 영미: 마이클 씨, 아침 안 먹었어요?
    마이클: _____, 먹었어요.
(3) 영미: 샌디 씨는 한국 사람 아니세요?
    샌디: _____, 중국 사람이에요.

TASK/FUNCTION

1. Talking about weekend plans: 주말에 뭐 할 거예요?

Choose what you are going to do this weekend, and expand your narration by responding to the questions.

(1) 파티할 거예요   무슨 파티예요?
                                      언제예요?
                                      누가 와요?

(2) 영화보러 갈 거예요   무슨 영화를 볼 거예요?
                              누구하고 보러 갈 거예요?
                              영화에 누가 나와요?

(3) 친구를 만날 거예요   친구 이름이 뭐예요?
                              친구는 한국 사람이에요,
                              미국 사람이에요?
                              친구 집이 어디예요?
                              어디(에)서 만나요?
                              친구하고 자주 만나요?
                              친구하고 뭐 할 거예요?

(4) 월요일에 시험이 있어요. 그래서   무슨 시험이 있어요?
    주말에 공부할 거예요.   몇 시간 공부할 거예요?
                              일요일에도 공부할 거예요?

(5) 놀러갈 거예요   어디에 놀러갈 거예요?
                              누구하고 같이 갈 거예요?
                              어떻게 갈 거예요?
                              얼마나 멀어요?

2. Giving and receiving; making and receiving phone calls; sending and receiving letters

(1) 샌디: 린다 씨, 어제 생일파티 재미있었어요?
    린다: 네, 재미있었어요. 그런데 왜 안 왔어요?
    샌디: 좀 바빴어요. 선물 많이 **받았어요**?
    린다: 네, 꽃하고 책을 **받았어요**.
    샌디: 누가 **줬어요**?
    린다: 마이클이 **줬어요**.

(2) 마이클: 영미 씨, 스티브한테 **전화했어요/전화 걸었어요?**

영미: 네, 했어요.

마이클 씨는요?

마이클: 저는 편지 **보냈어요.**

(3) 영미: 스티브 씨, 마이클한테서 크리스마스 (Christmas) 카드 **받았어요?**

스티브: 네, **받았어요.**

영미: 스티브 씨도 마이클한테 카드 **보냈어요?**

스티브: 아니오, 주소를 몰라요. 그래서 못 **보냈어요.**

(4) 린다: 영미 씨, 부모님께 편지 자주 **드려요?**

영미: 아니오, 자주 못 **드려요.** 전화는 자주 **드려요.**

Giving or sending versus receiving:

Giving or sending	Receiving
N한테 선물을 주다	N한테서 선물을 받다
N한테 전화(를) 하다/걸다	N한테서 전화(를) 받다
N한테 편지(를) 쓰다/보내다	N한테서 편지(를) 받다
N한테 편지(를) 보내다	N한테서 편지(를) 받다

[연습] Give a description in answer to the following questions.

(1) 생일날 무슨 선물을 받았어요?

(2) 이번 토요일이 친구 생일이에요. 무슨 선물을 줄 거예요?

(3) 누구한테 자주 전화하세요?

(4) 부모님께 언제 전화했어요?

(5) 부모님한테서 언제 전화 받았어요?

(6) 누구한테 크리스마스 카드를 보낼거예요?

(7) 작년에 누구한테서 크리스마스 카드를 받았어요? (작년 'last year')

(8) 부모님께 편지 자주 쓰세요?

3. Dates, days, and schedules

일	월	화	수	목	금	토
	3:00 P.M. 한국어 랩 1	2	3	4	5	3:30 P.M. 풋볼: vs. UCLA 6
7	3:00 P.M. 한국어 랩 8	9:00 A.M. 한국어 복습 9	10	9:00 A.M. 한국어 시험 11	12	13
14	8:00–10:00 한국어 Final exam 15	16	12:30 경제학 Final exam 17	Semester ends 18	19	1:30 P.M. 풋볼: vs. Michigan 20
21	22	23	24	*Christmas* 25	26	11:00 A.M. 보스톤 27
28	29	30	31	*New Year's Day* 1	2	3

오늘 며칠이에요?   <u>오늘은 2001년 1월 7일이에요.</u>

(1) 한국어 랩은 무슨 요일에 있어요? 몇 시에 있어요?

(2) 한국어 복습은 언제 해요? (복습 'review')

(3) 한국어 구두 시험은 언제 있어요? (구두 시험 'oral exam')

(4) 지난 주말에는 UCLA하고 풋볼 시합이 있었어요. 다음 주말에는
    누구하고 해요? 몇 시에 해요? (풋볼 시합 'football game')

(5) 다음 주일은 무슨 시험이 있어요? 한국어 시험은 몇 시간 걸려요?

(6) 경제학 시험은 언제예요?

(7) 이번 학기는 며칠에 끝나요? (끝나다 'to end')

(8) 보스톤에는 언제 가요? 보스톤에 어떻게 가요?

(9) 올해 크리스마스는 무슨 요일이에요? (올해 'this year')

(10) 내년은 몇 년이에요?

4. Talking about likes and dislikes

좋아해요/좋아하세요, 싫어해요/싫어하세요

(1) 스티브: 린다 씨는 무슨 선물을 좋아해요?
린다: 저는 꽃을 좋아해요.
스티브: 무슨 꽃을 좋아해요?
린다: 장미꽃을 좋아해요.
(2) 린다: 영미 씨는 주말에 뭐 해요?
영미: 저는 영화를 좋아해요. 그래서, 보통 영화 보러 가요.
린다: 무슨 영화를 좋아해요?
영미: 코미디를 좋아해요. 그리고 공포 영화도 좋아해요.
(코미디 'comedy', 공포 영화 'horror movie')
린다 씨 공포 영화 좋아하세요?
린다: 아니오, 저는 싫어해요.

[연습] Talk about your favorite person, place, thing, activity, and so on, with your partner for each of the following items:

(1) 오락 'leisure': 영화 'movie', 음악 'music', 운동 'sports', 연극 'play', 책 'book', 여행 'travel'

(2) 영화: 액션 영화 'action movie', 코미디 'comedy', 드라마 'drama', 드릴러 'thriller', 공포 영화 'horror movie'

(3) entertainers: 영화배우 'movie star', 남자 배우 'actor', 여자 배우 'actress', 코미디언 'comedian', 가수 'singer', 운동 선수 'athlete'

(4) 음악: 팝 'pop', 록 'rock', 재즈 'jazz', 소울 'soul', 발라드 'ballads', 블루스 'blues', 클래식 'classical', 가스펠 'gospel'

(5) 운동 경기 'sports': 농구 'basketball', 축구 'soccer', 야구 'baseball', 풋볼 'football', 배구 'volleyball', 아이스하키 'ice hockey', 육상 'track and field', 골프 'golf', 테니스 'tennis', 복싱 'boxing', 레슬링 'wrestling'

(6) 책 'books':   소설 'novels', 시 'poetry', 만화 'comic books'

(7) 음식 'food':   한식 'Korean', 일식 'Japanese', 중국식 'Chinese', 양식 'Western'

(8) 꽃 'flowers':   장미 'rose', 카네이션 'carnation', 난초 'orchid', 튤립 'tulip'

(9) 과목'subjects':   문학 'literature', 정치학 'political science', 경제학 'economics', 음악 'music', 언어학 'linguistics', 역사 'history'

(10) 언어 'languages': 한국어 'Korean', 일본어 'Japanese', 영어 'English', 중국어 'Chinese'

5. Organizing a birthday party

[Small-group activity] You are organizing a birthday party. Divide the class into several groups of three or four students. Each group prepares for the birthday party. Include the following:

(1) Whose birthday is it?

(2) When is it?

(3) Date, time, and place of party

(4) Sending out invitations

(5) Deciding on birthday presents

(6) Things to bring for the party

(7) Sending out thank-you notes

Lesson 6   The Weekend

CONVERSATION

1

(Linda and Steve see each other on Monday and talk about the past weekend.)

Steve:	Linda, what did you do over the weekend?
Linda:	I had a birthday party. Saturday was my birthday.
Steve:	Oh, really? I didn't know. Happy birthday!
Linda:	Thank you.
Steve:	Was it fun?
Linda:	Yes, it was. And I received a lot of presents, too.
Steve:	What did you get?
Linda:	I got flowers, books, and clothes.
Steve:	From whom did you receive the flowers?
Linda:	I received them from Michael. When is your birthday?
Steve:	My birthday is June 27.

2

(Linda and Steve talk about their weekend plans.)

Linda:	Steve, what are you going to do this weekend?
Steve:	I'm going to see a movie with a friend.
Linda:	What movie are you going to see?
Steve:	We're going to see the Charlie Chaplin movie.
Linda:	At which theater is it showing?
Steve:	At the Broadway Theater.
	What are you going to do, Linda?
Linda:	I'm just going to stay home. My older sister lives in Boston. It has been a while since I talked to her, so I'm going to give her a call.
Steve:	Don't you call your sister often?
Linda:	Not as often as I'd like to. Do you call your parents often?
Steve:	Not really. I call them once in a while.

제7과 서울에서

(Lesson 7: In Seoul)

OBJECTIVES:

CULTURE	1. Seoul
	2. The subway system in Seoul
GRAMMAR	G7.1 Deferential style: ~습니다/ㅂ니다, ~습니까/ㅂ니까?
	G7.2 The subject honorific ~(으)시
	G7.3 Seeking agreement: ~지요/죠?
	G7.4 Demonstrative expressions: 이/그/저 and 여기/거기/저기
	G7.5 The clausal connective ~고 (clause 1 and clause 2)
	G7.6 Direction: (으)로
	G7.7 The noun-modifying form: adjective stem + (으)ㄴ N
	G7.8 Irregular predicates in -ㄹ
TASK/FUNCTION	1. Conversing and inquiring about someone's background
	2. Talking about the weather
	3. Asking and giving directions

CONVERSATION

1

(Steve Wilson goes to Seoul to study Korean for a year, and in Korean class he meets Mark from Sydney.)

스티브   마크

스티브: 안녕하세요? 제 이름은 스티브 윌슨입니다.^{G7.1}

마크: 네, 안녕하세요? 저는 마크 스미스입니다.

           호주 시드니에서 왔어요.

           스티브 씨는 어디서 오셨어요?^{G7.2}

스티브: 저는 미국 뉴욕에서 왔어요.

           호주는 날씨가 좋지요?^{G7.3}

마크: 네, 좋아요.

스티브: 서울에 처음 오셨어요?

마크: 네, 처음이에요.

           서울이 너무 크고^{G7.5} 복잡해요.

스티브: 그래서 저는 책방에서 서울시 지도를 하나 샀어요.

           (Steve shows the map to Mark)

마크: 이 지도 어느 책방에서 사셨어요?

스티브: 우리 학교 책방에서 샀어요.

2

(Mark asks a passerby for directions to the post office.)

마크   지나가는 사람

마크: 저, 실례합니다.

                  말씀 좀 묻겠습니다.

지나가는 사람: 네.

마크: 이 근처에 우체국이 어디 있습니까?

지나가는 사람: 저기^{G7.4} 지하도 보이지요?

                  거기서 지하도로^{G7.6} 내려 가세요.

                  그리고 광화문쪽으로 나가세요.

                  그럼 왼쪽에 큰^{G7.7} 건물이 있어요.

                  우체국은 그 옆에 있어요.

마크: 감사합니다. 그런데 덕수궁은 어떻게 갑니까?

지나가는 사람: 지하철 1호선을 타세요.

                  그리고 시청역에서 내리세요.

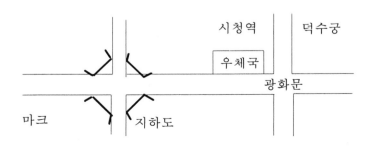

NARRATION

우리 동네

안녕하세요? 제 이름은 스티브 윌슨입니다. 저는 미국 뉴욕에서 왔습니다. 지금은 서울에서 한국어를 배웁니다. 저는 학교에서 가까운 아파트에서 삽니다.[G7.8] 아파트가 조용하고 깨끗합니다.

이게 우리 동네 지도입니다. 동네 가운데 초등 학교가 있습니다. 학교 앞에는 교회가 있습니다. 교회 옆에는 큰 백화점이 있습니다. 백화점 왼쪽에는 작고 예쁜 꽃집이 있습니다. 꽃집 옆에는 책방이 있고 책방 옆에는 식당이 있습니다. 극장은 약국 건너편에 있습니다. 우체국은 슈퍼 옆에 있습니다. 그리고 다방이 여러 군데 있습니다.

NEW WORDS AND EXPRESSIONS

NOUNS

가운데	the middle, center
건너편	the other side
건물	building
꽃집	flower shop
근처	the neighborhood, nearby
김치 (G7.3)	kimchi (Korean pickled cabbage)
교회	church
대학 생활 (G7.1)	college life
동네	neighborhood
말씀	words (honorific form of 말)
시	city (서울시 City of Seoul)
시청	city hall
약국	drugstore
역	station
오른쪽	right side
왼쪽	left side
우표 (G7.8)	stamp
의사 (G7.1)	doctor
제7과	lesson 7
지나가는 사람	passerby
지도	map
지하도	underpass (for pedestrians)
초등학교	elementary school

PROPER NOUNS

광화문	Kwanghwamun
뉴욕	New York
덕수궁	Tŏksugung/Tŏksu Palace (in Seoul)
마크	Mark

베이징 (G7.1)	Beijing
서울	Seoul
스미스	Smith
시드니	Sydney
종로 (G7.6)	Chongno area (in Seoul)
토쿄	Tokyo
호주	Australia

COUNTERS

군데	a place; a spot
호	identifies a number for apartment, subway line, bus line, and so on.

LOANWORDS

슈퍼	a store
슈퍼마켓	a supermarket

PRONOUNS

거기	there
그 분 (G7.4)	that person (honorific); he/she
이 분 (G7.4)	this person
저기	over there
저 분 (G7.4)	that person over there

VERBS

건너세요 (G7.4)	(건너다)	to cross
내려 가세요	(내려 가다)	to go down
내리세요	(내리다)	to get off
도세요 (G7.8)	(돌다)	to turn
만드세요 (G7.8)	(만들다)	to make
보이지요	(보이다)	to be seen, be visible (compare 보다 'to see')

실례합니다	(실례하다)	to be excused (lit. 'commit a rudeness')
삽니다	(살다)	to live
여세요(G7.8)	(열다)	to open
정했어요(G7.1)	(정하다)	to decide
타세요	(타다)	to get in (on), ride
파세요(G7.8)	(팔다)	to sell

ADJECTIVES

감사합니다	(감사하다)	to be thankful; to thank
긴(G7.7)	(길다)	to be long
깨끗합니다	(깨끗하다)	to be clean
미안합니다(G7.1)	(미안하다)	to be sorry (an apology)
복잡해요	(복잡하다)	to be crowded
어려운(G7.7)	(어렵다)	to be difficult
조용하고	(조용하다)	to be quiet, to be reserved
짧아요(G7.7)	(짧다)	to be short (not used for height)
흐렸어요(G7.5)	(흐리다)	to be cloudy

ADVERB

| 너무 | | too much |

PRE-NOUNS

그(G7.1)	that (near listener) (그것)
여러	many, several (여러 군데 'several/many places')
이	this (near speaker) (이것)
저(G7.4)	that over there (away from both speaker and listener) (저것)

PARTICLE

| (으)로 | toward, to [a place] (a direction) |

SUFFIXES

~(으)ㄴ	a noun-modifying form
~ㅂ니다/습니다	deferential ending for a statement
~ㅂ니까/습니까?	deferential ending for a question
~(으)시	subject honorific suffix
~지요?	isn't it? (for confirmation)

Pronunciation

교회	[교외]	약국	[약꾹], [야꾹]
깨끗합니다	[깨끄탐니다]	옆에	[여페]
꽃집	[꼳찝], [꼬찝]	작고	[자꼬]
묻겠습니다	[묻께씀니다]	종로	[종노]
	[무께씀니다]	좋다	[조타]
복잡해요	[복짜패요]	좋아요	[조아요]
실례합니다	[실레암니다]	좋지요	[조치요]

Vocabulary by Theme

Weather

날씨	weather		
날씨가 좋아요	the weather is good	좋은 날씨	good weather
날씨가 나빠요	the weather is bad	나쁜 날씨	bad weather
흐려요	it is cloudy	흐린 날씨	cloudy weather
추워요	it is cold	추운 날씨	cold weather
더워요	it is hot	더운 날씨	hot weather
맑아요	it is clear	맑은 날씨	clear weather
따뜻해요	it is warm	따뜻한 날씨	warm weather
비가 와요	it is raining	비	rain
눈이 와요	it is snowing	눈	snow
바람이 불어요	the wind is blowing	바람	wind

Places and Stores

우체국	post office	책방	bookstore
다방	tearoom	꽃집	flower shop
극장	movie theater	약국	drugstore
교회	church	백화점	department store
은행	bank	슈퍼	supermarket
역	(subway or railroad) station	버스 정류장	bus stop
가게	store	식당	informal restaurant, dining hall

Referring to a Location

여기	here	거기	there
저기	over there		

Directions

이 쪽	this side	그 쪽	that side
저 쪽	that side over there	오른쪽	right side
왼쪽	left side	건너편	other side

Subway Lines in Seoul

지하철 1호선	subway number 1	지하철 2호선	subway number 2
지하철 3호선	subway number 3	지하철 4호선	subway number 4
지하철 5호선	subway number 5	지하철 6호선	subway number 6
지하철 7호선	subway number 7	몇 호선	what line?

Counting Things without a Counter

지도 하나	one map	사과 하나	one apple

Verbs for Opening and Closing

열다	to open	닫다	to close

NOTES ON NEW WORDS AND EXPRESSIONS

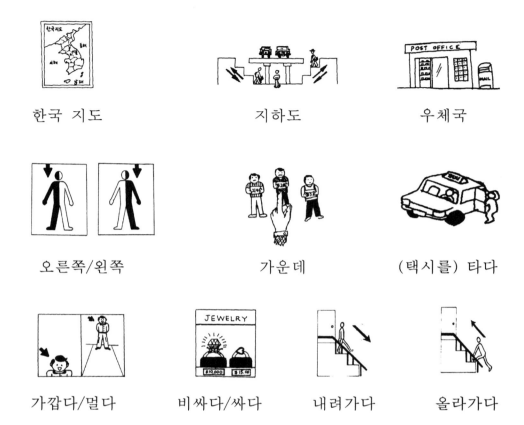

한국 지도   지하도   우체국

오른쪽/왼쪽   가운데   (택시를) 타다

가깝다/멀다   비싸다/싸다   내려가다   올라가다

Conversation 1

(1) **하나** in **서울 지도를 하나 샀어요** 'bought a/one map of Seoul' is the word for 'one'. **하나** is used without a counter.

지도 한 장 = 지도 하나   사과 한 개 = 사과 하나

Conversation 2

(1) **저** in **저, 실례합니다** 'excuse me' denotes the speaker's hesitation. **실례합니다** is a formulaic expression used when one asks a stranger about something. It is not used in the sense 'pardon me' when asking another person to repeat.

(2) 말씀 좀 묻겠습니다 'May I ask you a question?' (lit. I will ask you something) is used as a conversation opener for asking directions as well as for seeking information.

(3) 보이지요? means 'Can you see?' 보이다 'to be seen, be visible' is a passive form of 보다 'to see'. What you see is expressed as the subject of the sentence, as in 우체국이 보여요.

(4) 여기서 is a contracted form of 여기에서 (여기 'here' + 에서 'at'). The particle 에서 is often contracted to 서 after 여기, 저기, 거기, and 어디.

(5) 쪽 in 광화문 쪽으로 'in the direction of 광화문' means 'a direction, a side', as in 오른쪽 'right side', 왼쪽 'left side'.

Narration

(1) 조용하고 깨끗합니다 means 'It is quiet and clean.' Not all 하다 predicates are verbs. There are 하다-adjectives, e.g., 깨끗하다 'to be clean', 조용하다 'to be quiet'. These adjectives are negated by putting 안 before the whole predicate, as in 안 깨끗하다 and 안 조용하다.

(2) 이게 is a contracted form of 이것이 (이것 'this thing' + subject particle 이).

(3) In 여러 군데 'several places', 여러 means 'several' and 군데 is used as a counter for place (e.g., 한 군데, 두 군데, 세 군데, etc.)

CULTURE

1. Seoul

Situated on both sides of the Han River, Seoul, once the seat of the kings of the Chosŏn dynasty (1392-1910), is now the world's tenth largest city where past and present coexist in a most fascinating manner. Centuries-old palaces, gates, shrines, and priceless art objects at museums attest to the illustrious past of the city, while the glistening facades of soaring skyscrapers and the bustling traffic bespeak its vibrant present. With a population nearing twelve million, the city is not only the administrative capital of the republic, but also its political, economic, cultural, and educational center.

Kyŏngbokkung

There are four royal palaces in Seoul, all built during the Chosŏn dynasty: *Kyŏngbokkung, Tŏksugung, Changdŏkkung,* and *Changgyŏnggung.* There also is *Chongmyo,* the royal ancestral shrine of Chosŏn. *Piwŏn,* or the Secret Garden, which is adjacent to *Changdŏkkung,* is another noted palace with beautifully landscaped gardens and classical structures.

Changdŏkkung

2. The subway system in Seoul

The subway is probably the most convenient means of public transportation in Seoul. It is the seventh longest system in the world. Subway stations are decorated in a combination of traditional and contemporary motifs. The ticketing and fare collecting systems are fully automated. The major lines of the system carry two million passengers a day, which accounts for nearly 20 percent of the city's total traffic volume.

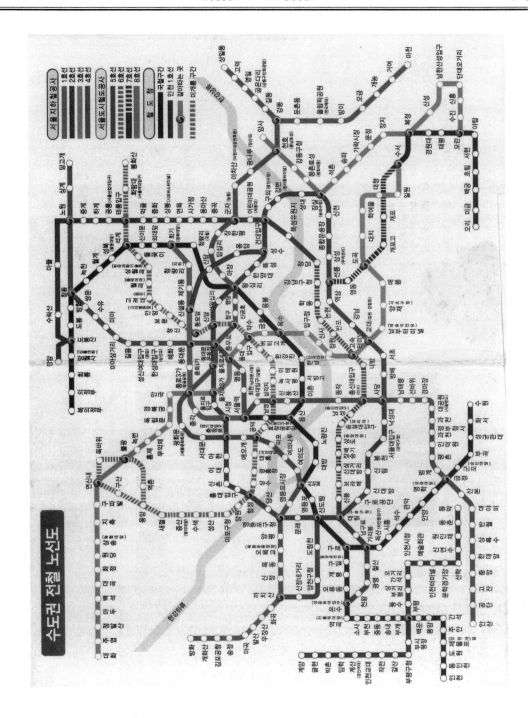

GRAMMAR

G7.1 Deferential style: ～습니다/ㅂ니다
～습니까/ㅂ니까?

Examples

(1) 스티브 윌슨: 처음 **뵙겠습니다.**
제 이름은 스티브 **윌슨입니다.**
마크 스미스: 저는 마크 **스미스입니다.**
(2) A: 언제 한국에 **갑니까?**
B: 이번 여름에 **갑니다.**
(3) A: 샌디 씨는 **한국 사람입니까?**
B: 아니오, **중국 사람입니다.**
(4) A: 지난 주말에 뭐 **했습니까?**
B: 친구하고 같이 테니스를 **쳤습니다.**

Notes

1. The deferential style is used mostly in formal settings, for example, news broadcasting, conferences, business meetings, public lectures, formal interviews, and so forth.

In general, male speakers tend to use the deferential style more than female speakers, who tend to use the polite ～어요/아요 style even in some formal situations. In broadcasting and conferences, however, both male and female speakers use the deferential style.

2. Even in formal conversational settings, the polite ～어요/아요 style may be used occasionally. This would give an effect of making the conversation sound less formal.

On the other hand, deferential style may be used in conversations before changing to polite style. In a first-time introduction, as in conversation 1 of this lesson, for example, identification of names is usually made in deferential style, particularly among male speakers. Once the communicators are introduced to each other, they may begin to use the polite style. This may be attributed to the idea that before names have been given, the situation is considered formal, because no personal relationship has been established. Likewise, one may use deferential style to speak to a stranger, although many people use polite style, as shown in conversation 2.

Some fixed expressions are almost always used in deferential style:

처음 뵙겠습니다.   감사합니다.

실례합니다.   미안합니다.

3. Deferential endings for statements and questions are formed as follows.

	Statement	Question
After a stem ending in a vowel	~ㅂ니다	~ㅂ니까?
After a stem ending in a consonant	~습니다	~습니까?

4. The following table compares deferential and polite endings for statements and questions.

Dictionary form	Speech style	Non-past		Past	
		Statement	Question	Statement	Question
가다	Deferential	갑니다	갑니까?	갔습니다	갔습니까?
	Polite	가요	가요?	갔어요	갔어요?
이다	Deferential	입니다	입니까?	이었습니다/였습니다	이었습니까?/였습니까?
	Polite	이에요/예요	이에요?/예요?	이었어요/였어요	이었어요?/였어요?
하다	Deferential	합니다	합니까?	했습니다	했습니까?
	Polite	해요	해요?	했어요	했어요?

Note that N이었습니다 is contracted to N였습니다 when the noun ends in a vowel, as in 그분은 의사였습니다 (이 + 었 + 습니다 → 였습니다). Compare 우리 어머니는 선생님이었습니다, where no contraction occurs.

[**연습** 1] Change the following conversation into deferential style and practice it with your partner.

샌디:　안녕하세요? 제 이름은 샌디 왕이에요.
영미:　안녕하세요? 저는 김영미예요. 샌디 씨는 어디서 왔어요?
샌디:　저는 홍콩에서 왔어요.
영미:　대학 생활이 재미있어요?
샌디:　네, 재미있어요. 영미 씨는 뭐 공부하세요?
영미:　경제학을 공부해요. 샌디 씨는 전공이 뭐예요?
샌디:　저는 아직 안 정했어요.

[**연습** 2]　Introduce yourself to classmates in deferential style, presenting the following information.

(1) Nice to meet you.
(2) My name is _____.
(3) I am _____. (nationality/ethnicity)
(4) My major is _____.

[**연습** 3] The following table shows a schedule for business trips. Based on the table, answer the questions, using deferential style.

Employees	Destination	Departure date
김철수	일본 토쿄	10/25
이상아	미국 로스앤젤레스	11/7
박기주 & 손인식	중국 베이징	12/8

(1) 김철수 씨는 언제 일본에 갑니까?

(2) 이상아 씨는 11월 7일 어디에 갑니까?

(3) 박기주 씨는 누구하고 중국에 갑니까?

G7.2 The subject honorific ~(으)시

Examples

(1)	제니:	마이클 씨, 안녕하**세**요?
	마이클:	어, 제니 씨. 오래간만이에요. 요즘 어떻게 지내**세**요?
	제니:	잘 지내요. 마이클 씨 이번 학기에도 한국어 들으**세**요?
	마이클:	아니오, 이번 학기에는 안 들어요.
(2)	마크:	스티브 씨 어디서 오**셨**어요?
	스티브:	저는 미국 뉴욕에서 왔어요.
(3)	마크:	저어, 이번 학기에 한국어를 누가 가르치**십**니까?
	동수:	이민수 선생님이 가르치**십**니다.
	마크:	지난 학기에도 이민수 선생님이 가르치**셨**습니까?
	동수:	아니오, 지난 학기에는 김영진 선생님이 가르치**셨**습니다.
(4)	마크:	저어, 실례합니다. 이민수 선생님 **계십**니까?
	동수:	지금 안 **계세**요. 오늘 안 나오셨어요.

Notes

1. ~(으)시 is added to a stem when the subject is honored by the speaker because he or she is older in age and/or higher in social rank, or simply out of courtesy.

2. ~(으)시 takes different forms depending on the suffix.

	Plain		Honorific		
	Non-past	Past	Non-past	Past	~(으)ㄹ 거예요
Polite style	~어요 ~아요	~었어요 ~았어요	~(으)세요	~(으)셨어요	~(으)실 거예요
Deferential style	~습니다 ~ㅂ니다	~었습니다 ~았습니다	~(으)십니다	~(으)셨습니다	~(으)실 겁니다

Examples

	Non-past		Past	
가다 가시다	가요 가세요	갑니다 가십니다	갔어요 가셨어요	갔습니다 가셨습니다
읽다 읽으시다	읽어요 읽으세요	읽습니다 읽으십니다	읽었어요 읽으셨어요	읽습니다 읽으셨습니다

3. ~(으)시 is already part of some honorific predicates, as in example (4).

Dictionary form	Polite style		Deferential style	
	Non-past	Past	Non-past	Past
계시다	계세요	계셨어요	계십니다	계셨습니다

[연습] Fill in the blank with an appropriate honorific form of the verb. Be consistent with the speech style in the conversation.

> 보기: 마크:　스티브 씨 어디서 <u>오셨어요</u> (오다)?
> 　　　 스티브: 저는 미국 뉴욕에서 왔어요.

(1) A:　　　실례합니다. 한국어 선생님 어디 _____ (계시다)?

　　 B:　　　지금 안 _____ (계시다).

　　　　　　수업에 _____ (들어가다).

(2) 스티브: 지난 학기에 몇 과목 _____ (듣다)?

　　 영미:　세 과목 들었어요.

　　 스티브: 이번 학기에는 몇 과목 _____ (듣다)?

　　 영미:　다섯 과목 들어요.

　　 스티브: 다음 학기에는 몇 과목 _____ (듣다)?

　　 영미:　네 과목 들을 거예요.

(3) 마크:　이 지도 어느 책방에서 _____ (사다)?

　　 스티브: 학교 책방에서 샀어요.

G7.3 Seeking agreement: ~지요/죠?

Examples

(1) A: 오늘 날씨 참 **좋지요/좋죠?**	The weather is very nice today, isn't it?
B: 네, 정말 좋아요.	Yes, it is really nice.
(2) A: 김 선생님, 내일 시험 **없지요/없죠?**	Prof. Kim, we don't have an exam tomorrow, do we?
B: 네, 없어요.	No, we don't.
(3) A: 오늘 학교에 안 **가지요/가죠?**	We don't go to school today, do we?
B: 네, 안 가요/아니오, 가요.	No, we don't/Yes, we do.
(4) A: 스티브 씨, 뉴욕에서 **왔지요/왔죠?**	Steve, you are from New York, aren't you?
B: 네, 뉴욕에서 왔어요.	Yes, I am from New York.

Notes

~지요? (often contracted to ~죠 in spoken Korean) is a request for confirmation or agreement about what the speaker believes to be true. The English equivalent is 'Is that right' or '. . . isn't it?' In contrast, ~어요/아요? is a regular question that asks for new information without any assumptions by the speaker.

[연습 1] Fill in the blanks with the ~지요 ending and practice with your partner.

A: 오늘 월요일 _____ (이다)?
B: 네, 월요일이에요.
A: 오늘 한국어 시험이 _____ (있다)?
B: 네, 있어요. 공부 많이 _____ (하다)?
A: 아니오, 많이 못 했어요.

[연습 2] Translate the following expressions into Korean using ~지요?

(1) You ate kimchi, didn't you? _____.
(2) You live in a dormitory, don't you? _____.
(3) You didn't do your homework, did you? _____.
(4) This coffee is delicious, isn't it? _____.

G7.4 Demonstrative expressions: 이/그/저 and 여기/거기/저기

Examples

Pointing to an object:
(1) 마크: **이** 지도 어느 책방에서 사셨어요?
     스티브: 우리 학교 책방에서 샀어요.
(2) 마크: (Looking at two books in front) 어느 책이 스티브 씨
              거예요?
     스티브: (Pointing to one of them) **이**게 제 책이에요.
     마크: (Pointing to one that is on the podium) **저**건 누구 책이에요?
     스티브: **저**건 선생님 책이에요.

(3) 마크: (Pointing to a book on Steve's desk) **그** 책 스티브 씨
           거예요?

     스티브: 아니오, **이**건 샌디 거예요. 제 거는 집에 있어요.

Pointing to a place:

(4) 마크: **여기** 우체국이 어디 있습니까?

     지나가는 사람: **저기** 지하도 보이지요?

                  거기서 길을 건너세요.

(5) 마크: 덕수궁은 **여기**서 어떻게 갑니까?

     지나가는 사람: 지하철 1호선을 타세요. 그리고 시청역에서

                  내리세요.

Notes

1. **이, 그,** and **저** indicate the physical or mental proximity of an item relative to
the speaker and the listener and are used to refer to something in terms of its
position in relation to that of the speaker and the listener.

이	'this' (near speaker)
그	'that' (near listener)
저	'that' over there (away from both speaker and listener)

이 책   그 책   저 책

2. **이, 그,** or **저** is always followed by a noun.

3. **이것/그것/저것** or **이거/그거/저거**

When a thing is mentioned again in the same conversation, there is no need to repeat the noun, which can be replaced with 것/거 (G3.2). 것/거, literally meaning 'thing', is always preceded by a modifier, as in 이것, 그것, and 저것, which correspond to 'this', 'that', and 'that over there', respectively.

것 is often shortened to ~거 in casual speech, and further contraction is made when the following particle begins with a vowel:

Full form	Contracted form
이것/그것/저것 'this/that/that over there'	이거/그거/저거
이것/그것/저것 + 은 (topic particle)	이건/그건/저건
이것/그것/저것 + 이 (subject particle)	이게/그게/저게
이것/그것/저것 + 을 (object particle)	이걸/그걸/저걸

4. 여기/거기/저기

For places, 여기, 거기, or 저기 is used, where 이/그/저 is built into these expressions, corresponding to 'here', 'there (close to you, the listener)', and 'over there' in English, respectively.

여기, 거기, and 저기 can be used as both pronouns and adverbs of place. The locative particle 에 is often omitted, but other particles should remain, as in 여기(에)서, 거기(에)서, and 저기(에)서.

5. Summary of demonstrative uses

	이	그	저
thing/object	이 + N	그 + N	저 + N
person	이 사람 이분 (honorific)	그 사람 그분 (honorific)	저 사람 저분 (honorific)
direction	이 쪽 'this side'	그 쪽 'that side'	저 쪽 'that side over there'
place	여기 'here'	거기 'there'	저기 'over there'

[**연습** 1] Practice the following dialogues with your partner, using real-life situations.

(1) A: 이게 뭐예요?
　　　그게 뭐예요?
　　　저게 뭐예요?
　　B: ＿＿＿＿＿＿ 이에요/예요.
(2) A: 이건 누구 가방이에요?
　　　그건 누구 가방이에요?
　　　저건 누구 가방이에요?
　　B: ＿＿＿＿＿＿ 가방이에요.

G7.5 The clausal connective ～고
(clause 1 and clause 2)

Examples

(1) 우리 아파트는 조용하고 깨끗해요. My apartment is quiet and clean.

(2) 어제는 흐리고 추웠어요.

(3) 스티브는 아파트에 살고
마크는 기숙사에 살아요.

(4) A: 저녁 먹고 보통 뭐 하세요?　　　What do you usually do after
　　　　　　　　　　　　　　　　　having dinner?

　　B: 텔레비전 좀 보고 공부해요.　　I watch TV a little and study.

(5) 점심을 먹고 기숙사에 갔어요.　　　I had lunch and then went to
　　　　　　　　　　　　　　　　　the dormitory.

(6) 우리 아파트는 싸고 조용하고　　　My apartment is cheap, quiet,
깨끗하고 학교에서 가까워요.　　　　clean, and close to school.

Notes

1. ~고 is used to link two clauses like 'and' in English. ~고 indicates that the event or state of clause 1 coexists with that of clause 2.

2. Clause 1 is usually not marked for any tense, especially when it is interpreted as being within the same time frame as clause 2. 어제는 흐리고 추웠어요, for example, sounds better than 어제는 흐렸고 추웠어요.

Note, in contrast to example (2), that with the conjunction 그리고, both sentences must be marked for tense:

어제는 흐렸어요. 그리고 추웠어요.

3. The two events or states in clause 1 and clause 2 may sometimes stand in contrast to each other, as in example (3) above.

4. ~고 is used to indicate a sequence of actions or events, as in example (4). When ~고 is used in this way, the past tense is expressed only in the final verb, as in example (5).

5. [Clause~고] may be used more than once in a sentence, as shown in example (6).

6. Compare 하고 and ~고. Both 하고 and ~고 are translated into 'and' in English. However, the particle 하고 is used to link two nouns (신문하고 책 'a newspaper and a book'), whereas ~고 links two clauses.

언니하고 오빠는 기숙사에 살아요.
언니는 기숙사에 살고 오빠는 아파트에 살아요.
언니는 기숙사에 살아요. 그리고 오빠는 아파트에 살아요.

[연습 1] Combine the two sentences using ~고, as shown in the example.

보기: 마이클은 테니스를 쳐요. 그리고 린다는 수영해요.
 → 마이클은 테니스를 치고 린다는 수영해요.

(1) 린다는 일학년이에요. 그리고 샌디는 삼학년이에요.

———————————————————————————————————————.

(2) 아파트가 깨끗해요. 그리고 싸요.

———————————————————————————————————————.

(3) 서울은 너무 커요. 그리고 사람이 많아요.

———————————————————————————————————————.

(4) 동생은 음악을 들어요. 그리고 언니는 텔레비전을 봐요.

———————————————————————————————————————.

(5) 우리 동네 약국은 7시에 닫아요. 그리고 책방은 10시에 닫아요.

———————————————————————————————————————.

[연습 2] Say the following expressions in Korean.

(1) I bought flowers and books.

———————————————————————————————————————.

(2) There is a newspaper and an umbrella on the desk.

———————————————————————————————————————.

(3) This watch is inexpensive and nice.

———————————————————————————————————————.

(4) Sandy majors in music, and Michael majors in economics.

———————————————————————————————————————.

[연습 3] Answer the following questions using ～고.

(1) 저녁 먹고 보통 뭐 하세요?

———————————————————————————————————————.

(2) 지난 주말에 뭐 했어요?

———————————————————————————————————————.

(3) 어제 저녁 집에서 뭐 했어요?

———————————————————————————————————————.

(4) 다음 주말에 뭐 할 거예요?

———————————————————————————————————————.

G7.6 Direction: (으)로

Examples

(1) A: 우체국이 어디 있어요?
    B: 종로에 있어요.
    A: 여기서 어떻게 가요?
    B: 저기 지하도 보이지요?
        거기서 오른쪽으로 가세요.   Go to the right.
(2) A: 여기 한국어 교실이 어디예요?
    B: 이층으로 가세요.   Please go to the second floor.
(3) 학생: 한국어 시험 어디서 봐요?
    선생님: 교실로 오세요.

Notes

1. Two uses of (으)로 are (i) means or instrument 'by means of' (G5.3), as in:

버스로 왔어요.   I came by bus.
한국말로 말하세요.   Please speak in Korean.

and (ii) direction 'toward, to (a place)' as in the examples above. In both uses, (으)로 indicates a choice made from several possibilities.

2. 으로 is used after a noun ending in a consonant (except ㄹ), and 로 after a noun ending in a vowel or the consonant ㄹ, as in 우체국으로, 버스로, 지하철로.

3. 에 and (으)로: 에 is used to indicate a specific destination, whereas (으)로 indicates a general direction.

이번 여름 방학에 서울에 갑니다.   I am going to Seoul this summer.
이번 여름 방학에 서울로 갑니다.   I am going to Seoul (over other
                                  possible cities I can go to).

오른쪽으로 가세요.   Turn to the right.

오른쪽에 가세요 is not acceptable because 오른쪽 is a direction, not a specific destination.

[연습] Fill in the blanks with 에 or (으)로.

(1) 여기서 오른쪽_____ 가세요.
(2) A: 영미 씨, 내일 뭐 할 거예요?
    B: 도서관_____ 갈 거예요.
(3) 빨리 4층_____ 오세요.
(4) 학교 책방 앞에서 왼쪽_____ 내려 가세요.

G7.7 The noun-modifying form: adjective stem + (으)ㄴ N

Examples

(1) 꽃집에서 **예쁜** 꽃을 많이 봤어요.
(2) 우체국은 **큰** 건물 안에 있어요.
(3) 린다는 백화점에서 **비싼** 옷을 샀어요.
(4) 저는 학교에서 **가까운** 아파트에   I live in an apartment
    살아요.   that is near school.
(5) 백화점 옆에 작고 **예쁜** 꽃집이 있습니다.

Notes

~(으)ㄴ occurs with adjectives and is used to modify nouns, as in:

modifier + noun
  큰   집

Examples of adjective stems that end in vowels:

stem + ㄴ		
Dictionary form	Meaning	Noun-modifying form
크다	to be big	큰　big
싸다	to be inexpensive, cheap	싼　inexpensive
예쁘다	to be pretty	예쁜　pretty

Examples of adjective stems that end in consonants:

stem + 은		
Dictionary form	Meaning	Noun-modifying form
좋다	to be good	좋은　good
많다	to be plentiful	많은　plentiful
작다	to be small	작은　small

Examples of irregular adjectives in -ㅂ:
If ㅂ is at the end of the adjective stem, it is changed to 우 before a vowel. **가깝 + 은 → 가까운** (G5.9).

Dictionary form	~(으)ㄴ form
가깝다　　to be close, near	가까운
춥다　　to be cold	추운
어렵다　　to be difficult	어려운
쉽다　　to be easy	쉬운

더운 날씨   추운 날씨   어려운 시험   쉬운 시험

Examples of regular adjectives in -ㅂ:

Dictionary form		~(으)ㄴ form
좁다	to be narrow	좁은
짧다	to be short	짧은

Examples of irregular adjectives in -ㄹ:

Dictionary form		~(으)ㄴ form
멀다	to be far	먼 far
길다	to be long	긴 long

2. **있다** and **없다** take ~는 instead of ~(으)ㄴ.

있는/없는			
Dictionary form		Noun-modifying form	
재미있다	to be interesting, fun	재미있는	interesting
재미없다	to be uninteresting, boring	재미없는	uninteresting
맛있다	to be tasty, delicious	맛있는	tasty
맛없다	not to be tasty, delicious	맛없는	bad-tasting

3. When you use more than one adjective, the adjectives are connected with ～고, and only the last adjective takes the noun-modifying form, as in 비싸고 좋은 옷, 싸고 맛있는 음식, and 크고 넓은 집.

[연습 1] Fill in the blanks with a noun-modifying form.

(1) ＿＿＿＿＿＿＿＿＿ 집
(2) ＿＿＿＿＿＿＿＿＿ 한국말
(3) ＿＿＿＿＿＿＿＿＿ 영화
(4) ＿＿＿＿＿＿＿＿＿ 동네

[연습 2] Say the following in Korean.

(1) Linda is a good student.

＿＿＿＿＿＿＿＿＿＿＿＿＿＿＿＿＿＿＿＿＿＿＿.

(2) I bought this present at a department store that is nearby.

＿＿＿＿＿＿＿＿＿＿＿＿＿＿＿＿＿＿＿＿＿＿＿.

(3) I bought a small and pretty watch.

＿＿＿＿＿＿＿＿＿＿＿＿＿＿＿＿＿＿＿＿＿＿＿.

(4) I live in a quiet and clean apartment.

＿＿＿＿＿＿＿＿＿＿＿＿＿＿＿＿＿＿＿＿＿＿＿.

G7.8 Irregular predicates in －ㄹ

Examples

(1) A: 한국 노래를 많이 **아세요?**	Do you know lots of Korean songs?
B: 네, 좀 알아요.	Yes, I know some.
(2) A: 부모님은 어디 **사세요?**	Where do your parents live?
B: 서울에 **사세요.**	They live in Seoul.
(3) A: 집이 여기서 **멉니까?**	Is your house far from here?
B: 네, 좀 멀어요.	Yes, it is rather far.

Notes

1. When an adjective or verb stem ending in ㄹ is followed by ㄴ, ㅂ, or ㅅ, the final ㄹ is omitted.

2. In this case, the vowel ~(으) is not inserted. (알 + ~으세요 → 아세요)

Dictionary form	~ㅂ니다	~(으)세요	~어요/아요	~었/았어요	~(으)ㄹ 거예요
알다 'to know'	압니다	아세요	알아요	알았어요	알 거예요
놀다 'to play'	놉니다	노세요	놀아요	놀았어요	놀 거예요
돌다 'to turn'	돕니다	도세요	돌아요	돌았어요	돌 거예요
살다 'to live'	삽니다	사세요	살아요	살았어요	살 거예요
만들다 'to make'	만듭니다	만드세요	만들어요	만들었어요	만들 거예요
팔다 'to sell'	팝니다	파세요	팔아요	팔았어요	팔 거예요
멀다 'to be far'	멉니다	머세요	멀어요	멀었어요	멀 거예요
열다 'to open'	엽니다	여세요	열어요	열었어요	열 거예요

[**연습** 1]   Change the polite style into the deferential style.

> 보기: 저는 기숙사에 살아요. → 저는 기숙사에 삽니다.

(1) 도서관에서 우체국까지 멀어요. → _____.

(2) 학교 책방에서 지도를 팔아요. → _____.

(3) 저는 그 선생님을 잘 알아요. → _____.

[**연습** 2] Answer the following questions using deferential style, as in the example.

> 보기:　A: 저 선생님을 아세요?
> 　　　　B: <u>네, 압니다.</u>

(1) 지금 어디서 사세요?

_____

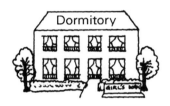

(2) 동생은 어디서 살아요?

_____

(3) 집이 학교에서 멀어요?

_____

(4) 어디서 우표를 팔아요?

_____

TASK/FUNCTION

1. Conversing and inquiring about someone's background

When you want to know about someone's background (for example, the town or country s/he comes from), the question 어디서 오셨어요? 'Where are you from?' is often used (어디서 is a shortened form of 어디에서). The response to this question is [place/location]에서 왔어요, as shown in the following model.

> A: 어디서 오셨어요?
> B: [Place/location]에서 왔어요.

(1)   스티브: 저는 미국에서 왔어요. 마크 씨는 어디서 오셨어요?
      마크: 저는 호주에서 왔어요.

When you specify a town or a city you came from along with the country, the larger unit (country) should precede the smaller (city). For example, (1) in the above can be made more specific as follows:

(2)   스티브: 저는 미국 뉴욕에서 왔어요. 마크 씨는 어디서 오셨어요?
      마크: 저는 호주 시드니에서 왔어요.

Instead of 어디서 오셨어요? 고향이 어디예요? 'Where is your hometown?' can be used.

> A: 고향이 어디예요?
> B: 서울이에요.

Note that 어디예요? and 어디 있어요? are sometimes interchangeable. However, in the case of 고향 'hometown', 고향이 어디 있어요? is unacceptable. In general, movable objects such as 책 'book' are not used in 어디예요? but they are used in the 어디 있어요? form.

[**연습** 1] Practice the following dialogue with your classmate.

스티브: 안녕하세요? 제 이름은 스티브 윌슨입니다.
마크: 네, 안녕하세요? 저는 마크 스미스입니다.
       호주 시드니에서 왔어요. 스티브 씨는 어디서 오셨어요?
스티브: 저는 미국 뉴욕에서 왔어요.
마크: 서울에 언제 오셨어요?
스티브: 8월 24일에 왔어요.

Now exchange the following information.

A: 안녕하세요? 제 이름은 _____.
B: 네, 안녕하세요? 저는 _____.
   _____에서 왔어요. _____ 씨는 어디서 오셨어요?
A: 저는 _____에서 왔어요.
B: _____ (the place you live in now)에 언제 오셨어요?
A: _____년 (year) _____월 _____일에 왔어요.

Practice the conversation again, using deferential style.

[**연습** 2] Let's find out where each student in the chart below comes from.
Play both roles according to the sample dialogue.

Student	Country	State/Town
스티브	미국	뉴욕
샌디	중국	베이징
노리코	일본	오사카
마크	호주	시드니

스티브: 샌디 씨, 어디서 왔어요?

샌디:　　중국에서 왔어요.

스티브: 아, 그래요? 중국 어디서 왔어요?

샌디:　　베이징에서 왔어요.

2. Talking about the weather

날씨가 어때요?　　　　　　　　　How's the weather?

추워요　　　　　　흐려요　　　　　더워요　　　　눈이 와요

비가 와요　　　　바람이 불어요　　　좋아요/맑아요

[**연습** 1] You are a weather reporter for an international weather channel.
Give the weather for January 16, 2001.

2001년 1월 16일

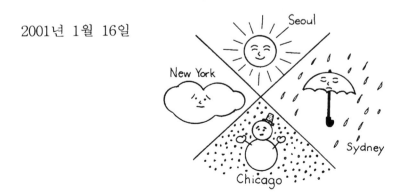

3. Asking and giving directions

When you want to ask for directions on the street in Korea, it is best to start with 실례합니다 'excuse me', a polite way to seek someone's attention. People will expect this expression to be followed by a question about directions and will be ready for it. 말씀 좀 묻겠습니다 (lit. I will ask you something) can immediately follow 실례합니다.

(1)   A: 저, 실례합니다. 말씀 좀 묻겠습니다.
      B: 네.
      A: 이 근처에 우체국이 어디 있어요?
      B: 저기 은행 옆에 있어요.

(Note: 저 . . . is used at the beginning of conversation to get the other person's attention, and also for hesitation.)

For more specific directions, you may ask 어떻게 가요? For instance:

(2)   A: 여기서 어떻게 가요?   How do I go from here?
      B: 이 길로 쭉 가세요.   Go straight.
         그럼 오른쪽에 있어요.   Then it is on your right side.
      A: 감사합니다.

(으)로 가세요 'Go toward the direction of . . .' is often used to give directions. More expressions about directions follow.

로터리	rotary (circular intersection)	오른쪽으로 도세요	turn right
똑바로 (쭉)	straight	왼쪽으로 도세요	turn left
건너편	across the street	길을 건너세요	cross the street
건너가다	to cross the street	똑바로 가세요	go straight
왼쪽	left side	돌다(도세요)	turn
오른쪽	right side	돌아가세요	make a turn
네거리 (사거리)	intersection	신호등	traffic light

[**연습** 1] (Pair work) Ask and give directions for each location on the basis of dialogues (1) and (2) above.

(1) 은행
(2) 우체국
(3) 극장
(4) 약국
(5) 다방

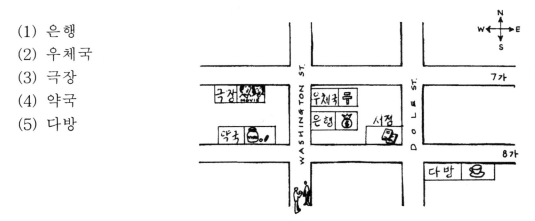

[**연습** 2] (Pair work) Use real-life information from this campus.
It is your first day on campus. You want to go to _____, but you don't know how to get there. Ask your classmates for directions to the following places: cafeteria, library, bookstore, post office, Korean professor's office, bank.

Lesson 7   In Seoul

CONVERSATION

1

(Steve Wilson goes to Seoul to study Korean for a year, and in Korean class he meets Mark from Sydney.)

Steve: Hi, my name is Steve Wilson.

Mark: Hi, I'm Mark Smith. I'm from Sydney, Australia. Where are you from?

Steve: I'm from New York, America. The weather's nice in Australia, isn't it?

Mark: Yes, it is.

Steve: Is this your first time in Seoul?

Mark: Yes, it's my first visit. Seoul is so big and crowded.

Steve: That's why I bought a Seoul city map at a bookstore.
         (Steve shows the map to Mark)

Mark: At which bookstore did you buy this map?

Steve: I bought it at the campus bookstore.

2

(Marks asks a passerby for directions to the post office.)

Mark: Excuse me, may I ask you something?

Passerby: Sure.

Mark: Where is a post office around here?

Passerby: Do you see that underpass over there? Go under it and then go out toward the Kwanghwamun exit. And there's a tall building on your left. The post office is next to that building.

Mark: Thank you. By the way, how do I get to Tŏksu Palace from here?

Passerby: Take the number 1 subway, and get off at the City Hall station.

APPENDICES

Appendix 1-1. Copula, Adjective, and Verb Conjugations

Lesson	Dictionary form / Patterns	이다	아니다	있다	계시다	되다	하다 adjective: 깨끗하다 / verb: 공부하다
10 11	~겠어요 conjecture, intention	—	—	있겠어요	계시겠어요	되겠어요	깨끗하겠어요 / 공부하겠어요
7	~고 clausal connective	(이)고	아니고	있고	계시고	되고	깨끗하고 / 공부하고
13	V.S.~고 나서 clausal connective	—	—	—	—	되고 나서	— / 공부하고 나서
8	V.S.~고 싶다/싶어하다 expressing desire	—	—	있고 싶다/싶어하다 (want to stay)	계시고 싶어 하다	되고 싶다/싶어하다	— / 공부하고 싶다/싶어하다
9	V.S.~고 있다 progressive	—	—	—	—	되고 있다	— / 공부하고 있다
14	~기 때문에 clausal connective	(이)기 때문에	아니기 때문에	있기 때문에	계시기 때문에	되기 때문에	깨끗하기 때문에 / 공부하기 때문에
15	V.S.~기로 하다 'plan to/decide to'	—	—	있기로 하다	계시기로 하다	되기로 하다	— / 공부하기로 하다
15	V.S.~기 시작하다 'begin to'	—	—	—	—	되기 시작하다	— / 공부하기 시작하다
15	V.S.~기 전에 clausal connective 'before ~ing'	—	—	있기 전에	계시기 전에	되기 전에	— / 공부하기 전에
7	A.S. ~(으)ㄴ noun modifier	인	아닌	—	—	—	깨끗한 / —
10	V.S.~(으)ㄴ noun modifier (past/completed)	—	—	—	계신	된	— / 공부한
8	A.S.~(으)ㄴ데 background information	(이)ㄴ데	아닌데	—	계신데	—	깨끗한데 / —
8	V.S.~는 (present) noun modifier	—	—	있는	계시는	되는	— / 공부하는

Lesson	Dictionary form / Patterns	이다	아니다	있다	계시다	되다	하다 adjective: 깨끗하다 / verb: 공부하다
8	v.s.~는데 background information	—	—	있는데	계시는데	되는데	— / 공부하는데
10	~네요 sentence ending	(이)네요	아니네요	있네요	계시네요	되네요	깨끗하네요 / 공부하네요
10	~(으)ㄹ noun modifier (prospective)	일	아닐	있을	계실	될	— / 공부할
6	~(으)ㄹ 거예요 probability	(이)ㄹ 거예요	아닐 거예요	있을 거예요	계실 거예요	될 거예요	깨끗할 거예요 / 공부할 거예요
11	v.s.~(으)ㄹ게요 willingness	—	—	있을게요	—	될게요	— / 공부할게요
8	~(으)ㄹ까요? asking opinion	(이)ㄹ까요?	아닐까요?	있을까요?	계실까요?	될까요?	깨끗할까요? / 공부할까요?
13	v.s.~(으)ㄹ까 하다 'think of ~ing'	—	—	있을까 하다	—	될까 하다	— / 공부할까 하다
15	~(으)ㄹ 때 'when'	일 때	아닐 때	있을 때	계실 때	될 때	깨끗할 때 / 공부할 때
9	v.s.~(으)ㄹ래요 intention	—	—	있을래요 있을래요?	계실래요?	될래요 될래요?	— / 공부할래요
15	~(으)ㄹ 수 있다/없다 potential	일 수 있다	아닐 수 있다	있을 수 있다 (can stay)	계실 수 있다/없다	될 수 있다/없다	— / 공부할 수 있다/없다
15	v.s.~(으)ㄹ 줄 알다/모르다 'know/not know how to'	—	—	—	—	—	— / 공부할 줄 알다/모르다
4	v.s.~(으)러 purpose	—	—	—	—	—	— / 공부하러
15	~(으)면 conditional	(이)면	아니면	있으면	계시면	되면	깨끗하면 / 공부하면

Lesson	Dictionary form / Patterns	이다	아니다	있다	계시다	되다	하다 adjective: 깨끗하다 / verb: 공부하다
13	v.s.~(으)면서 'while ~ing' clausal connective	—	—	있으면서	계시면서	—	— / 공부하면서
2	~(으)세요 honorific polite	(이)세요	아니세요	있으세요	—	되세요	깨끗하세요 / 공부하세요
7	~(으)셨어요 honorific polite (past)	(이)셨어요	아니셨어요	있으셨어요	—	되셨어요	깨끗하셨어요 / 공부하셨어요
7	~(으)셨습니다 honorific deferential (past)	(이)셨습니다	아니셨습니다	있으셨습니다	—	되셨습니다	깨끗하셨습니다 / 공부하셨습니다
7	~습니다/ㅂ니다 ~습니까/ㅂ니까? deferential	입니다 입니까?	아닙니다 아닙니까?	있습니다 있습니까?	계십니다 계십니까?	됩니다 됩니까?	깨끗합니다 깨끗합니까? / 합니다 합니까?
7	~(으)십니다 honorific deferential	(이)십니다	아니십니다	있으십니다	—	되십니다	깨끗하십니다 / 공부하십니다
14	v.s.~어/아 보다 'try doing'	—	—	있어 보다	계셔 보다	되어 보다 /돼 보다	— / 공부해 보다
8 10 12	~어서/아서 (causal, sequential) clausal connective	(이)라서 이어서/ 여서	아니라서/ 아니어서	있어서	계셔서	되어서/ 돼서	깨끗해서 / 공부해서
2	~어요/아요 polite	이에요/ 예요	아니에요	있어요	계세요	되어요 돼요	깨끗해요 / 공부해요
11	~어/아야 되다/하다 obligation, necessity	이어야 되다/ 여야 되다	아니어야 되다	있어야 되다	계셔야 되다	되어야 되다 /돼야 되다	깨끗해야 되다 / 공부해야 되다

Lesson	Dictionary form / Patterns	이다	아니다	있다	계시다	되다	하다 adjective: 깨끗하다 / verb: 공부하다
11 14	V.S.~어/아 드리다/주다 benefactive	—	—	있어 드리다 있어 주다	계셔 주다	되어 드리다 되어 주다	해 드리다 해 주다
8	~었/았는데 background information	이었는데/ 였는데	아니었는데	있었는데	계셨는데	되었는데	깨끗했는데 공부했는데
8	~었/았습니다 past deferential	이었습니다 /였습니다	아니었습니다	있었습니다	계셨습니다	되었습니다	깨끗했습니다 공부했습니다
5	~었/았어요 past	이었어요/ 였어요	아니었어요	있었어요	계셨어요	되었어요	깨끗했어요 공부했어요
12	V.S.~지 마세요 negative command	—	—	있지 마세요	계시지 마세요	되지 마세요	— 공부하지 마세요
13	~지만 'but, although' clausal connective	(이)지만	아니지만	있지만	계시지만	되지만	깨끗하지만 공부하지만
12	~지 못하다 long negation, 'cannot'	—	—	있지 못하다	계시지 못하다	되지 못하다	깨끗하지 못하다 공부하지 못하다
14	~지 않다 long negation	—	—	있지 않다	계시지 않다	되지 않다	깨끗하지 않다 공부하지 않다
7	~지요? seeking agreement	(이)지요?	아니지요?	있지요?	계시지요?	되지요?	깨끗하지요? 공부하지요?

Appendix 1-2. Conjugation of Irregular Adjectives and Verbs

Lesson	Dictionary form / Patterns	-ㄷ 듣다 걷다 묻다	-ㄹ ADJ: 멀다 / 길다 V: 열다, 팔다, 놀다, 돌다 / 만들다, 살다, 알다	-ㅂ ADJ: : 춥다, 덥다 / 쉽다, 어렵다 / 반갑다, 즐겁다 V: 돕다
10 11	~겠어요 conjecture, intention	듣겠어요	멀겠어요 열겠어요	춥겠어요 돕겠어요
7	~고 clausal connective	듣고	멀고 열고	춥고 돕고
13	v.s.~고 나서 clausal connective	듣고 나서	— 열고 나서	— 돕고 나서
8	v.s.~고 싶다 v.s.~고 싶어하다 desire	듣고 싶다 듣고 싶어하다	— 열고 싶다 열고 싶어하다	— 돕고 싶다 돕고 싶어하다
9	v.s.~고 있다 progressive	듣고 있다	— 열고 있다	— 돕고 있다
14	~기 때문에 clausal connective	듣기 때문에	멀기 때문에 열기 때문에	춥기 때문에 돕기 때문에
15	v.s.~기로 하다 'plan to/decide to'	듣기로 하다	— 열기로 하다	— 돕기로 하다
15	v.s.~기 시작하다 'begin to'	듣기 시작하다	— 열기 시작하다	— 돕기 시작하다
15	v.s.~기 전에 clausal connective 'before ~ing'	듣기 전에	— 열기 전에	— 돕기 전에
7	A.S.~(으)ㄴ noun modifier	—	먼 —	추운 —
10	v.s.~(으)ㄴ noun modifier (past/completed)	들은	산	도운
8	A.S.~(으)ㄴ데	—	먼데 —	추운데 —

Lesson	Dictionary form / Patterns	-ㅅ ADJ: 낫다 V: 짓다 낫다	-ㅎ 그렇다 이렇다 저렇다 빨갛다 노랗다 파랗다 하얗다	-으 ADJ: 크다 바쁘다 V: 쓰다	-르 ADJ: 다르다 빠르다 V: 부르다 모르다
10 11	~겠어요 conjecture, intention	낫겠어요 짓겠어요	그렇겠어요	크겠어요 바쁘겠어요 쓰겠어요	다르겠어요 빠르겠어요 부르겠어요
7	~고 clausal connective	낫고 짓고	그렇고	크고 바쁘고 쓰고	다르고 부르고
13	V.S.~고 나서 clausal connective	— 짓고 나서	—	— 쓰고 나서	— 부르고 나서
8	V.S.~고 싶다 V.S.~고 싶어하다 expressing desire	— 짓고 싶다 짓고 싶어하다	—	— 쓰고 싶다 쓰고 싶어하다	— 부르고 싶다/싶어하다
9	V.S.~고 있다 progressive	— 짓고 있다	—	— 쓰고 있다	— 부르고 있다
14	~기 때문에 clausal connective	낫기 때문에 짓기 때문에	그렇기 때문에	크기 때문에 바쁘기 때문에 쓰기 때문에	다르기 때문에 빠르기 때문에 부르기 때문에
15	V.S.~기로 하다 'plan to/decide to'	— 짓기로 하다	—	— 쓰기로 하다	— 부르기로 하다
15	V.S.~기 시작 하다 'begin to'	— 짓기 시작하다	—	— 쓰기 시작하다	— 부르기 시작하다
15	V.S.~기 전에 clausal connective 'before ~ing'	— 짓기 전에	—	— 쓰기 전에	— 부르기 전에
7	A.S.~(으)ㄴ noun modifier	나은 —	그런	큰 바쁜 —	다른 빠른 —
10	V.S.~(으)ㄴ noun modifier (past/completed)	— 지은	—	— 쓴	— 부른
8	A.S.~(으)ㄴ데 background information	나은데 —	그런데	큰데 바쁜데	다른데 빠른데

Lesson	Dictionary form \ Patterns	-ㄷ 듣다 걷다 묻다	-ㄹ ADJ: 멀다 길다 / V: 열다, 팔다, 놀다,돌다 만들다, 살다, 알다	-ㅂ ADJ: 춥다, 덥다 쉽다, 어렵다 반갑다, 즐겁다 / V: 돕다
8	V.S.~는 (present) noun modifier	듣는	— / 여는	— / 돕는
8	V.S.~는데 background information	듣는데	— / 여는데	— / 돕는데
10	~네요 sentence ending	듣네요	머네요 기네요 / 여네요	춥네요 / 돕네요
10	~(으)ㄹ noun modifier (prospective)	들을	멀 길 / 열	추울 / 도울
6	~(으)ㄹ 거예요 probability	들을 거예요	멀 거예요 길 거예요 / 열 거예요	추울 거예요 / 도울 거예요
11	V.S.~(으)ㄹ게요 willingness	들을게요	— / 열게요	— / 도울게요
8	~(으)ㄹ까요? asking opinion	들을까요?	멀까요? 길까요? / 열까요?	추울까요? / 도울까요?
13	V.S.~(으)ㄹ까 하다 'thinking of ~ing'	들을까 하다	— / 열까 하다	— / 도울까 하다
15	V.S.~(으)ㄹ 수 있다/없다 potential	들을 수 있다/없다	— / 열 수 있다/없다	— / 도울 수 있다/없다
15	V.S.~(으)ㄹ 줄 알다/모르다 'know/not know how to'	들을 줄 알다/모르다	— / 열 줄 알다/모르다	— / 도울 줄 알다/모르다
4	V.S.~(으)러 purpose	들으러	— / 열러	— / 도우러

Lesson	Dictionary form / Patterns	－ㅅ ADJ: 낫다 v: 짓다 낫다	－ㅎ 그렇다 이렇다 저렇다 빨갛다 노랗다 파랗다 하얗다	－으 ADJ: 크다 바쁘다 v: 쓰다	－르 ADJ: 다르다 빠르다 v: 부르다 모르다
8	V.S. ~는 (present) noun modifier	— 짓는	—	— 쓰는	— 부르는
8	V.S. ~는데 background information	— 짓는데	—	— 쓰는데	— 부르는데
10	~네요 sentence ending	낫네요 짓네요	그러네요	크네요 바쁘네요 쓰네요	다르네요 부르네요
10	~(으)ㄹ noun modifier (prospective)	나을 지을	그럴	클 바쁠 쓸	다를 부를
6	~(으)ㄹ 거예요 probability	나을 거예요 지을 거예요	그럴 거예요	클 거예요 바쁠 거예요 쓸 거예요	다를 거예요 부를 거예요
11	V.S. ~(으)ㄹ게요 willingness	— 지을게요	—	— 쓸게요	부를게요
8	~(으)ㄹ까요? asking opinion	나을까요? 지을까요?	그럴까요?	클까요? 바쁠까요? 쓸까요?	다를까요? 부를까요?
13	V.S. ~(으)ㄹ까 하다 'thinking of ~ing'	— 지을까 하다	—	— 쓸까 하다	— 부를까 하다
15	A.S./V.S. ~(으)ㄹ 수 있다/없다 potential	나을 수 있다 지을 수 있다/없다	그럴 수 있다	클 수 있다 바쁠 수 있다 쓸 수 있다/없다	다를 수 있다 부를 수 있다/없다
15	V.S. ~(으)ㄹ 줄 알다/모르다 'know/not know how to'	— 지을 줄 알다/모르다	—	— 쓸 줄 알다/모르다	— 부를 줄 알다/모르다
4	V.S. ~(으)러 purpose	— 지으러	—	— 쓰러	— 부르러

Lesson	Dictionary form / Patterns	-ㄷ 듣다 걷다 묻다	-ㄹ ADJ: 멀다 길다 / V: 열다, 팔다, 놀다, 돌다 만들다, 살다, 알다	-ㅂ ADJ: 춥다, 덥다 쉽다, 어렵다 반갑다, 즐겁다 / V: 돕다
15	~(으)면 conditional	들으면	멀면 / 열면	추우면 / 도우면
13	v.s.~(으)면서 'while ~ing' clausal connective	들으면서	— / 열면서	— / 도우면서
2	~(으)세요 honorific polite	들으세요	머세요 / 여세요	추우세요 / 도우세요
7	~(으)셨어요 honorific polite (past)	들으셨어요	머셨어요 / 여셨어요	추우셨어요 / 도우셨어요
7	~(으)셨습니다 honorific deferential (past)	들으셨습니다	머셨습니다 / 여셨습니다	추우셨습니다 / 도우셨습니다
7	~습니다/ㅂ니다 ~습니까?/ㅂ니까? deferential	듣습니다 듣습니까?	멉니다 / 엽니까?	춥습니다 / 돕습니까?
7	~(으)십니다 honorific deferential	들으십니다	머십니다 / 여십니다	추우십니다 / 도우십니다
14	v.s.~어/아 보다 'try doing'	들어 보다	— / 열어 보다	— / 도와 보다
8 10	~어서/아서 (causal, sequential) causal connective	들어서	멀어서 / 열어서	추워서 / 도와서
2	~어요/아요 polite	들어요	멀어요 / 열어요	추워요 / 도와요
11	~어/아야 되다/하다 obligation, necessity	들어야 되다 들어야 하다	멀어야 되다 / 열어야 되다	추워야 되다 / 도와야 되다

Lesson	Patterns \ Dictionary form	－ㅅ ADJ: 낫다 / V: 짓다 낫다	－ㅎ 그렇다 이렇다 저렇다 빨갛다 노랗다 파랗다 하얗다	－으 ADJ: 크다 바쁘다 / V: 쓰다	－르 ADJ: 다르다 빠르다 / V: 부르다 모르다
15	~(으)면 conditional	나으면 / 지으면	그러면	크면 바쁘면 / 쓰면	다르면 / 부르면
13	V.S. ~(으)면서 'while ~ing' clausal connective	— / 지으면서	—	— / 쓰면서	— / 부르면서
2	~(으)세요 honorific polite	나으세요 / 지으세요	그러세요	크세요 바쁘세요 / 쓰세요	다르세요 / 부르세요
7	~(으)셨어요 honorific polite (past)	나으셨어요 / 지으셨어요	그러셨어요	크셨어요 바쁘셨어요 / 쓰셨어요	다르셨어요 / 부르셨어요
7	~(으)셨습니다 honorific deferential (past)	나으셨습니다 / 지으셨습니다	그러셨습니다	크셨습니다 바쁘셨습니다 / 쓰셨습니다	다르셨습니다 / 부르셨습니다
7	~습니다/ㅂ니다 ~습니까?/ㅂ니까? deferential	낫습니다 / 짓습니다	그렇습니다 그렇습니까?	큽니다 바쁩니다 / 씁니다	다릅니다 / 부릅니다
7	~(으)십니다 honorific deferential	나으십니다 / 지으십니다	그러십니다	크십니다 바쁘십니다 / 쓰십니다	다르십니다 / 부르십니다
14	V.S. ~어/아 보다 'try doing'	— / 지어 보다	—	— / 써 보다	— / 불러 보다
8 10	~어서/아서 (causal, sequential) causal connective	나아서 / 지어서	그래서	커서 바빠서 / 써서	달라서 / 불러서
2	~어요/아요 polite	나아요 / 지어요	그래요	커요 바빠요 / 써요	달라요 / 불러요
11	~어/아야 되다/하다 obligation, necessity	나아야 되다 / 지어야 되다	그래야 되다	커야 되다/하다 바빠야 되다/하다 / 써야 되다 써야 하다	달라야 되다 달라야 하다 / 불러야 되다 불러야 하다

Lesson	Patterns / Dictionary form	-ㄷ	-ㄹ	-ㅂ
	Dictionary form	듣다 걷다 묻다	ADJ: 멀다 길다 V: 열다, 팔다, 놀다, 돌다 만들다, 살다, 알다	ADJ: 춥다, 덥다 쉽다, 어렵다 반갑다, 즐겁다 V: 돕다
11 14	v.s. ~어/아 드리다 v.s. ~어/아 주다 benefactive	들어 드리다 들어 주다	— 열어 드리다 열어 주다	— 도와 드리다 도와 주다
8	~는데/(으)ㄴ데 background information	들었는데	멀었는데 열었는데	추웠는데 도왔는데
8	~었/았습니다 deferential (past)	들었습니다	멀었습니다 열었습니다	추웠습니다 도왔습니다
5	~었/았어요 past/completed	들었어요	멀었어요 열었어요	추웠어요 도왔어요
12	v.s. ~지 마세요 negative command	듣지 마세요	— 열지 마세요	— 돕지 마세요
13	~지만 'but, although' clausal connective	듣지만	멀지만 열지만	춥지만 돕지만
12	~지 못하다 'cannot' long negation	듣지 못하다	— 열지 못하다	— 돕지 못하다
14	~지 않다 'not' long negation	듣지 않다	멀지 않다 열지 않다	춥지 않다 돕지 않다
7	~지요? seeking agreement	듣지요?	멀지요? 열지요?	춥지요? 돕지요?

Lesson	Dictionary form / Patterns	－ㅅ ADJ: 낫다 V: 짓다 낫다	－ㅎ 그렇다 이렇다 저렇다 빨갛다 노랗다 파랗다 하얗다	－으 ADJ: 크다 바쁘다 V: 쓰다	－르 ADJ: 다르다 빠르다 V: 부르다 모르다
11 14	V.S. ～어/아 드리다 V.S. ～어/아 주다 benefactive	— 지어 드리다 지어 주다	—	— 써 드리다 써 주다	— 불러 드리다 불러 주다
8	～는데/(으)ㄴ데 background information	나았는데 지었는데	그랬는데	컸는데 바빴는데 썼는데	달랐는데 불렀는데
8	～었/았습니다 deferential (past)	나았습니다 지었습니다	그랬습니다	컸습니다 바빴습니다 썼습니다	달랐습니다 불렀습니다
5	～었/았어요 past/completed	나았어요 지었어요	그랬어요	컸어요 바빴어요 썼어요	달랐어요 불렀어요
12	V.S. ～지 마세요 negative command	— 짓지 마세요	—	— 쓰지 마세요	— 부르지 마세요
13	～지만 'but, although' clausal connective	낫지만 짓지만	그렇지만	크지만 바쁘지만 쓰지만	다르지만 부르지만
12	～지 못하다 'cannot' long negation	— 짓지 못하다	그렇지 못하다	크지 못하다 쓰지 못하다	빠르지 못하다 부르지 못하다
14	～지 않다 'not' long negation	낫지 않다 짓지 않다	그렇지 않다	크지 않다 바쁘지 않다 쓰지 않다	다르지 않다 부르지 않다
7	～지요? seeking agreement	낫지요? 짓지요?	그렇지요?	크지요? 바쁘지요? 쓰지요?	다르지요? 부르지요?

Appendix 1-3. The Three Types of Conjugation

Conjugations for adjectives and verbs can be classified into the following three types:

    A. Stem + 어/아

    B. Stem + (으)

    C. No change in stem

A. Stem + 어/아	B. Stem + (으)	C. No change in stem
~어요/아요 ~어서/아서 ~어/아 보다 ~어/아 주다/드리다 ~어/아야 되다/하다	~(으)ㄴ ~(으)ㄴ데 ~(으)ㄹ ~(으)ㄹ 거예요 ~(으)ㄹ 때 ~(으)ㄹ 수 있다/없다 ~(으)ㄹ 줄 알다/모르다 ~(으)ㄹ게요 ~(으)ㄹ까 하다 ~(으)ㄹ까요? ~(으)ㄹ래요 ~(으)러 ~(으)면 ~(으)면서 ~(으)세요 ~(으)셨습니다 ~(으)셨어요 ~(으)십니다	~겠 ~고 ~고 나서 ~고 싶다/싶어하다 ~고 있다 ~기 ~기 때문에 ~기 시작하다 ~기 전에 ~기로 하다 ~네요 (except for stems in -ㄹ) ~는 (except for stems in -ㄹ) ~는데 (except for stems -ㄹ) ~지 마세요 ~지 못하다 ~지 않다 ~지만 ~지요

Appendix 2. Honorific and Humble Expressions

		Plain form	Honorific form	Humble form
Nouns	age name birthday word house meal counter for people	나이 이름 생일 말 집 밥 사람/명	연세 성함 생신 말씀 댁 진지 분	말씀
Pronouns	he/she I my we	그/사람 나는/내가 내 우리	그 분	저는/제가 제 저희
Verbs	see/meet exist, stay die be well, fine sleep eat give speak ask	보다/만나다 있다 죽다 잘 있다 자다 먹다/들다 주다 말하다 물어 보다	보시다/만나시다 계시다 돌아가시다 안녕하시다 주무시다 잡수시다/드시다 주시다 말씀하시다 물어 보시다	뵙다 드리다 말씀드리다 여쭈어 보다
Particles	subject topic goal	이/가 은/는 한테/에게	께서 께서는 께	
Suffixes	～님 Mr., Ms.	교수 부모 선생	교수님 부모님 선생님	

Appendix 3.   Kinship Terms

1. 가족 'family'; 식구 'member of a family'

부모	parents	딸	daughter (plain)
부모님	parents (honorific)	따님	daughter (honorific)
아버지	father	맏딸	first daughter
아버님	father (honorific)	외딸	only daughter
어머니	mother	형제	sibling(s)
어머님	mother (honorific)	형	male's older brother
할아버지	grandfather	형님	male's older brother (honorific)
할머니	grandmother	누나	male's older sister
남편	husband	누님	male's older sister (honorific)
아내	wife (plain)	오빠	female's older brother
부인	wife (honorific)	언니	female's older sister
아들	son (plain)	남동생	younger brother
아드님	son (honorific)	여동생	younger sister
맏아들	first son	막내	youngest child
외아들	only son		

2. 친척 'relative(s)'

아저씨	uncle
아주머니	aunt
큰아버지	uncle (who is one's father's older brother)
큰어머니	aunt (who is the wife of one's father's older brother)
작은아버지	uncle (who is one's father's younger brother)
작은어머니	aunt (who is the wife of one's father's younger brother)
삼촌	uncle (who is one's father's younger brother)
숙모	aunt (who is the wife of one's father's younger brother)
외삼촌	uncle (who is one's mother's brother)
외숙모	aunt (who is the wife of one's mother's brother)
고모	aunt (who is one's father's sister)
이모	aunt (who is one's mother's sister)
사촌	cousin

Appendix 4. Color Terms

Dictionary form	Color	Color noun	Noun modifier	-(아/어)요
노랗다	yellow	노랑 / 노란색	노란 N	노래요
하얗다 (희다)	white	하양 / 하얀색	하얀 N	하얘요
까맣다	black	까망 / 까만색	까만 N	까매요
빨갛다	red	빨강 / 빨간색	빨간 N	빨개요
파랗다	blue	파랑 / 파란색	파란 N	파래요

Additional Colors

초록색 green
갈색 light brown
밤색 brown
회색 gray

보라색 purple
주황색 orange
분홍색 pink

Appendix 5. Numbers

Arabic number	Sino-Korean	Native Korean	Native Korean with counters
0	영 or 공	—	—
1	일	하나	한
2	이	둘	두
3	삼	셋	세
4	사	넷	네
5	오	다섯	다섯
6	육	여섯	여섯
7	칠	일곱	일곱
8	팔	여덟	여덟
9	구	아홉	아홉
10	십	열	열
11	십일	열하나	열한
12	십이	열둘	열두
13	십삼	열셋	열세
14	십사	열넷	열네
15	십오	열다섯	열다섯
16	십육 [심뉴]	열여섯	열여섯
17	십칠	열일곱	열일곱
18	십팔	열여덟	열여덟
19	십구	열아홉	열아홉
20	이십	스물	스무
30	삼십	서른	서른
40	사십	마흔	마흔
50	오십	쉰	쉰
60	육십	예순	예순
70	칠십	일흔	일흔
80	팔십	여든	여든
90	구십	아흔	아흔
100	백		
1,000	천		
10,000	만		

Large Numbers

100	백	200	이백
1,000	천	2,000	이천
10,000	만	20,000	이만
100,000	십만	200,000	이십만
1,000,000	백만	2,000,000	이백만
10,000,000	천만	20,000,000	이천만
100,000,000	억	200,000,000	이억
1,000,000,000	십억	2,000,000,000	이십억
10,000,000,000	백억	20,000,000,000	이백억
100,000,000,000	천억	200,000,000,000	이천억
1,000,000,000,000	조	2,000,000,000,000	이조

Appendix 6. Counters

A. With Sino-Korean Numbers

Counter	층	분	과	년	월	일
What is being counted	floors of a building	minutes	lesson (in order)	years	months	days
1	일 층	일 분	일 과	일 년	일월	일 일
2	이 층	이 분	이 과	이 년	이월	이 일
3	삼 층	삼 분	삼 과	삼 년	삼월	삼 일
4	사 층	사 분	사 과	사 년	사월	사 일
5	오 층	오 분	오 과	오 년	오월	오 일
6	육 층	육 분	육 과	육 년	유월	육 일
10	십 층	십 분	십 과	십 년	시월	십 일
12	십이 층	십이 분	십이 과	십이 년	십이월	십이 일

Counter	달러(불)	원	마일	학년	번	주일
What is being counted	dollars	won (Korean currency)	mile	school years	numbers (serial)	weeks
1	일 달러	일 원	일 마일	일 학년	일 번	일 주일
2	이 달러	이 원	이 마일	이 학년	이 번	이 주일
3	삼 달러	삼 원	삼 마일	삼 학년	삼 번	삼 주일
4	사 달러	사 원	사 마일	사 학년	사 번	사 주일
5	오 달러	오 원	오 마일	오 학년	오 번	오 주일
6	육 달러	육 원	육 마일	육 학년	육 번	육 주일
10	십 달러	십 원	십 마일	십 학년	십 번	십 주일
12	십이 달러	십이 원	십이 마일	십이 학년	십이 번	십이 주일

B. With Native Korean Numbers

Counters	명/사람	분	시	시간	달	마리	살	과목
What is being counted	people	people (honorific)	point of time: 'the hour'	duration: 'hours'	duration: 'months'	animals	age: 'years old'	academic subjects
1	한 명 한 사람	한 분	한 시	한 시간	한 달	한 마리	한 살	한 과목
2	두 명 두 사람	두 분	두 시	두 시간	두 달	두 마리	두 살	두 과목
3	세 명 세 사람	세 분	세 시	세 시간	세 달	세 마리	세 살	세 과목
4	네 명 네 사람	네 분	네 시	네 시간	네 달	네 마리	네 살	네 과목
5	다섯 명 다섯 사람	다섯 분	다섯 시	다섯 시간	다섯 달	다섯 마리	다섯 살	다섯 과목
6	여섯 명 여섯 사람	여섯 분	여섯 시	여섯 시간	여섯 달	여섯 마리	여섯 살	여섯 과목
10	열 명 열 사람	열 분	열 시	열 시간	열 달	열 마리	열 살	열 과목

Counters	과	개	권	장	병	잔	번	대
What is being counted	number of lessons	items	volumes	sheets (of paper)	bottles	cups and glasses	times	vehicles, cars
1	한 과	한 개	한 권	한 장	한 병	한 잔	한 번	한 대
2	두 과	두 개	두 권	두 장	두 병	두 잔	두 번	두 대
3	세 과	세 개	세 권	세 장	세 병	세 잔	세 번	세 대
4	네 과	네 개	네 권	네 장	네 병	네 잔	네 번	네 대
5	다섯 과	다섯 개	다섯 권	다섯 장	다섯 병	다섯 잔	다섯 번	다섯 대
6	여섯 과	여섯 개	여섯 권	여섯 장	여섯 병	여섯 잔	여섯 번	여섯 대
10	열 과	열 개	열 권	열 장	열 병	열 잔	열 번	열 대

Grammar Index

L = lesson, C = conversation, N = narration, G = grammar

Korean–English Glossary

가게	store
가깝다	to be close, near
가끔	once in a while, sometimes
가다	to go
가르치다	to teach
가방	bag
가볍다	to be light
가수	singer
가슴	chest
가운데	middle, center
가위 바위 보	rock, paper, scissors
가을	autumn, fall
가장	the most
가족	family
가지고 가다	to take
가지고 다니다	to carry around
가지고 오다	to bring
가지다	to have, possess (=갖다)
간장	soy sauce
갈비	*kalbi* (barbecued spareribs)
갈색	light brown
갈아입다	to change (clothes)
갈아타다	to change (vehicles)
감기	a cold
감기(에) 걸리다	to catch a cold
감사하다	to be thankful
갑자기	suddenly
값	price
갖고 가다	to take (short form)
갖고 다니다	to carry around (short form)
갖고 오다	to bring (short form)
갖다 놓다	to bring and put down somewhere
갖다 드리다	to bring or take (humble)
갖다 주다	to bring or take
갖다	to have, possess (=가지다)
같다	to be the same
같이	together
개	item (counter)
거	thing (contraction of 것)
거기	there
거스름돈	change
건강	health
건강하다	to be healthy
건너다	to cross
건너편	other side
건물	building
걷다	to walk
걸리다	to take (time)
걸어 가다	to walk (to a place)
걸어 다니다	to walk (regularly)
걸어 오다	to come on foot
게이트	airport gate
게임	game
겨울	winter
겨울 방학	winter (school) vacation
결혼	marriage
결혼하다	to get married
경제학	economics
계산서	check (restaurant), bill
계시다	to exist, stay (honorific)
계획	plan
계획을 세우다	to make a plan
계획하다	to plan
고기	meat
고등 학교	high school
고등 학생	high school student
고맙다	to be thankful
고장이 나다	to be out of order; to be broken
고추	red-pepper
고추장	red-pepper paste
고춧가루	red-pepper powder
고향	hometown
골프	golf
곳	place
공부하다	to study
공원	park
공책	notebook

공항	airport
과[1]	lesson (in order), number of lessons
과[2]	department
과목	subject, course
과일 가게	fruit store
광화문	Kwanghwamun
괜찮다	to be all right, okay
굉장히	very much
교과서	textbook
교수	professor
교수님	professor (honorific)
교실	classroom
교통	traffic
교포	an ethnic Korean living abroad (=동포)
교회	church
구월	September
구경	sightseeing
구두	dress shoes
구두 가게	shoe store
국내선	domestic flight
국수	noodle
국제선	international flight
군데	place; spot (counter)
권	volume(s) (counter)
권투	boxing
귀	ear
귀걸이	earring(s)
그동안	during that time
그 쪽	that side
그것	that (thing) (near listener)
그냥	just, without any special reason
그래서	so, therefore
그런데	by the way, but then
그럼	if so, then
그렇다	to be that way
그렇지만	but, however
그룹	(music) group
그리고	and
그리고 나서	and then
그리다	to draw

그림	picture
그만	without doing anything further
그저께	the day before yesterday
극장	movie theater
근처	neighborhood; nearby
글쎄요	well; it's hard to say
금년	this year
금요일	Friday
기다리다	to wait
기분	feeling
기사	driver
기숙사	dormitory
기차	train
길	street, road
길다	to be long
김치	*kimch'i* (Korean pickled cabbage)
까만색	black (=까망)
까망	black (=까만색)
까맣다	to be black
깨끗하다	to be clean
꼭	without fail, by all means
꽃	flower
꽃집	florist, flower shop
꿈을 꾸다	to dream
끝	end
끝나다	to be over
끼다	to put on, wear (glasses, gloves)
나	I (plain)
나가다	to go out
나라	country
나쁘다	to be bad
나오다	to come out
나이	age (plain)
나이아가라 폭포	Niagara Falls
나중에	later
낚시 가다	to go fishing
낚시하다	to fish
날	day
날마다	every day
날씨	(the) weather

남동생	younger brother	누구(의)	whose?
남자	male	누나	male's older sister
남자 친구	boyfriend	누님	male's older sister
남쪽	south side		(honorific)
남편	husband	눈¹	snow
남학생	male student	눈²	eye
낮	daytime, day	뉴스	news
낮다	to be low	뉴욕	New York
내	my (plain)	뉴욕 대학	New York University
내년	next year	뉴욕 케네디	New York's Kennedy
내다	① to turn in, hand in;	공항	Airport
	② to pay	뉴저지	New Jersey
내려 가다	to go down	느리다	to be slow
내려 오다	to come down	늦게	late
내리다	to get off	늦다	to get late, become late,
내일	tomorrow		be late
냉면	*naengmyŏn* (cold noodle		
	dish)	다	all
냉수	cold water	다니다	to attend
냉장고	refrigerator	다르다	to be different
너무	too much	다리	leg
넓다	to be spacious, wide	다섯	five
네¹	① yes; ② I see	다시	again
네²	four (with a counter)	다음	next, following
넥타이	tie	다음부터(는)	from next time
넷	four	단어	word; vocabulary
넷이서	four people (together)	닫다	to close
년	years	달	months
노란색	yellow (=노랑)	달다	to taste sweet
노랑	yellow (=노란색)	달러	dollar (=불)
노랗다	to be yellow	달리다	to run
노래	song	닭고기	chicken
노래방	karaoke room	닮다	to resemble
노래하다	to sing a song	담배	cigarette
놀다	① to play, enjoy oneself;	담배를 피우다	to smoke
	② to not work	답	answer
놀러가다	to go out to play	당근	carrot
농구	basketball	대단히	very much
농구하다	to play basketball	대통령	president of a country
높다	to be high	대학	college
놓다	to put down, lay down	대학 생활	college life
놓아 주다	to put something down	대학 캠퍼스	campus
	for someone	대학교	college, university
누가	who? (누구 + particle 가)	대학생	college student
누구	who?	대학원	graduate school

대학원생	graduate student	된장	(fermented) soybean paste
대한극장	Daehan Theater		
댁	home, house (honorific)	된장찌개	*toenjang tchigae*
댄서	dancer		(soybean-paste stew)
댄스	dance	두	two (with a counter)
더	more	둘	two
더럽다	to be dirty	둘이서	two people (together)
덕수궁	Tŏksu Palace	뒤	back, behind
덜	less	뒷줄	back row
덥다	to be hot	드리다	to give (humble)
데	place	듣다	to listen; to take
데이트하다	to date (someone), go out		a course
	(with someone)	들다¹	to cost (money), hold up
도서관	library	들다²	to eat (polite form of
도시	city		먹다)
도요다	Toyota	들리다	to be heard, be audible
도착	arrival	들어오다	to come in
도착하다	to arrive	등	back
독서	reading	등산	hiking, mountain climbing
돈	money	등산 가다	to go hiking
돈이 들다	to cost money	등산하다	to go hiking
돈을 내다	to pay	디스코	disco
돈을 벌다	to earn money	디즈니	Disney
돌다	to turn	따님	daughter (honorific)
돌려 드리다	to return (something)	따뜻하다	to be warm
	(humble)	딸	daughter
돌려 주다	to return (something)	땀을 흘리다	to sweat
돌아가시다	to die, pass away	때	time
	(honorific)	떠나다	to leave
돌아오다	to return, come back	떠들다	to make a noise
돕다	to help	또	and, also, too
동네	neighborhood	똑똑	knock-knock; sound of
동부	the East Coast (of the		knocking (at a door)
	United States)	뛰어서	(by) running
동생	younger sibling	뜨겁다	to be hot
동수	Dongsoo (masculine		
	name)	라디오	radio
동안	during	라면	instant noodles (ramen)
동양학	Asian studies	랩	lab(oratory)
동쪽	east side	러시아워	rush hour
동포	an ethnic Korean living	럿거스 대학	Rutgers University
	abroad (=교포)	레모네이드	lemonade
돼지고기	pork	레몬	lemon
되다	to become, get,	레슬링	wrestling
	turn into	레인코트	raincoat

로미오와 줄리엣	Romeo and Juliet	머리(가) 아프다	to have a headache
로스앤젤레스	Los Angeles	머리방	hair salon
록 (음악)	rock music	먹다	to eat
록펠러 센터	Rockefeller Center	멀다	to be far
롤러블레이드	rollerblade	메뉴	menu
롤러블레이드 타다	to rollerblade	메시지	message
		메일	mail
룸메이트	roommate	며칠	what day of the month?
린다	Linda	명	person (counter)
		몇	how many? what? (with a counter)
마리	counter for animals		
마시다	to drink	모두	all
마음	heart, nature	모레	the day after tomorrow
마일	mile	모르다	to not know, be unaware of, not understand
마중 나오다	to come out to greet someone		
		모자	hat, cap
마치다	to finish	목	neck
마흔	forty	목걸이	necklace
막내	youngest child	목소리	voice
막히다	to be blocked, congested	목요일	Thursday
		몸조리	care of health
만¹	only	몸조리하다	to take care of one's health
만²	ten thousand		
만나다	to meet	못	not (possibly), can't
만들다	to make	못 하다	to be unable to do; cannot do
만 원	₩10,000		
만 원짜리 돈	10,000-won bill	무	radish
많다	to be many/much	무겁다	to be heavy
많이	much, many	무섭다	to be afraid
말	language; words	무슨	what?, what kind of?
말다	to stop, cease	무엇	what?
말씀	words (honorific and humble)	무용가	dancer
		무척	very much
맑다	to be clear	문	door
맛	taste, flavor	문방구점	stationery store
맛(이) 없다	to be tasteless	문화	culture
맛(이) 있다	to taste good, be tasty, be delicious	물	water
		물가	cost of living
매달	every month	물어 보다	to inquire
매일	every day (=날마다)	뭐	what? (contraction of 무엇)
매주	every week		
맨하탄 호텔	Manhattan Hotel	뮤지컬	musical
맵다	to taste spicy	미국	America
머리	hair; head	미국 사람	an American

미술	art
미술가	painter, artist
미시시피강	Mississippi River
미식축구	football (=풋볼)
미안하다	to be sorry
미장원	beauty shop
밑	beneath, below, under
바꾸다	to switch, change
바나나	banana
바닷가	beach
바람	wind
바람이 불다	the wind is blowing
바로	right (there)
바쁘다	to be busy
바이올린	violin
바지	pants
박물관	museum
반	half
반갑다	to be glad, happy
반바지	short pants
반지	ring
반찬	side dish
받다	to receive
발	foot
발레	ballet
밤	night
밤색	brown
밥	meal; cooked rice
방	room
방금	just now
방송국	broadcasting station
방학	school vacation
배[1]	stomach
배[2]	pear
배(가) 고프다	to be hungry
배(가) 부르다	to be full, sated
배구	volleyball
배우	actor, actress
배우다	to learn
배추	cabbage
백	one hundred
백 살	one hundred years old (=백 세)
백 세	one hundred years old
백만 달러	one million dollars
백화점	department store
밴쿠버	Vancouver
버스	bus
버스 정류장	bus stop
번	number of times (counter)
번호	number
벗다	to take off (clothes)
베이징	Beijing
벤치	bench
벨트	belt
별로	(not) really, (not) particularly
별일	special event
병	bottles
병원	hospital
보내 주다	to send
보내다	① to spend (time); ② to send mail
보다	to see, look, watch
보라색	purple
보리차	barley tea
보스톤	Boston
보이다	to be seen, be visible
보통	usually, commonly
복	blessing
복도	hallway
복잡하다	to be crowded
볼링	bowling
볼펜	ballpoint pen
봄	spring
봄 방학	spring vacation
뵙다	to see (a social superior)
부모	parents
부모님	parents (honorific)
부산	Pusan (city in South Korea)
부엌	kitchen
부인	wife (honorific)
부치다	to send (a letter)
부탁하다	to ask a favor
북쪽	north side
분[1]	counter for people (honorific form of 명)

분²	minutes	사이	relationship, between
불	dollar (=달러)	사이다	soda
불고기	*pulgogi* (roast meat)	사전	dictionary
불친절하다	to be unkind	사진	picture, photograph
불편하다	to be uncomfortable, inconvenient	사촌	cousin
		사층	fourth floor
붓글씨	calligraphy	사학년	senior year in college
브로드웨이	Broadway	산	mountain
블루밍턴	Bloomington	살다	to live
비	rain	삼	three
비가 오다	it is raining	삼십 분	thirty minutes
비디오	video	삼월	March
비디오 게임	video game	삼학년	junior year in college
비빔밥	*pibimpap* (rice dish with vegetables and beef)	상자	box
		상점	store
비싸다	to be expensive	상추	lettuce
비타민	vitamin	새	new
비행기	airplane	새로	newly
빌딩	building	새해	New Year
빌려 드리다	to lend, rent (humble)	색	color (=색깔)
빌려 주다	to lend, rent	색깔	color (=색)
빌리다	to borrow	샌드위치	sandwich
빠르다	to be fast	생각하다	to think
빨간색	red (=빨강)	생물학	biology
빨강	red (=빨간색)	생선	fish (for food)
빨갛다	to be red	생신	birthday (honorific)
빨래하다	to wash (laundry)	생일	birthday
빨리	fast, quickly	생활	life, living
빵	bread	샤워하다	to take a shower
빵집	bakery (=제과점)	서로	each other
빼다	to take off (gloves)	서른	thirty
		서비스	service
사	four	서울	Seoul
사 가다	to go carrying something bought	서울대학	Seoul National University
		서점	bookstore (=책방)
사거리	intersection	서쪽	west side
사과	apple	선물	present, gift
사귀다	to make friends	선생님	teacher
사다	to buy	선수	athlete, player
사랑하다	to love	설거지하다	to do the dishes
사모님	teacher's wife	설명하다	to explain
사십	forty	설탕	sugar
사 오다	to come carrying something bought	성함	name (honorific)
		세	three (with a counter)
사월	April	세수하다	to wash one's face

세우다	to stop, park (a vehicle)	스포츠	sports
세일	sale	스포츠 카	sports car
센트 (=전)	cents (=전)	슬프다	to be sad
셋	three	시¹	city
셋이서	three people (together)	시²	the hour, o'clock (time)
셔츠	shirt	시간	① time; ② hours
소고기	beef		(counter for duration)
소금	salt	시계	clock, watch
소나타	sonata	시계방	watchmaker's
소리	sound	시금치	spinach
손	hand	시끄럽다	to be noisy
손님	guest, customer	시내	downtown
손을 씻다	to wash one's hands	시다	to taste sour
쇼핑	shopping	시드니	Sydney
쇼핑하다	to do shopping	시드니	University of Sydney
수고하다	to put forth effort, take	대학교	
	trouble	시월	October
수도	capital	시어즈	Sears (department store)
수박	watermelon	시작하다	to start, begin
수업	class	시장	market
수영	swimming	시장 보다	to go grocery shopping
수영 선수	swimmer	시장 보러	to go grocery shopping
수영장	swimming pool	가다	
수영하다	to swim	시청	city hall
수요일	Wednesday	시카고	Chicago
숙제	homework; assignment	시키다	to order (food in a
숙제하다	to do homework		restaurant), make
술	liquor		someone do something
숫자	number	시험	test, exam
쉬다	to rest	시험 때	exam period
쉰	fifty	시험을 보다	to take an examination
쉽다	to be easy	식구	(members of) a family
슈퍼	store	식다	to cool off
슈퍼마켓	supermarket	식당	restaurant
스무	twenty (with a counter)	식사	meal
스미스	Smith	식초	vinegar
스웨터	sweater	신	shoe (=신발)
스케이트	skating	신기하다	to be novel, new, exciting
스키	skiing; ski(s)	신나다	to be excited, to be
스키 타다	to ski		exciting
스키장	ski resort	신다	to put on, wear
스타워즈	*Star Wars*		(footwear)
스트레스	stress	신문	newspaper
스티브 윌슨	Steve Wilson	신발	shoe (=신)
스페인	Spain	신호등	traffic light

실례하다	to be excused (lit. commit a rudeness)	안²	not
		안경	(eye)glasses
싫다	to be not likable	안경점	optician('s)
싫어하다	to hate, dislike	안녕하다	to be well; feel well
심심하다	to be bored	안녕히	peacefully, safely
심포니	symphony	안부	regards
십	ten	안부 전하다	to give regards to
십이월	December		someone
십일월	November	안테나	antenna
싱겁다	to taste bland	앉다	to sit (down)
싶다	to want to	않다	to not-be, not do
싸다	to be cheap	알다	to know, understand
쓰다¹	to use	알아보다	to find out, check (out)
쓰다²	to write	앞	front
쓰다³	to put on, to wear (hats)	앞으로(는)	from now on, in the
쓰다⁴	to taste bitter		future
		애인	boyfriend, girlfriend
아	ah	애플 컴퓨터	Apple computer
아까	a while ago	야구	baseball
아내	wife	야구하다	to play baseball
아니다	to not be	야채 가게	vegetable store; grocer
아니오	no	약국	pharmacy (=약방)
아드님	son (honorific)	약방	pharmacy (=약국)
아들	son	약속	appointment, promise
아래	under, below, down	양말	sock, stocking
아르바이트	part-time job	양식집	Western-style restaurant
아마	probably, perhaps	얘기하다	to talk
아버님	father (honorific)	어	oh
아버지	father	어깨	shoulder
아이	child	어느	which?
아이구	oh my! my goodness	어디	where?
아이비엠 컴퓨터	IBM computer	어떤	which?, what kind of?
		어떻게	how?, in what way?
아주	very much	어렵다	to be difficult
아직	still, yet	어머	oh! oh my! dear me!
아침	① breakfast; ② morning	어머니	mother
아트 빌딩	art building	어머님	mother (honorific)
아프다	to be sick	어서	please
아파트	apartment	어제	yesterday
아파트 생활	living in an apartment	어젯밤	last night
아프리카	Africa	언니	female's older sister
아홉	nine	언제	when?
아흔	ninety	얼굴	face
악기	musical instrument	얼마	how much?
안¹	in, inside	얼마나	how long?, how much?

얼마나 자주	how often?	옆	beside, next to, side, nearby
엄마	mom		
없다	to not exist, not have, not own	예쁘다	to be pretty, beautiful
		예순	sixty
엘리베이터	elevator	오	five
엘에이	L.A., Los Angeles	오늘	today
엠파이어 스테이트 빌딩	the Empire State Building	오다	to come
		오래간만	for the first time in a while
여기	here		
여덟	eight	오랫동안	for a long time
여동생	younger sister	오렌지	orange
여든	eighty	오렌지 주스	orange juice
여러	many; several	오른쪽	right side
여름	summer	오빠	female's older brother
여름 방학	summer vacation	오월	May
여보	Honey (in addressing one's spouse)	오이	cucumber
		오전	A.M.
여보세요	hello	오케스트라	orchestra
여섯	six	오페라	opera
여자	female	오후	P.M.
여자 친구	girlfriend	올라오다	to come up
여학생	female student	올림	sincerely yours (in letters)
여행	travel		
여행 가다	to travel	올해	this year
여행사	travel agency	옷	clothes
여행하다	to travel	옷가게	clothing store
역	(subway or railroad) station	옷집	clothing store
		왜	why?
역사	history	외국	foreign country
연구실	professor's office	왼쪽	left side
연락	contact	요리	cooking
연락하다	to keep in touch (with)	요즘	these days
		용평	Yongp'yŏng ski resort area (in Kangwŏn Province)
연세	age (honorific)		
연습	exercise, practice		
연습 문제	exercises	우리	we, us, our
연습(을) 하다	to practice	우산	umbrella
연하다	to be tender	우유	milk
열	ten	우체국	post office
열다	to open	우표	stamp
열심히	diligently	운동장	field, playground
영국	England	운동하다	to exercise
영어	English	운동화	sports shoes, sneakers
영화	movie	운전하다	to drive
영화(를) 보다	to see a movie	워크맨	Walkman

원	won (Korean currency)	이월	February
월	month	이 쪽	this side
월요일	Monday	이젠	now
월츠	waltz	이층	second floor
웬일	what matter?	이학년	sophomore
위	top, above	인구	(human) population
유월	June	인디애나 대학	Indiana University
유니온 빌딩	Union Building	인사	greeting
유럽	Europe	인사하다	to greet
유자차	citron tea	인삼차	ginseng tea
육개장	*yukkaejang* (hot shredded beef soup)	인형	doll
		일¹	one
육교	pedestrian overpass	일²	date (day of the month)
은행	bank	일³	event, thing
음료수	beverage	일⁴	work
음식	food	일곱	seven
음식점	restaurant (=식당)	일본 음식점	Japanese restaurant
음악	music	일식집	Japanese restaurant
음악가	musician	일어나다	to get up
음악(을) 듣다	to listen to music	일요일	Sunday
음악회	concert	일월	January
의사	doctor	일찍	early
의자	chair	일층	first floor
이¹	subject particle	일하다	to work
이²	two	일학년	freshman
이³	this (near speaker)	일흔	seventy
이⁴	tooth	읽다	to read
이거	this (thing) (contraction of 이것)	잃어버리다	to lose
		입	mouth
이기다	to win	입고 가다	to go wearing something
이다	to be	입고 다니다	to go wearing something (regularly)
이따가	little later		
이렇다	to be this way	입고 오다	to come wearing something
이를 닦다	to brush teeth		
이름	name	입다	to wear, put on (clothes)
이만	this much, this only	입술	lips
이메일을 보내다	to send e-mail	있다	to exist
		잊어버리다	to forget
이민 가다	to emigrate		
이발소	barbershop	자다	to sleep
이번	this time	자라다	to grow up
이사하다	to move, change residence	자리	seat
		자전거	bicycle
이스트 홀	East Hall	자전거(를) 타다	to ride a bicycle
이야기하다	to talk (with someone)		

자주	frequently, often	점원	clerk, salesperson
작년	last year	정말	really
작다	to be small	정치학	political science
잔	glass(es), cup(s)	정하다	to decide
잘	well	제	my (humble)
잘라 드리다	to cut (for someone) (humble)	제과점	bakery (=빵집)
잘라 주다	to cut (for someone)	제일	the first, the most
잠	sleep	조각	sculpture
잠깐만	for a short time, for a while	조금	little
		조깅하다	to jog
잠을 자다	to sleep	조용하다	to be quiet
잡다	to catch, grab	졸업하다	to graduate
잡수시다	to eat (honorific)	좀	① a little; ② please
장	sheet(s) (counter)	좁다	to be narrow
장갑	glove(s)	종로	Chongno area (in Seoul)
재미 교포	an ethnic Korean living in the United States	종업원	waiter, waitress
		종이	paper
재미없다	to be no fun, to be boring	좋다	to be good
		좋아하다	to like, be fond of
재미있다	to be fun	죄송하다	to be sorry
저¹	I (humble)	주다	to give
저²	(저것) that over there (away from both speaker and listener)	주말	weekend
		주무시다	to sleep (honorific)
		주문하다	to order
		주소	address
저 쪽	that side over there	주스	juice
저기	over there	주일	week
저녁	① evening; ② supper, dinner	주황색	orange (color)
		죽다	to die
저렇다	to be that way	줄	row
저어	expression of hesitation	중국	China
적다	to be few, scarce	중국 사람	Chinese (person)
적어도	at least	중국집	Chinese restaurant
전	cents (=센트)	중학교	middle school
전(에)	before	중학생	junior high school student
전공	major	즐겁다	to be pleasant, enjoyable
전공하다	to major in	즐기다	to enjoy
전부	all together, totol	지갑	wallet
전하다	to pass, convey	지금	now
전화	telephone	지나가는 사람	passerby
전화국	telephone company	지난	last
전화를 걸다	to make a call	지내다	to pass by, spend days
전화 번호	telephone number	지다	to be defeated
전화하다	to make a phone call	지도	map
점심	lunch	지하도	pedestrian underpass

지하철	subway	춥다	to be cold
직접	directly	취미	hobby
진지	meal, cooked rice (honorific)	층	floor; layer (counter)
질문	question	치다	to play (tennis, piano, guitar)
질문하다	to ask	치마	skirt
집	home, house	친구	friend
짜다	to taste salty	친절하다	to be kind, considerate
짧다	to be short	칠월	July
쪽	side, direction	칠판	blackboard
쯤	about, around	카드	card
찍다	to take (a photograph)	카메라 가게	camera shop
차¹	car, automobile	카운터	cash register, counter
차²	tea	카페	cafe, coffee shop
차다¹	to put on, to wear (a wristwatch)	캐나다	Canada
		캠퍼스	campus
차다²	to be cold	커피	coffee
참	① very, really; ② by the way	컴퓨터	computer
		케이크	cake
참기름	sesame oil	코	nose
창문	window	콘서트	concert
찾다	① to withdraw money (from the bank); ② to look for, find, search	크다	to be big
		크리스마스	Christmas
		큰아버지	uncle (father's older brother)
채소 가게	vegetable store		
책	book	클라리넷	clarinet
책방	bookstore (=서점)	클래스	class
책상	desk	클래스메이트	classmate
처음	for the first time	클래식 (음악)	classical music
천	one thousand	키	height (of a person or a plant)
천천히	slowly		
첫	first	키가 작다	to be short (height)
청소하다	to clean	키가 크다	to be tall
첼로	cello	타고 가다	to go riding ((in a vehicle)
초등 학교	elementary school		
초등 학생	elementary school student	타고 다니다	to ride (regularly)
초록색	green	타고 오다	to come riding
추천서	letter of recommendation	타다	to get in (on), ride
축구	soccer	탁구	table tennis, pingpong
축하하다	to congratulate	탈춤	t'alch'um (Korean mask dance)
출구	exit		
출발	departure	태권도	T'aekwŏndo (Korean martial art)
춤	dance(s)		
춤을 추다	to dance	태어나다	to be born

태워 주다	to give a ride	피자	pizza
택시	taxi		
택시비	taxi fare	하나	one
턱	chin	하다	to do
테니스	tennis	하루	day
테니스 코트	tennis court	하얀색	white
테이프	audio tape	하얗다	to be white
텍사스	Texas	하와이	Hawai'i
텔레비전	television	하키	hockey
텔레비전(을)	to watch TV	학교	school
보다		학교 식당	school cafeteria
토론토	Toronto	학기	semester, academic term
토요일	Saturday	학년	academic year
토쿄	Tokyo	학생	student
통화중이다	the line is busy	한	one (with a counter)
트럭	truck	한국	Korea
특히	particularly	한국말	Korean (language)
			(=한국어)
파	scallion	한국 사람	Korean (person)
파란색	blue (=파랑)	한국어	Korean (language)
파랑	blue (=파란색)		(=한국말)
파랗다	to be blue	한글	Korean alphabet
파인애플	pineapple	한번	once, one time
파티	party	한복	hanbok (traditional
팔	arm		Korean dress)
팔월	August	한식집	Korean restaurant
팔다	to sell	할머니	grandmother
팝송	pop music	할머님	grandmother (honorific)
팩스를 보내다	to send a fax	할아버님	granadfather (honorific)
펜	pen	할아버지	grandfather
폭스바겐	Volkswagen	핫도그	hotdog
편리하다	to be convenient	해장국	haejangkuk (soup to eat
편지	letter (of correspondence)		to relieve a hangover)
편하다	to be comfortable	햄버거	hamburger
표	ticket	행복하다	to be happy
푹	deeply	허리	waist
풀다	① to take off (tie, belt,	헤드폰	headphones, earphones
	watch); ② to solve a	형	male's older brother
	problem	형님	male's older brother
풋볼	football		(honorific)
풋볼 시합	football game	형제	sibling(s)
플룻	flute	호	(with Sino-Korean
피곤하다	to be tired		number) classifier for
피아노	piano		apartment numbers,
피우다	to smoke (담배 피우다)		subway and bus lines, etc.

호주	Australia	회색	gray
혼자(서)	alone, by oneself	후	after
홍차	black tea	후추 (가루)	black pepper (powder)
홍콩	Hong Kong	휴게실	lounge
화가 나다	to get angry	휴일	holiday, day off
화랑	art gallery	흐리다	to be cloudy
화요일	Tuesday	힘들다	to be difficult
화장실	restroom		

English-Korean Glossary

10,000-won bill	만 원짜리 돈	ask	질문하다
about	쯤	ask a favor	부탁하다
above	위	assignment	숙제
academic term	학기	athlete	선수
academic year	학년	attend	다니다
actor	배우	audible	들리다
actress	배우	August	팔월
address	주소	Australia	호주
afraid	무섭다	automobile	차
after	후	autumn	가을
again	다시		
age	나이; (honorific) 연세	back	① 뒤; ② 등
ah	아	back row	뒷줄
airplane	비행기	bad	나쁘다
airport	공항	bag	가방
all	다, 모두	bakery	빵집, 제과점
all right	괜찮다	ballpoint pen	볼펜
all together	전부	banana	바나나
alone	혼자(서)	bank	은행
also	또	barbecued spareribs	갈비
A.M.	오전	barbershop	이발소
America	미국	barley tea	보리차
and	그리고	baseball	야구
and then	그리고 나서	basketball	농구
(get) angry	화가 나다	be	이다
animals (counter)	마리	beach	바닷가
answer	답	beauty shop	미장원
antenna	안테나	become	되다
apartment	아파트	beef	소고기
apple	사과	before	전(에)
Apple computer	애플 컴퓨터	begin	시작하다
		behind	뒤
appointment	약속	below	밑, 아래
April	사월	belt	벨트
arm	팔	bench	벤치
around	쯤	beneath	밑
arrival	도착	beside	옆
arrive	도착하다	between	사이
art	미술	beverage	음료수
art gallery	화랑	bicycle	자전거
artist	미술가	big	크다
Asian studies	동양학	bill	계산서

biology	생물학	bus stop	버스 정류장
birthday	생일; (honorific) 생신	busy	바쁘다
bitter	쓰다 (of taste)	but	그렇지만
black	① 까만색; ② 까망; ③ 까맣다	buy	사다
		by all means	꼭
black tea	홍차	by the way	그런데, 참
blackboard	칠판		
black pepper (powder)	후추	cabbage	배추
		cafe	카페
bland	싱겁다 (of taste)	cake	케이크
blessing	복	calligraphy	붓글씨
blocked	막히다	camera shop	카메라 가게
blue	① 파란색; ② 파랑; ③ 파랗다	campus	캠퍼스
		cannot do	못 하다
book	책	can't	못
bookstore	책방 (=서점)	cap	모자
bored	심심하다	capital	수도
born	태어나다	car	차
borrow	빌리다	card	카드
bottle	병	care of one's health	몸조리
bowling	볼링		
box	상자	carrot	당근
boxing	권투	carry (something) around	가지고 다니다
boyfriend	남자 친구, 애인		
bread	빵	catch	잡다
breakfast	아침	catch a cold	감기에 걸리다
bring and put down somewhere	갖다 놓다	cease	말다
		cello	첼로
bring or take (something to a person)	갖다 주다; (humble) 갖다 드리다	cent(s)	센트, 전
		center	가운데
		chair	의자
bring (something)	가지고 오다	change	① 거스름돈; ② 바꾸다
broadcasting station	방송국		
		change (clothes)	갈아 입다
broken	고장이 나다	change residence	이사하다
brown	밤색	change (vehicles)	갈아 타다
brother	① 오빠 (female's older brother); ② 형, (honorific) 형님 (male's older brother); ③ 남동생 (younger brother)	cheap	싸다
		check (at a restaurant)	계산서
		check (out)	알아 보다
		chest	가슴
		chicken	닭고기
brush teeth	이를 닦다	child	아이
building	건물, 빌딩	chin	턱
bus	버스	China	중국

Chinese (person) 중국 사람
Chinese restaurant 중국집
church 교회
cigarette 담배
citron tea 유자차
city 시, 도시
city hall 시청
clarinet 클라리넷
class 수업, 클래스
classical music 클래식 (음악)
classmate 클래스메이트
classroom 교실
clean ① 청소하다;
② 깨끗하다
clear 맑다
clock 시계
close ① 가깝다; ② 닫다
clothes 옷
clothing store 옷가게, 옷집
cloudy 흐리다
coffee 커피
coffee shop 카페
cold ① 차다; ② 춥다;
③ 감기
cold water 냉수
cold noodle dish, 냉면
  naengmyŏn
college 대학
college life 대학 생활
college student 대학생
color 색/색깔
come 오다
come carrying 사 오다
  something bought
come down 내려오다
come in 들어오다
come on foot 걸어오다
come out 나오다
come out to greet 마중 나오다
  someone
come riding 타고 오다
come up 올라오다
come wearing 입고 오다
  something
comfortable 편하다

commonly 보통
computer 컴퓨터
concert 음악회, 콘서트
congested 막히다
congratulate 축하하다
considerate 친절하다
contact ① 연락; ② 연락하다
convenient 편리하다
convey 전하다
cooking 요리
cool off 식다
cost (money) (돈이) 들다
cost of living 물가
counter 카운터
country 나라
course 과목
cousin 사촌
cross 건너다
crowded 복잡하다
cucumber 오이
culture 문화
cup 잔
customer 손님
cut for someone 잘라 주다

Daehan Theater 대한극장
dance ① 춤, 댄스; ② 춤을
추다
dancer 무용가, 댄서
date (day of the 일
  month)
date (someone) 데이트하다
daughter 딸; (honorific) 따님
day ① 낮; ② 하루;
③ 날
day after tomorrow 모레
day before 그저께
  yesterday
daytime 낮
December 십이월
decide 정하다
deeply 푹
defeated 지다
delicious 맛(이) 있다
department 과

department store	백화점	eight	팔; 여덟
departure	출발	eighty	여든
desk	책상	elementary school	초등 학교
dictionary	사전	elementary school student	초등 학생
die	죽다	elevator	엘리베이터
different	다르다	emigrate	이민 가다
difficult	어렵다, 힘들다	end	끝
diligently	열심히	England	영국
dinner	저녁	English language	영어
direction	쪽	enjoy	즐기다
directly	직접	enjoyable	즐겁다
dirty	더럽다	ethnic Korean living abroad	교포, 동포
dislike	싫다, 싫어하다	ethnic Korean in the United States	재미 교포
do	하다		
doctor	의사	evening	저녁
doll	인형	event	일
dollar	달러, 불	every day	매일, 날마다
domestic flight	국내선	every month	매달
door	문	every week	매주
dormitory	기숙사	exam	시험
down	아래	exam period	시험 때
downtown	시내	excited	신나다
draw	그리다	exciting	① 신나다; ② 신기하다
dream	꿈을 꾸다		
dress shoes	구두	excused	실례하다
drink	마시다	exercise	① 연습; ② 운동하다; ③ 연습문제
drive	운전하다		
driver	기사	exist	있다;
during	동안		(honorific) 계시다
during that time	그 동안		
		exit	출구
each other	서로	expensive	비싸다
ear	귀	explain	설명하다
early	일찍	eye	눈
earn (money)	돈을 벌다		
earrings	귀걸이		
East Coast (of the United States)	동부	face	얼굴
		family	가족; 식구
East Hall	이스트 홀	far	멀다
east side	동쪽	fast	① 빨리; ② 빠르다
easy	쉽다	father	아버지
eat	먹다;	February	이월
	(honorific) 잡수시다;	feel well	안녕하다
	(polite) 들다	feeling	기분
economics	경제학	female	여자

female student	여학생	fruit store	과일 가게
few	적다	full (not hungry)	배(가) 부르다
field	운동장	fun	재미있다
fifty	쉰		
find	찾다	game	게임
find out	알아 보다	gate (at an	게이트
finish	마치다	airport)	
first	① 제일; ② 첫	get	되다
first floor	일층	get in (on)	타다
fish (food)	생선	get married	결혼하다
fish, go fishing	낚시하다,	get off	내리다
	낚시 가다	get up	일어나다
five	오; 다섯	gift	선물
flavor	맛	ginseng tea	인삼차
floor	층	girlfriend	여자 친구, 애인
florist	꽃집	give	주다;
flower	꽃		(humble) 드리다
flower shop	꽃집	give a ride	태워 주다
flute	플룻	give regards	안부 전하다
following	다음	to someone	
fond of	좋아하다	glad	반갑다
food	음식	glass	잔
foot	발	glasses	안경
football	미식축구, 풋볼	gloves	장갑
football game	풋볼 시합	go	가다
for a long time	오랫동안	go carrying	사가다
for a short time	잠깐만	go down	내려 가다
for the first time	처음	go grocery	시장 보다; 시장
for the first time	오래간만	shopping	보러 가다
in a while		go hiking	등산하다, 등산 가다
foreign country	외국	go out	나가다
forget	잊어버리다	go out to play	놀러가다
forty	마흔; (Sino-Korean)	go out (with	데이트하다
	사십	a boy- or	
four	사; 넷, (with a	girlfriend)	
	counter) 네	go riding (a	타고 가다
four people	넷이서	vehicle)	
(together)		go wearing	입고 가다
fourth floor	사층	something	
frequently	자주	golf	골프
freshman	일학년	good	좋다
Friday	금요일	grab	잡다
friend	친구	graduate	졸업하다
from now on	앞으로(는)	graduate school	대학원
front	앞	graduate student	대학원생

grandfather	할아버지; (honorific) 할아버님	home	집
		hometown	고향
grandmother	할머니; (honorific) 할머님	homework	숙제
		do homework	숙제하다
gray	회색	hospital	병원
green	초록색	hot	① 덥다;
greet	인사하다		② 뜨겁다
greeting	인사	hour (time)	시
group	그룹	hours (counter	시간
grow up	자라다	for duration)	
guest	손님	house	집; (honorific) 댁
		how?	어떻게
hair	머리	how long?	얼마나
hair salon	머리방	how many?	몇
half	반	how much?	얼마(나)
hallway	복도	how often?	얼마나 자주
hamburger	햄버거	however	그렇지만
hand	손	hundred	백
hand in	내다	hungry	배(가) 고프다
happy	① 행복하다; ② 반갑다	husband	남편
hat	모자	I	(humble) 저; (plain) 나
hate	싫어하다		
have	갖다, 가지다	if so	그럼
have a headache	머리(가) 아프다	in	안
head	머리	in the future	앞으로(는)
health	건강	in toto	전부
healthy	건강하다	in what way?	어떻게
heard	들리다	inconvenient	불편하다
heart	마음	inquire	물어 보다
heavy	무겁다	inside	안
height (of a person or a plant)	키	instant noodles (ramen)	라면
hello	여보세요	international flight	국제선
help	돕다	intersection	사거리
here	여기	item (counter)	개
high	높다		
high school	고등 학교	January	일월
high school student	고등 학생	Japanese restaurant	일식집, 일본 음식점
hike, go hiking	등산하다, 등산 가다	jog	조깅하다
hiking	등산	juice	주스
history	역사	July	칠월
hobby	취미	June	유월
holiday	휴일	junior	삼학년

junior high school student	중학생
just	그냥
just now	방금
karaoke room	노래방
kimch'i	김치 (Korean pickled cabbage)
kind	친절하다
kitchen	부엌
knocking	똑똑
know	알다
Korea	한국
Korean alphabet	한글
Korean (language)	한국어, 한국말
Korean mask dance	탈춤
Korean (person)	한국 사람
Korean restaurant	한식집
lab	랩
language	말; (honorific) 말씀
last	지난
last night	어젯밤
last year	작년
late	① 늦게; ② 늦다
later	나중에
layer (counter)	층
learn	배우다
at least	적어도
leave	떠나다
left side	왼쪽
leg	다리
lemon	레몬
lemonade	레모네이드
lend	빌려 주다
less	덜
lesson (counter)	과
letter	편지
letter of recommendation	추천서
lettuce	상추
library	도서관
life	생활
light	가볍다

light brown	갈색
like	좋아하다
the line is busy	통화중이다
lips	입술
liquor	술
listen	듣다
listen to music	음악(을) 듣다
a little	조금
a little later	이따가
live	살다
living	생활
long	길다
look	보다
look for	찾다
lose	잃어버리다
lounge	휴게실
love	사랑하다
low	낮다
lunch	점심
mail	메일
major	전공
major in	전공하다
make	만들다
make a noise	떠들다
make a phone call	전화하다, 전화를 걸다
make a plan	계획을 세우다
make an effort	수고하다
make friends	사귀다
make someone do something	시키다
male	남자
male student	남학생
Manhattan Hotel	맨하탄 호텔
many	① 많다; ② 많이; ③ 여러
map	지도
March	삼월
market	시장
marriage	결혼
May	오월
meal	밥, 식사
meat	고기
meet	만나다
menu	메뉴

message	메시지	next to	옆
middle	가운데	next year	내년
middle school	중학교	night	밤
mile	마일	nine	구; 아홉
milk	우유	ninety	아흔
minute(s)	분	no	아니오
mom	엄마	no fun	재미없다
Monday	월요일	noisy	시끄럽다
money	돈	noodle	국수
month	월; 달	north side	북쪽
more	더	nose	코
morning	아침	not	① 안; ② 않다
most	가장, 제일	not be	아니다
mother	어머니;	not do	않다
	(honorific) 어머님	not exist	없다
mountain	산	not have	없다
mountain climbing	등산	not know	모르다
mouth	입	not (be) likable	싫다
move to a new	이사하다	not own	없다
home		not particularly	별로
movie	영화	not possibly	못
movie theater	극장	not really	별로
much	① 많다; ② 많이	not work	놀다
museum	박물관	notebook	공책
music	음악	novel	신기하다
musical	뮤지컬	November	십일월
musical instrument	악기	now	① 이젠; ② 지금
musician	음악가	number	① 숫자; ② 번호
my	(humble) 제;		
	(plain) 내	o'clock (point of	시
		time)	
name	이름; (honorific) 성함	October	시월
narrow	좁다	often	자주
nature	마음	oh!	어머
near	가깝다	okay	괜찮다
nearby	근처	once	한번
neck	목	once in a while	가끔
necklace	목걸이	one	일; 하나, (with a
neighborhood	근처, 동네		counter) 한
new	① 새; ② 신기하다	one hundred	백 살, 백 세
New Year	새해	years old	
newly	새로	one million dollars	백만 달러
news	뉴스	one time	한번
newspaper	신문	only	만
next	다음	open	열다

opera	오페라	play baseball	야구하다
optician('s)	안경점	play basketball	농구하다
orange (color)	주황색	player	선수
orchestra	오케스트라	playground	운동장
order	주문하다	pleasant	즐겁다
order (food in a restaurant)	시키다	please	① 어서; ② 좀
		P.M.	오후
other side	건너편	political science	정치학
our	우리	population	인구
out of order	고장이 나다	pork	돼지고기
over	끝나다	possess	갖다, 가지다
over there	저기	post office	우체국
overpass (for pedestrians)	육교	practice	① 연습; ② 연습(을) 하다
		present	선물
painter	미술가	president (of a country)	대통령
pants	바지		
paper	종이	pretty	예쁘다
parents	부모	price	값
park	공원	probably	아마
park (a vehicle)	세우다	professor	교수
part-time job	아르바이트	professor's office	연구실
particularly	특히	promise	약속
party	파티	purple	보라색
pass	전하다	put down	놓다
pass away, die	(honorific) 돌아가시다	pur forth effort	수고하다
pass by	지내다	put on (clothes)	입다
passerby	지나가는 사람	put on (footwear)	신다
pay	(돈을) 내다	put on (glasses, gloves)	끼다
peacefully	안녕히		
pear	배	put on (hats, caps)	쓰다
pen	펜		
perhaps	아마	put on (wristwatch)	차다
person (counter)	명; (honorific) 분		
pharmacy	약국, 약방		
photograph	사진	question	질문
piano	피아노	quickly	빨리
picture	① 사진; ② 그림	quiet	조용하다
pineapple	파인애플		
ping-pong	탁구	radio	라디오
place	① 곳; ② 데	radish	무
plan	① 계획; ② 계획하다	rain	비
play	놀다	raincoat	레인코트
play (tennis, piano, guitar)	치다	read	읽다
		reading	독서

really	정말, 참	Saturday	토요일
receive	받다	scallion	파
red	① 빨간색; ② 빨강;	school	학교
	③ 빨갛다	school cafeteria	학교 식당
red pepper	고추	school vacation	방학
red-pepper paste	고추장	sculpture	조각
red-pepper	고춧가루	search	찾다
powder		seat	자리
refrigerator	냉장고	second floor	이층
regards	안부	see	보다; (humble) 뵙다
register	카운터	see a movie	영화(를) 보다
relationship	사이	(be) seen	보이다
rent (out)	빌려 주다	sell	팔다
resemble	닮다	semester	학기
rest	쉬다	send	보내 주다
rest room	화장실	send a fax	팩스를 보내다
restaurant	음식점, 식당	send (a letter)	부치다
return	돌아오다	send (an) e-mail	이메일을 보내다
return something	돌려 주다	send mail	보내다
(cooked) rice	밥; (honorific) 진지	senior	사학년
ride	타다; (regularly) 타고	September	구월
	다니다	service	서비스
ride a bicycle	자전거(를) 타다	sesame oil	참기름
right side	오른쪽	seven	칠; 일곱
right (there)	바로	seventy	일흔
ring	반지	several	여러
road	길	sheet(s) (counter)	장
roast meat	불고기	shirt(s)	셔츠
rock, paper,	가위 바위 보	shoe(s)	신, 신발
scissors		shoe store	구두 가게
rollerblade	롤러블레이드 타다	shopping	쇼핑
room	방	do shopping	쇼핑하다
roommate	룸메이트	short	짧다
row	줄	short (of height)	키가 작다
run	달리다	short pants	반바지
(by) running	뛰어서	shoulder	어깨
rush hour	러시아워	sibling	① 형제; ② 동생
			(younger sibling)
sad	슬프다	sick	아프다
safely	안녕히	side	① 옆; ② 쪽
salesperson	점원	side dish	반찬
salt	소금	sightseeing	구경
salty	짜다	sincerely yours	올림
same	같다	(in letters)	
sandwich	샌드위치	sing a song	노래하다

singer	가수	spend days	지내다
sister	① 언니 (female's older sister); ② 누나, (honorific) 누님 (male's older sister); ③ 여동생 (younger sister)	spend (time)	보내다
		spicy	맵다
		spinach	시금치
		sport shoes	운동화
		spot	군데
		spring	봄
sit (down)	앉다	spring vacation	봄 방학
six	육; 여섯	stamp	우표
sixty	예순	start	시작하다
skating	스케이트	station (subway or railroad)	역
ski	스키 타다		
ski resort	스키장	stationery store	문방구점
skiing	스키	stay	있다; (honorific) 계시다
skirt(s)	치마		
sleep	① 잠; ② 잠을 자다; (honorific) 주무시다	still	아직
		stomach	배
slow	느리다	stop	말다
slowly	천천히	stop (a vehicle)	세우다
small	작다	store	가게, 상점, 슈퍼
smoke	(담배를) 피우다	street	길
sneakers	운동화	student	학생
snow	눈	study	공부하다
so	① 그래서; ② 그렇다	subject	과목
soccer	축구	subject particle	이
sock(s)	양말	subway	지하철
soda	사이다	suddenly	갑자기
solve (a problem)	풀다	sugar	설탕
someone	누구	summer	여름
sometimes	가끔	summer vacation	여름 방학
son	아들	Sunday	일요일
sonata	소나타	supermarket	슈퍼마켓
song	노래	supper	저녁
sophomore	이학년	sweat	땀을 흘리다
sorry	죄송하다, 미안하다	sweet	달다
sound	소리	swim	수영하다
sour	시다	swimmer	수영 선수
south side	남쪽	swimming	수영
soybean paste (fermented)	된장	swimming pool	수영장
		switch	바꾸다
soybean-paste stew	된장찌개	symphony	심포니
soy sauce	간장	table tennis	탁구
spacious	넓다	take (a course)	듣다
special event	별일	take (a picture)	찍다

take a shower	샤워하다	then	그럼
take (a test)	보다	there	거기
take (time)	걸리다	therefore	그래서
take care of one's	몸조리하다	these days	요즘
health		thing	① 거 (contraction of
take off (a tie,	풀다		것); ② 일
belt, watch)		think	생각하다
take off (clothes)	벗다	thirty	서른
take off (gloves)	빼다	thirty minutes	삼십 분
take something	가지고 가다	this much, this	이만
take trouble	수고하다	only	
talk	애기하다	this (near speaker)	① 이 ; ② 이것
talk (with a	이야기하다	this side	이 쪽
person)		this (thing)	이거 (contraction of
tall (height)	키가 크다		이것)
tape	테이프	this time	이번
taste	맛	this way	이렇다
tasteless	맛(이) 없다	this year	올해, 금년
taxi	택시	thousand	천
taxi fare	택시비	three	삼; 셋, (with a
tea	차		counter) 세
teach	가르치다	Thursday	목요일
teacher	선생님	ticket	표
teacher's wife	사모님	tie	넥타이
telephone	전화	time	① 시간; ② 때
telephone company	전화국	times (counter)	번
telephone number	전화번호	tired	피곤하다
television	텔레비전	today	오늘
ten	십; 열	together	같이
tender	연하다	tomorrow	내일
tennis	테니스	too	또
ten thousand	만	too much	너무
ten thousand won	만 원	tooth	이
test	시험	top	위
textbook	교과서	traditional Korean	한복
thankful	감사하다, 고맙다	dress	
that (near listener)	① 그; ②그것	traffic	교통
that over there	① 저; ②저것	traffic light	신호등
(away from both		train	기차
speaker and		travel	① 여행; ② 여행하다,
listener)			여행 가다
that side	그 쪽	travel agency	여행사
that side over	저 쪽	truck	트럭
there		Tuesday	화요일
that way	저렇다	turn	돌다

turn in	내다	wait	기다리다
turn into	되다	waiter	종업원
twenty	스물, (with a counter) 스무	waitress	종업원
		walk	걷다
two	이; 둘, (with a counter) 두	Walkman	워크맨
		walk (regularly)	걸어 다니다
two people (together)	둘이서	walk (to a place)	걸어 가다
		wallet	지갑
		waltz	월츠
umbrella	우산	want to	싶다
unable to do	못 하다	warm	따뜻하다
uncle	① 큰아버지 (father's elder brother); ② 작은아버지 (father's younger brother); ③ 삼촌 (father's brother)	wash (laundry)	빨래하다
		wash the dishes	설거지하다
		wash face	세수하다
		wash hands	손을 씻다
		watch	① 시계; ② 보다
		watchmaker's	시계방
uncomfortable	불편하다	watch TV	텔레비전(을) 보다
under	아래, 밑	water	물
underpass (for pedestrians)	지하도	watermelon	수박
		we	우리
understand	알다	wear (clothes)	입다
uninteresting	재미없다	wear (footwear)	신다
university	대학교	wear (glasses, gloves)	끼다
unkind	불친절하다		
us	우리	wear (hats, caps)	쓰다
use	쓰다	wear (wristwatch)	차다
usually	보통	weather	날씨
		Wednesday	수요일
Vancouver	밴쿠버	week	주일
vegetable store, grocer	야채 가게, 채소 가게	weekend	주말
		well	① 글쎄요; ② 안녕 하다; ③ 잘
very	참		
very much	굉장히, 무척, 대단히, 아주	west side	서쪽
		Western-style restaurant	양식집
vinegar	식초		
violin	바이올린	what?	무슨 (pre-noun); 무엇, 뭐 (contraction of 무엇)
vitamin	비타민		
vocabulary	단어		
voice	목소리	what day of the month?	며칠
volleyball	배구		
volume(s) (counter)	권	what kind of?	무슨; 어떤
		what matter?	웬일
		when?	언제
waist	허리	where?	어디

which?	어느, 어떤	without doing	그만
(a) while (ago)	아까	anything further	
white	① 하얀색; ② 하얀;	without fail	꼭
	③ 하얗다	won (Korean	원
who?	누구; (with particle	currency)	
	가) 누가	word	단어; 말;
whose?	누구(의)		(honorific) 말씀
why?	왜	work	① 일; ② 일하다
wide	넓다	wrestling	레슬링
wife	아내; (honorific) 부인	write	쓰다
win	이기다		
wind	바람	year(s)	년, 연
(the) wind is	바람이 불다	yellow	① 노란색; ② 노랑;
blowing			③ 노랗다
window	창문	yes	네
winter	겨울	yesterday	어제
winter vacation	겨울 방학	yet	아직
withdraw money	찾다	youngest child	막내
(from the bank)			